D0429530

JOYCE'S GRANDFATHERS

JOYCE'S GRANDFATHERS

Myth and History in

Defoe, Smollett, Sterne, and Joyce

JOHN M. WARNER

THE UNIVERSITY OF GEORGIA PRESS

Athens and London

© 1993 by the University of Georgia Press
Athens, Georgia 30602
All rights reserved
Set in Sabon with Neuland display
by Tseng Information Systems, Inc.
Printed and bound by Thomson–Shore, Inc.
The paper in this book meets the guidelines for
permanence and durability of the Committee on
Production Guidelines for Book Longevity of the
Council on Library Resources.

Printed in the United States of America

97 96 95 94 93 C 5 4 3 2 1

Library of Congress Cataloging in Publication Data

Warner, John M., 1935–
Joyce's grandfathers : myth and history in Defoe, Smollett,
Sterne, and Joyce / John M. Warner.
p. cm.
Includes bibliographical references and index.
ISBN 0-8203-1495-1
1. English fiction—18th century—History and criticism.
2. Smollett, Tobias George, 1721–1771—Criticism and interpretation.
3. Sterne, Laurence, 1713–1768—Criticism and interpretation.
4. Defoe, Daniel, 1661?–1731—Criticism and interpretation.
5. Influence (Literary, artistic, etc.) 6. Joyce, James,
1882–1941. Ulysses. 7. History in literature. 8. Myth in
literature. I. Title.
PR851.W28 1993
823.009'005—dc20 92–15587
CIP

British Library Cataloging in Publication Data available

He was and felt himself the father of all his race, the father of his own grandfather, the father of his unborn grandson . . .

the library scene, *Ulysses*

Contents

Preface

When I began this study, Ian Watt's thesis about the rise of the novel, though beleaguered, remained predominant. Separating the "novel" from romance, Watt argued that the genre could be defined aesthetically in terms of its "formal realism" and ideologically through its relation to the rising middle class. A persistent argument raised against Watt's thesis was its failure to take account of the "many non-rationalistic, non-empirical, non-'realistic' aspects of the major novels of the century" (Hunter 523). On the other hand, archetypalist theories of genre, based on the separability of history and mythic structure, saw the novel as simply a displaced version of romance. What was missing at that time was a theory of the novel which would mediate between the ahistoricity of myth and the failure of the historical approach to take into account the persistence of romance elements.

During the long gestation of this study, Michael McKeon published *The Origins of the English Novel 1600–1740*, a work which seems likely to become for the next twenty-five years the central critical text on the eighteenth-century novel that Ian Watt's *The Rise of the Novel* was for the last quarter century. Through a dialectical reconceptualization of the idea of genre and its relation to history, McKeon is enabled also to refigure the relation of the English novel to its precursor genres. While my more textually oriented study shares few methodological features with McKeon's broad-ranging goals and strategies, his study does provide a more congenial frame for my work than had Watt's hypothesis about the novel. With my interest in myth, I could only share the growing consensus that Watt's emphasis on realism distorted our sense of the eighteenth-century novel. On the other hand, my definition of myth as a historical phenomenon that could only be evoked rather than re-created precluded my understanding the novel as simply a displaced form of romance. McKeon's historical analysis, formulated in Marxist terms, seeks to overcome the disjuncture between myth and history found in both Watt and Northrop Frye. "A dialectical theory of genre," as McKeon points out, "so far from rejecting the archetypalist insight into the relationship of 'romance' and 'the novel,' would aim to make it truly comprehensible by grounding it in the history of literary and material forms" (19).

If McKeon's model in constructing a mode of literary history is Karl Marx, mine might seem to be David Lodge. Like Persse McGarrigle, the hero of *Small World* who writes a critical study of Eliot's influence on Shakespeare, I may seem to be reversing the dialectical process. Although I had done my doctoral dissertation on Smollett's relation to the minor comic novelists of his period, departmental exigencies led to my teaching modern British literature as well as that of the eighteenth century. What I began to notice in Joyce's *Ulysses* was a pattern of mediation between history and myth. This mediation occurred in the use of language and plot as well as in the treatment of time. Teaching the eighteenth-century novel concurrently with *Ulysses*, I began to see how fruitfully they could be read in light of one another. Traditional literary history dictates, of course, that one find traces of earlier works in the later, and it was possible to draw a number of connections of this sort. More interesting to me, however, was finding foreshadowings of *Ulysses*'s mediation of mythic and historic tensions in earlier eighteenth-century works. Having become attuned to this pattern in the later work, I began to discover not any exact parallels to Joyce's novel but anticipations of its dialectical processes.

Hence in my title, *Joyce's Grandfathers*, I deliberately evoke a double perspective on literary tradition. Its surface meaning suggests how three eighteenth-century novelists, Defoe, Smollett, and Sterne, can function in some ways as models, if not precise sources, for Joyce's later achievement. The title also alludes, however, to Stephen Dedalus's theory, developed in the library scene of *Ulysses*, that Shakespeare "was and felt himself the father of all his race, the father of his own grandfather, the father of his unborn grandson" (171). Following Stephen's idea that the artist *creates* his own forefathers, another thrust of my study will be to show how a sense of Joyce's dialectical response to history and myth can yield for us a deeper appreciation of artistic and intellectual strategies which have been overlooked in these three eighteenth-century novelists.

Stephen's notion that the artist is the creator of his grandfather has parallels, of course, with T. S. Eliot's idea, developed in "Tradition and the Individual Talent," that the introduction of a really new work alters the ideal order of previously existing works of art. The "new" work helps us to see elements of theme and technique in older artifacts differently. The insight of the truly original creative artist lifts up features in his or her work to our attention in ways that do alter our perception of the medium. It is in this way that Eliot can say that the past may be "altered by the present as much as the present is directed by the past." A Renaissance sonnet does not, certainly, alter literally in terms of its physical appearance; but the technical freedoms and innovations of *The Waste Land* inevitably affect our sense of the role of convention in poetry. It does not necessarily make us think convention good or bad; it simply alters our sense of possibilities within the medium.

We ought, however, to remember that Joyce both shares in and dissociates himself from Stephen's theory of artistic grandparenting, just as he both continues and refuses to project himself into Stephen in *Ulysses*. (Ralph Rader has insightfully, and I think correctly, argued that "whereas Stephen in *Ulysses* is to be understood as the real young Joyce imagined in his own body as if he were another, Bloom is to be understood finally as the mature Joyce imagining another in a different body as himself" ["Exodus and Return" 155].) As my reading of *Ulysses* will suggest, it can be most fruitfully approached as mediating opposing historical and mythic thrusts, as working not on one or the other but on both diachronic and synchronic axes. Thus, without abandoning Eliot's insight into the synchronic nature of literature, I would want—parallel to the way Michael McKeon has so tellingly grounded romance in the history of both literary and material forms—to place it within a historical context.

In her admirable *Paradise Lost as "Myth"* (1959), Isabel MacCaffrey noted that "the critical undertaking that follows will be quite unlike the tracing of mythological 'motifs' as can be found, for example, in the works of Maud Bodkin" (18). Writing in a context that still largely defines myth in Northrop Frye's terms, I need to stress that I work with a different conception of myth. Emphasizing the importance of the archetype, Frye apparently rejects the idea that myth represents an earlier, different mode of consciousness. He says, in *Spiritus Mundi*, that "all attempts to deal with mythological thinking as 'primitive' based on hazy analogies to biological evolution, are in my view totally mistaken" (ix).

There is, nevertheless, a long tradition of myth theory that assumes that myth flourished in an early, if not necessarily "primitive," time. My own introduction to such thought was through the work of Owen Barfield. From him I moved to Ernst Cassirer, whose conception of myth energizes MacCaffrey's work on Milton, and to Eric Voegelin. Only later did I become aware of the looming importance of Vico's theory of myth for my own interest in Joyce and his relation to certain eighteenth-century novelists. Much of this book was written before I encountered the work of Donald Verene both on Vico and on Joyce's relationship to Vico. Thus the view of myth developed herein is a conflation of ideas from Barfield, Cassirer, Voegelin, and Vico. While eclectic, it agrees in most major points with Verene's sense not only of Vico but of Vico's importance for James Joyce.

Perhaps Vichian waters affect critics like Verene and me with achronicity, for Verene's main ideas can be found in an essay in which he imagines Vico as a reader of Joyce. What, he asks, would Vico make of what Joyce made of him? While most critics interested in these matters have emphasized the impact of Vico's cyclical theory of history on Joyce's work, Verene, like me, sees Vico's theory of the imagination as a more significant influence on the novelist. As old as Plato's discussion of the forms of the state in the *Republic*, the theory of cycles is "not the most important thing in Vico's thought" but "simply the most obvious." Vico did, however, "invent a new view of language in his conception of imaginative universals [and] Vico as reader of Joyce would be most impressed with Joyce's sense of language" (*Vico and Joyce* 225). Distressed by the modern Cartesian age with its "barbarie della riflessione, 'barbarism of reflection'" (224), Vico had sought to rehabilitate the imagination by turning back to the earlier world of myth. Instead of dismissing, on the basis of reason and logic, the exaggerations of early myths as untruths, Vico made the leap to see that these stories reflected how different from ours was the way early humans related to, not conceived, their world. They did not "conceive" their world, for the split between subject and object on which conceptualization would depend had not yet occurred. Thus, every person was not consciously a poet yet spoke out of a oneness with nature and therefore, as we might put it, "imaginatively."

Language becomes, then, a key to a "sensus communis" common to all humanity in the age of myth. In ages that overvalue reason, the appeal of such mythic vision seems obvious: one finds in the age of "giants" all those warm feelings that alleviate the "nightmare" of history, whether in its incipient or developed phase. The danger of this kind of myth, as critics have been quick to point out, is its substitution of authority for reason. A book on the impact of interest in such mythic thinking on high modernist literature needs to be written, but that is not my intention here. We must note, however, that Joyce from my view exhibits no trace of a sympathy for that authority we can trace in the modernist movement's occasional flirtation with modes of fascism.

Along with Vico, Joyce recognized that this "primordial common sense of mankind, once lost, can never be recovered in actual historical life" (*Vico and Joyce* 227). The writer cannot take humanity back to its origin point in history; he or she can only use language imaginatively as a way to evoke those meanings out of which it arose. For Joyce, much of the appeal of myth lay in the opportunities it gave for verbal play rather than in any authoritarian answer it might give to the problem of history.

Moreover, Joyce's own attitude toward authority was so ambivalent as to preclude any easy acceptance of myth as an "answer" to the complex problems of historical existence. What allows Joyce to constitute these eighteenth-century novelists as his "grandfathers" is his perception of their similar ambivalence. Each generates in novelistic terms the same tensions that Vico conceptualizes in the *Scienza Nuova*: a clash between modern empirical, positivist thought and a "revolutionary nostalgia" for the world of myth. By lifting up this dialectical pattern *Ulysses* "alters" our approach to these eighteenth-century novels as much as they have "directed" how we should read it.

Acknowledgments

As my bibliography indicates, my debts to scholars of Defoe, Smollett, Sterne, and Joyce are many. Owen Barfield's visits to Drew University sparked my interest in myth and led me into a field of inquiry that has proved consistently fascinating; my obligations to those others who have become beguiled with the idea of myth as a mode of knowing will be apparent.

A number of people have generously read, either in part or in full, manuscript versions of this study. I thank the following for their advice and help: Paul Alkon, Janet Burstein, Robert Adams Day, William C. Dowling, Violet Halpert, Laura Kendrick, Michael McKeon, Nadine Ollman, Barry V. Qualls, and John Richetti.

The staffs of the Rose Memorial Library at Drew University, of Widener Library at Harvard University, and of the British Library provided generous assistance. I thank Drew University for a release-time grant that helped in the writing of this book. Parts of chapter 3 were first published as "Smollett's Development as a Novelist," *Novel: A Forum on Fiction* 5 (Winter 1972): 148–61. Part of chapter 5 was published as "Myth and History in Joyce's 'Nauiscaa' Episode," *James Joyce Quarterly* 24 (Fall 1986): 19–31. I thank the editors of these journals for their support. I owe a special debt to Nancy Grayson Holmes, an editor whose advice and encouragement I would wish to have encountered earlier in the long evolution of this project.

Abbreviations

UL Richard Ellmann, *Ulysses on the Liffey* (New York: Oxford University Press, 1972).

JJ Richard Ellmann, *James Joyce*, revised edition (New York: Oxford University Press, 1982).

Life Henri Focillon, *The Life of Forms in Art*, trans. Charles Beecher Hogan (New York: Wittenborn, Schultz, Inc., 1948).

NS Giambattista Vico, *The New Science of Giambattista Vico*, trans. from the third edition (1744) by Thomas Goddard Burgin and Max Harold Fisch (Ithaca, N.Y.: Cornell University Press, 1948).

JOYCE'S GRANDFATHERS

1

Myth, History, and Mediation

In Joyce's *Ulysses* tiny elements exfoliate and become keys to the vast, complex structure of the novel. One such element is the newspaper ad that Bloom tries to secure in the Aeolus section: "—Like that, see. Two crossed keys here. A circle. Then here the name. Alexander Keyes, tea, wine and spirit merchant. So on" (99). The emphasis on the word *key,* and the fact that it is part of a wider symbolic pattern within the novel,[1] suggest the importance of the ad as a clue to deeper levels within *Ulysses.* The implications of the ad expand in the Ithaca episode where Bloom ponders "the infinite possibilities hitherto unexploited of the modern art of advertisement if condensed in triliteral monoideal symbols, vertically of maximum visibility (divined), horizontally of maximum legibility (deciphered) and of magnetizing efficacy to arrest involuntary attention, to interest, to convince, to decide" (559). If we take the ad as a symbol of "modern" art (at least as it reveals itself to Bloom), this gloss from Ithaca suggests that we can find in art both a vertical level of implication—which is "divined" or understood more intuitively, perhaps irrationally—and a horizontal one—which is "deciphered" more by our minds in logical acts. Further, the symbols of such art are curiously both "triliteral" and "monoideal," which suggests not only that art is three and one, but also that it is material, or tangible ("literal"), as well as spiritual, or beyond matter ("ideal"). Lastly, having arrested the reader/viewer's involuntary attention, the work of art can yield not only interest, but also conviction and decision.

The distinction between deciphering and divining reality is central not just to our understanding of *Ulysses* but to our understanding of its relation to the works of Joyce's "grandfathers": Defoe, Smollett, and Sterne. Writing in an era of epistemological dislocation, they "divined" that in the synchronisms of myth they could find ways to resist the pressures of an encroaching positivism and empiricism. Yet they were very much "decipherers" of their age; each shows, along with a revolutionary nostalgia for myth, a clear responsiveness to historical circumstances. The consequent tension in their works between what can be deciphered and what can be divined was what Joyce found useful in his grandfathers. He worked in *Ulysses* with the relation between myth and history in ways that are immediately apparent to us. The usual mode of the literary historian is to decipher—along the horizontal line of history—the influence of the earlier work on the later. In this instance, we will work equally fruitfully by "divining" how Joyce fathers his own grandfathers. Looking at these earlier writers through the lens of *Ulysses*, we can discover a similar tension in their fiction which had not been so immediately apparent to us before. In my reading, Joyce both uses *and* creates a tradition for his novel. This chapter will demonstrate what it means, first, to divine and, then, to decipher reality.

The Novel and Vico's World of Myth

This study's view of myth is essentially an epistemological one concerned with myth as a mode of knowing. It draws not upon Northrop Frye, but upon Cassirer, Barfield, Eliade, and Voegelin. Ultimately its origins are found in the work of Vico. The basic premise of this epistemological view is that myth arose in a period of early or even preconsciousness (Voegelin defines it as a period of "compact" as opposed to modern man's "differentiated" consciousness) where different conceptions of language, time, and space held sway. Obviously, Defoe, Smollett, and Sterne, to say nothing of Joyce 150 years later, did not write myths out of a prerational consciousness. But, I argue, similar ideas about myth were abroad at the time that they wrote, and these writers *simulated* the manner of myth as an alternative to the mode of historical consciousness they also used. Why they should do so is a question best answered by turning to a historical survey of ideas about myth since the Renaissance. This survey suggests the analogous epistemological crises all of these writers faced.

A variation on an epistemological explanation of myth existed in the Renaissance. As Isabel MacCaffrey has pointed out, the mythographers of the Renaissance thought that the "myths of other cultures reflected, dimly and in distorted outlines, larger more portentous figures. They were, in Raleigh's pregnant phrase, 'crooked images of some one true history.' The nature of that *one* was never in doubt; it was the Christian version of human destiny" (11–12). Myths, then, were conceived as distorted visions or versions of the Christian story of creation, the story of the Garden. As mythographers understood them, myths were shadowy repetitions of the "one true history." Associated with this vision of myth was a typological view of history. History was not interpreted as a linear, cause and effect pattern extending chronologically in time. Instead, as Elizabeth Deeds Ermarth points out, the "unifying principles of history were past patterns that repeated themselves in the arena provided by time, and the interpretation of even the most trivial action could only be sought in some typological pattern" (6–7).

Just when historiography gave up such typological thinking for the linear, chronological patterns of modern empirical history cannot be clearly stated; every scholar can find examples to support his or her date. As Ermarth indicates, the seventeenth century seems to be the watershed in the development of modern history. She cites, however, a number of authorities who argue for the "persistence of medieval methods well past the seventeenth century" (29). Perhaps we can simply agree with Ermarth that the "more humanism proved to be a solvent for scholasticism, the more typological thinking lost its primacy" (9). By the time Milton wrote *Paradise Lost*, undoubtedly many had broken away from the older view that classical myths were shadowy images of the "one true history." Indeed, for some thinkers these supposedly shadowy reflections had become another sort of historical phenomenon that could call the one true story itself into question. Nevertheless, MacCaffrey believes, and makes a very convincing case for her belief, that Milton was *creating* a true myth in writing his epic. For MacCaffrey, Milton is not simulating the manner of myth but is using every resource of language and structure to create a "mythological content, the Christian paradigm of history" (30). Not asking us to believe in

Milton's myth, she does feel that we must understand that he is *writing* myth if we are "to read *Paradise Lost* properly" (22).[2]

I am not asking my readers to believe that for these eighteenth-century novelists myth is "a structured and epistemological principle, reflecting accurately . . . the real nature of our first world" (MacCaffrey 209). The authors whom I am exploring will simulate the mode of myth in order to express dissatisfaction with discursive modes of expression, to extend the possibilities of language and structure, to enrich characterization, to find literary—narrative—solutions to the crisis in epistemology they confronted. Yet, while their interest in myth will thus tend to relate more to possibilities for narrative than to the regaining of paradise, one cannot entirely dismiss the moral and even ontological implications of their mythic simulations. Instead of trying to reclaim Christian paradises, they seek more, as in Smollett's search for the ideal society, to reconcile mythic vision and historic reality.[3]

If that vision was not the Christian idea of myth, what was it? Scholars have surveyed Vico's sixteenth- and seventeenth-century predecessors; and, more relevant to my concerns, Frank E. Manuel has impressively explored eighteenth-century responses in *The Eighteenth Century Confronts the Gods*.[4] In "Myth and Language in Vico," Gianfranco Cantelli describes the ideas about myth established by Jean Leclerc before Vico. These essentially convert myth from a typological to a historical study (48). Mythographers who, "on the model of Leclerc, wished to resolve mythology into profane history" nevertheless found it impossible "to conceive an allegorical meaning for the fables different from that consecrated by tradition" (Cantelli 55); as an alternative, consequently, they began to offer narrowly euhemeristic readings of myth well before Milton wrote his poem. Manuel further describes how such mythographers tried to make myth palatable for an eighteenth century that was largely hostile to myth itself.[5] Mythography came, he says, "to be conceived as a historical science using linguistic and even astronomic data, following the method of hypothesis and verification precisely as did other sciences" (105). This effort to apply logical and rationalistic principles to the study of myth would sink Milton's efforts to re-create the religious origins of human life beneath a plethora of euhemerist explanations that the gods had indeed only been ordinary human beings about whose worldly deeds tales had been spun which raised these mortals to godlike status. Manuel richly summarizes how the disrobing of pagan deities soon led to the disrobing even of the country parsons. " 'Greek religion not mysterious' was the manifesto of Euhemerist abbés and bishops. 'Christianity not mysterious' was the Deist echo. In fact, 'Nothing is mysterious' soon became the credo of the age, and all truths were assumed to be self-evident" (125).

Concurrent with this demystification of myth arose a counterimpulse. As Manuel points out, the euhemerist explanations had a built-in disadvantage; the myths for which they sought earthly models were so ancient as to be "removed from any individual identifiable action attached to a real person and a specific place" (111). The Christian interpretation of myth as shadowy reflections of the "one true history" perhaps prepared the way for the idea that began to develop that there was a distinctive primitive mind. As Manuel notes, Fontenelle, one of the first commentators to psychologize myth at the turn of the century, "had still regarded the differences between the primitive mind and the contemporary principally as one of degree"; for later writers, however, "the mentality of the primitive became more distinct, individualized to the point where a different human nature was recognized" (141).

A key figure behind this changed view of the nature of early man is Giambattista Vico, who will prove equally significant for our sense of Joyce's ideas about myth. The first edition of the *New Science* was published in 1725, with second and third editions published in 1730 and 1744. Vico is perhaps best known for his cyclic view of history in which theocratic, aristocratic, and democratic ages succeed one another only to end in a return to the beginning of another cycle. But as Donald Verene has shown, Vico's theory of knowledge is an equally important element of his philosophy, for his "theory of poetic wisdom is the basis for the *New Science*" ("Vico's Science" 302). Based on the idea that ancient primitives, contemporary savages, children, and peasants share a common form of mentality (Verene 302), this theory of poetic wisdom posits an age of myth in which consciousness was different from that of contemporary man. "Hence poetic wisdom, the first wisdom of the gentile world, must have begun with a metaphysic not rational and abstract like that of learned men now, but felt and imagined as that of these first men must have been, who, without the power of ratiocination, were all robust sense and vigorous imagination" (Vico NS 104 §375). On the basis of this insight, Vico established his analogy between primitive thought and poetic (or figurative) language. But, as

Hayden White has observed, there is a crucial difference: the modern poet uses figurative language self-consciously while "primitive man is presumed to have been able at first to speak only figuratively and to think in allegories and to have taken these figures and allegories as literal truths, or denotative representations, of the world external to himself" ("Tropics" 75). Or, as Verene has more succinctly put it, the "distinctive characteristic of mythic or primordial thought is its power to assert *identities* not *similarities*" ("Vico's Science" 307).

The parallels between Vico's and Cassirer's basic premises are significant. These have been explored carefully by Verene in his essay "Vico's Science of Imaginative Universals and the Philosophy of Symbolic Forms." Here, he sees Vico and Cassirer as speaking directly to "the separation that Descartes enacted in his own thought between the reason of the intellect and the forms of the humanistic imagination" (317). Although volume 2 of *The Philosophy of Symbolic Forms* is entitled *Mythical Thought*, Cassirer raises the question of how appropriate it is even to use the term *thought* in relation to myth: "For is it not a *petitio principii,* a false rationalization of myth, to attempt to understand it through its *form of thought*? Admitted even that such a form exists—is it anything more than an outward shell which conceals the core of myth? Does myth not signify a unity of intuition, an *intuitive* unity preceding and underlying all the explanations contributed by *discursive* thought?" (*Mythical Thought* 69). Since this earliest stage of myth precedes discursive reasoning and is utterly alien to our analytic modes, Cassirer spends the larger portion of his study analyzing later phases of myth where we can speak of "mythic thinking." Even here, however, we need to recognize the difference between the way reality is experienced by mythic and by post-mythic man. If we examine "myth itself, what it is and what it *knows* itself to be, we see that this separation of the ideal from the real, this distinction between a world of immediate reality and a world of mediate signification, this opposition of 'image' and 'object' is alien to it." Since we do not live in myth but reflect upon it, we are likely to read such distinctions into myth. But, Cassirer observes, "where we see mere 'representation,' myth, insofar as it has not deviated from its fundamental and original form, sees real identity. The 'image' does not represent the 'thing'; it *is* the thing; it does not merely stand for the object, but has the same actuality, so that it replaces the thing's immediate presence" (*Mythical Thought* 38).

From this basic insight into the difference between mythic "thinking" and discursive thought, Cassirer develops fundamental notions about mythic conceptions of time, space, and number. Despite the importance which the "universal intuition of time" possesses for the mythic world, Cassirer understands why the idea of mythical consciousness has been called a timeless consciousness. "For compared with objective time, whether cosmic or historical, mythic time is indeed timeless" (*Mythical Thought* 106). Historical consciousness of time "is based on a fixed chronology, a strict distinction of the earlier and the later, and the observation of a determinate, unequivocal order in the sequence of the moments of time." But myth "is aware of no such division of the stages of time, no such ordering of time into a rigid system where any particular event has one and only one position" (*Mythical Thought* 110). Full exploration of the implications of these ideas for the novels I will be discussing must await a more appropriate moment; but Isabel MacCaffrey aptly states the main point that mythical narrative, consequent on its view of time, "slights chronology in favor of a folded structure which continually returns upon itself, or a spiral that circles around a single center" (45).[6]

In *Poetic Diction*, Owen Barfield offers a twentieth-century reflection of Vico's ideas about language similar to Cassirer's mirroring of Vico's ideas on time.[7] Poetic diction, as Barfield defines it, has nothing to do with the classic use of periphrasis in the eighteenth century; rather, it is an effort by the poet to use, or better to *re*use, language in such a way as to recapture its lost emotional overtones and meanings. Language in its earliest state, which for Barfield is the period of myth, was not the abstract, emotionally neutered instrument it became in the age of logical, historical thought. Barfield suggests that such a word as *cut*, which is highly abstract and emotionally neutral, derives from earlier words (cut-with-joy-for-sacrifice) which are both highly emotive and concrete.

Most modern linguistic theory (like that on which deconstruction is based) sees the relation between name and thing as purely arbitrary. Barfield, like Cassirer, suggests that the relation is necessary; naming occurs in the prelogical era of myth when there is less, if any, differentiation between spirit and body. Our words for spirit and breath postulate both a spiritual *and* a material reality, but the word from which they etymologically derive does not postulate but simply assumes a reality in which there is no differentiation between what we see as two states (Barfield 80). In such a field of being, our logical differentiation between subject and object does not exist, and the name's relation to its object is necessary as expressive of the spiritual reality in which both subject and object participate.

Anticipating Barfield, Vico fits specifically into the mythic paradigm I have been establishing in his views of language. The needs of abstract thought have led to the creation of a language which he sees as unresponsive to ultimate realities: "But the nature of our civilized minds is so detached from the senses, even in the vulgar, by abstractions corresponding to all the abstract terms our languages abound in, and so refined by the art of writing, and as it were spiritualized by the use of numbers, because even the vulgar know how to count and reckon, that it is naturally beyond our power to form the vast image of this mistress called 'Sympathetic Nature.' Men shape the phrase with their lips but have nothing in their minds" (Vico NS 106 §378). Manuel suggests that we can parallel Vico's ideas on language with those of other eighteenth-century etymologists who also felt that "language more than any other human creation had encased and preserved the spiritual history of mankind. What distinguished them from their arid seventeenth-century predecessors was the novel idea that words bore with them a set of emotive terms which were clues to the true temper of antiquity" (218). Losing touch with antiquity and mythic language had, according to these mythographers, impoverished modern rational man.[8]

Before moving on to explore how Joyce absorbed these notions about myth, it seems wise to pause and ask what relation these ideas developed by eighteenth-century mythographers could have had to these eighteenth-century novelists. To what extent could they have been influenced by these ideas about myth? The art historian Henri Focillon has theorized that the artist may "be thoroughly contemporary with his age, and may even, because of this fact, adapt himself to the artistic activities going on around him. With equal consistency he may select examples and models from the past, and create from them a new and complete environment" (*Life* 62). But Focillon adds, "A sudden shift in the equilibrium of his ethnic values may bring him into violent opposition with his environment and hence with the moment, and arouse a nostalgia in him that is highly revolutionary" (*Life* 63). The three novelists whom I discuss have all been considered very much of their age; yet all three have also been considered in some ways revolutionary. Defoe, after all, is often credited as being the founder of a new genre; and Sterne created a unique anti-novel before the novel itself had become fully established. Smollett's *Humphry Clinker* is also a radical innovation, perhaps so radical that its significance has not yet been grasped. The value of Focillon's insight is that it makes us consider that the "revolutionary" aspect of these writers derives from their nostalgia for the past—for that primitive sense of being which the mythographers contemporary with them were finding in myth.

That nostalgia appears differently as we proceed further into the century, and it is most ambiguous with the earlier Defoe. Are his myths Christian like Milton's or reflective of earlier pagan forms? How consciously did Defoe incorporate mythic elements into his work? In *God's Plot and Man's Stories*, Leopold Damrosch explicitly equates myth with Christianity (7). In tracing how "fiction finally broke free from myth" (71), he argues that *Robinson Crusoe* embodies "a remarkable reconciliation of myth with novel" (212). His reading of the novel thus has parallels with MacCaffrey's of *Paradise Lost*. Damrosch argues that only *Crusoe* reconciles myth and novel form, for Defoe's other novels not only fail to conform to the logic of providential plan but fail "to develop an inner logic at all" (211). The later novels do, however, develop the same antithetical pattern of tensions as *Robinson Crusoe*; and, if we associate Defoe's concept of myth not with Milton's Christian idea but with that developing in the mythographers of the period, we can account for this tension not just in Defoe's first novel but in them all. I shall argue later that Defoe parallels Crusoe's experiences on the island to the Hebrews' temptation to turn aside to pagan worship as they wander in the wilderness. As Eliade and others have theorized, the Judaeo-Christian tradition is associated with the rise of history, not myth; thus, we may interpret Crusoe's return to belief as his triumph over pagan mythological thinking.[9] The tension that structures the novel, then, is the clash between Christian historical time and the timeless world of pagan myth.

Defoe had trouble sustaining the Christian vision of an orderly history. Faced with the same sense of the potential chaos of a modern naturalistic world as were Pope and Swift, he took increasing recourse to mythic modes as means of structuring his fictions. Was this use of myth simply a convenient solution to a narrative problem or the product of belief? I think it was what Focillon has called revolutionary nostalgia which earned Defoe the contempt of his more traditional contemporaries. It was not just his new, unsanctified forms or his descriptions of low life which they detested but the appeal to the pre-rational, anti-intellectual modes of being envisioned in his novels. Part of Defoe shares in that Puritan tradition that extends from Bunyan to Blake and Lawrence. Another part, of course, is more firmly grounded in history. My own belief is that this tension between myth and history works itself out unconsciously in Defoe as he searches for patterns that could help him organize the stories he created as something quite different from the tracts, pseudobiographies, and "histories" that he had been writing.

With Smollett and Sterne the situation is much more straightforward. Even though Sterne is an Anglican clergyman, there is no question here of trying to re-create a Christian myth. Smollett's ideal states are not religious ones, and Sterne's Shandy Hall seems more a parody of Eden than anything else. Nor does either author believe in recovering the mythic attitudes contemporary mythographers were exploring. But Smollett and Sterne could have shared the fascination of their age for these new understandings of myth. Their extensive travels on the Continent would have given them ample opportunity to familiarize themselves with theories of myth developed in France and Italy. As sophisticated men of letters of their time, they would be aware of the differences between a mythic consciousness and a historic one. As revolutionary artists in the Focillon mode, they could even express a good deal of nostalgia for earlier, more harmonious relations between self and world. One thinks particularly of Smollett's pictures of tranquil rural retreats in *Humphry Clinker*; Sterne also evokes scenes of idyllic peasant life in the Languedoc. Such evocations of myth are, however, clearly simulations rather than replications of earlier more unified modes of seeing. These simulations in part answered emotional needs as these writers faced both the eighteenth-century equivalent of the "nightmare of history" and also the personal traumas of their ill-health and ever-threatening death. Perhaps more importantly, such simulations also fulfilled certain narratological needs, enabling a more complex language, richer modes of characterization, a fuller sense of structure, as well as a more forgiving awareness of time.

More crucial still, narrative became an epistemological issue for these writers. Like Vico, these novelists faced the problem of a massive dislocation of their epistemological universe. Under the pressure of an encroaching positivism and empiricism, Vico and these novelists wanted to *salvage* or *rescue* something of the older mythic way of seeing reality, and did so in related and representative ways. Vico constructed a system that gives a central place to ideas about myth as I am using that term. He is the philosopher who gives conceptual status to what these novelists, and Joyce after them, try to rescue in *narrative* terms. These writers tell stories in ways that refuse to relinquish altogether the older "mythic" perception of the world.

Joyce is the twentieth-century writer who experiences anew the epistemological problem these writers are trying to solve, and who makes it *and* their response to it central to his own writing. Reading *Ulysses* compels us to see both Joyce's work and that of his "grandfathers" through the lens of revolutionary nostalgia. A myriad of sources suggest how Joyce might have absorbed this idea of myth and its narrative implications.[10] Among other relevant texts, Joyce's personal library contained Jane Harrison's *Mythology*, Renan's *Les Apôtres*, Lucien Lévy-Bruhl's *L'Âme primitive* and *L'expérience mystique et les symboles chez les primitifs* (Connolly 15 et passim). Of these, the Lévy-Bruhl texts are perhaps most significant as sources for this conception of myth (as the Harrison would be for an archetypal mode of analysis). As Janet Burstein has shown in her work on Victorian mythography,[11] Karl Otfried Müller and George Grote kept alive the idea that "myths originated among men who had not yet differentiated themselves from their natural and social worlds; myths, therefore, were understood to express a fundamental coherence of man and world, and to represent a better integrated perception of the world than the self-conscious modern mind could achieve" (Burstein "Journey" 500). While Joyce may have known Grote and Müller's work, he probably picked up these, or very similar, ideas from John Addington Symonds and, more especially, from Walter Pater. Symonds's "Nature Myths and Allegories," in *Essays Speculative and Suggestive*, was published in 1890. In it he speaks of myth's "suggestive way of regarding the universe as a spiritual whole, and man in relation to it as a part thereof" (I 130). Pater felt that myth had a "unifying or identifying power" (29) which had been lost in the evolution of mind beyond its earliest stages.

Primarily, Joyce would have acquired his ideas about myth from

Vico's *New Science*. According to A. Walton Litz, Joyce read Vico soon after 1905; and *Ulysses* reveals a number of specific Vichian influences ("Vico and Joyce" 249). Until relatively recently Joyce scholars had emphasized only his use of Vico's theory of history (developed in books 4 and 5 of the *New Science*). Litz's prediction (254) that we would come to see other influences than that of the cyclic theory of history as our knowledge of *Finnegans Wake* grew has come true in the collection of essays *Vico and Joyce*, particularly in the work of the book's editor Donald Verene. But even Verene underplays the Vichian elements in *Ulysses* which, he thinks, "have the form of allusions, not direct references" (222). *Finnegans Wake*, he says, can "be seen as what results when a linguistic genius of the first order sets out to write his way back to Vico's common mental language. The imaginative manipulation of language causes it to yield up memories out of which language itself is made" (226–27). I shall be arguing that one aspect of *Ulysses* is precisely its wish to evoke, through its manipulation of time and structure, as well as language, the primordial reality of myth.

Early critical response to Joyce's use of myth tended to be conditioned by a famous statement by T. S. Eliot. In this pronouncement, Eliot did not see (or at least has not been understood as seeing) that Joyce's use of myth was anything more than a technical expedient used to achieve structure. "In using the myth, in manipulating a continuous parallel between contemporaneity and antiquity, Mr. Joyce is pursuing a method which others must pursue after him. . . . It is simply a way of controlling, of ordering, of giving shape and a significance to the immense panorama of futility and anarchy which is contemporary history. . . . It is, I seriously believe, a step toward making the modern world possible for art" (*The Dial*, November 1923, quoted in Beebe 182). Whatever Eliot's intention, the common assumption that students of high modernism took from this passage was that Joyce used myth only as "an arbitrary means of ordering art" (Beebe 175). Deciphering the impact of Joyce's grandfathers on him will convince us that his use of myth is considerably more complex. Sharing their investment in historical processes, Joyce also shared their revolutionary nostalgia for a unified mythic vision that could solace the epistemological crises to which those processes had given rise.[12]

The Novel and the Idea of History

Although critics have often applied the myth/history dyad to Joyce's *Ulysses*,[13] they have more rarely related it to the eighteenth-century novel, preferring more narrowly focused antitheses like romance versus history, ancient versus modern, pastoral Golden Age versus modern leaden age, etc. As valuable, and sensibly scaled, as these formulations are, they are too restrictive to encompass the relationship between Joyce and his grandfathers, which invokes a formal synchrony of the past and present as well as a substantive contextual diachrony. Milton A. Goldberg's emphasis on primitivism versus progress, for example, can illuminate *Humphry Clinker*, but it does not illuminate that novel's relation to *Ulysses*. Nor, ultimately, can terms more exact, and more modest, than *myth* and *history* illuminate the questions of narrative form raised by the relationship of Joyce to his grandfathers.

Robert Scholes and Robert Kellogg have addressed such questions in *The Nature of Narrative*, which demonstrates the importance of ideas about myth and history in the evolution of narrative forms from the epic to the novel. Epic and the novel are the most admired narrative forms because they combine "most powerfully and copiously" the various aspects of narrative. "The epic, dominated by its mythic and traditional heritage, nevertheless included fictional, historical, and mimetic materials in its powerful amalgam. The novel, dominated by its growing realistic conception of the individual in actual society, nevertheless has drawn upon mythic, historical, and romantic patterns for its narrative articulation" (232). In this view, the novel is a synthesizing form in the same fashion as was the earlier epic. One aspect of this synthesis is the bringing together of mythic and historic attitudes.

Although my specifically Vichian conception contextualizes myth much more exactly than Scholes and Kellogg do, I intend to hew closely to their common-sense, empirical use of the term *history*. When they speak of the historical aspect of the great Homeric epics, I assume they mean precisely what Erich Kahler says: "These early epics are not mere fictions in our sense of the word, that is to say, not pure inventions. Rather, along with their ancient mythic materials they reproduce, at the core, real happenings, or at least *believed* realities" (9–10). Kahler's qualification about "*believed* realities" reflects not so much a doubt that fiction *can* reflect a historical reality as a doubt about the reality

Homer thought he was reflecting. Similarly, we might question the "one true history" around which medieval historians constructed their typological narratives without questioning that they *believed* their stories reflected historical realities.

This sort of typological historiography gradually yielded to linear, chronological thinking throughout the sixteenth and seventeenth centuries. History continued, however, to be conceived as dealing with real happenings: "the facts of a time, the articulable relationships of a time, the ways of knowing of a time, the ideological interpretations of a time" (Bradbury 13). Recognizing that history as practiced was a narrative form, one still thought it a basically empirical mode. The term *history,* Warner Berthoff says, "is reserved for that species of narrative in which we try to describe something that happened according to the discoverable testimony about it and by means of certifiable techniques for gathering and identifying such testimony" (270). These ideas would seem to define that sense of history which has, until very recently, been one of the defining characteristics of our modern age.

Berthoff adds that the "practice of history, so defined, seems a more recent development than myth and fiction" (270). If fiction preceded this kind of history, one particular form of fiction—the novel—quickly adopted history as its special venue. As we shall see, the line between Defoe's histories and his novels can be a thin one. The habit of calling novels by the title "The History of . . ." only suggests the affinity between fiction and history commonly accepted throughout the eighteenth century. In the nineteenth century we reach the apogee of the assimilation of the novel to history with George Eliot. She hated the idea of fiction because of the implied sense of lying and frivolity. She wanted the novel to be wedded to an idea of history so that it might be a carrier of cultural and moral values in a world that had no other assurances. With George Eliot, the "one true history" is not the God of Christian revelation but the processes and progresses of history itself.

These sweeping generalizations can serve as the prolegomena to my own sense of what history meant for these writers. Since the complications in modern analyses of history deal with its narrative aspects, it is easiest to begin with the sense of history as a source of data rather than "story." *Humphry Clinker*, for example, is filled with references to real persons (including to Smollett himself), places, and events. A large portion of the novel serves as a social history, a tour guide to the various cities the characters visit in their expedition. Similarly, Sterne's novel contains many documents drawn directly into it from the outside world. While the characters' responses to it serve a narrative function, Sterne's own sermon on "The Abuses of Conscience" (preached at York on 29 July 1750) is directly incorporated as a document into his text. Similarly, he uses such other public records as the Excommunication document and the "Memoire presenté à Messieurs les Docteurs de Sorbonne." While Defoe's use of specific reference to real persons, places, and events is more rare, that of Smollett and Sterne is unusually profuse and could have served as Joyce's model for his well-known, even notorious, dependence on historical data in his reconstruction (one might say) of Dublin in *Ulysses*. Like Smollett and Sterne, Joyce uses in his fiction historically verifiable accounts of his family life (his father and his father's friends, for instance), of place (as in his inquiry to his aunt of the actual distance of the drop from the area railing at 7 Eccles Street), and document (as in the use of speeches in Aeolus). These works are surely unusual, if not unique in the history of the novel, in the way they incorporate historical data into their structures.

When these writers use historical data as narrative, more complex issues arise. Lady Vane's history, which is interpolated directly into Smollett's *Peregrine Pickle*, is not exactly a document, for it may have been written at least in part by Smollett himself, not by Lady Vane; still, it is not a fiction either since the parameters of its story line are determined by the real-life circumstances of its subject. The story of the Annesley claimant in the same novel makes no pretense of being written in another voice than that of the narrator; but it raises the interesting question of whether that narrator is Smollett as "author" of his fiction or Smollett as historian of his friend's "story." Similarly, the "travel-notes" (New 171) Sterne incorporated in volume 7 of *Tristram Shandy* seem all the more like history when we compare how he transformed the same material into fiction in *A Sentimental Journey*. While Joyce transformed his own chance encounter with Albert Hunter into the fiction of *Ulysses* (Ellmann UL xvi), the "stories" he tells of many of the real people he brought into his novel seem as historically determined as that of Lady Vane. Simon Dedalus, for example, cannot transcend the shape given him by John Joyce.[14]

In addition to these narratives based on, or drawn from, actual historical circumstances, we have narratives that are "historical" in that they emulate reports of the real world. In *Defoe and the Uses of Narrative*, Michael M. Boardman shows how Defoe "always clung tenaciously to the older historical and pseudohistorical traditions from which they drew sustenance" (5). Even when dealing with fabricated material, Defoe, often to the disadvantage of his art, Boardman argues, tries to make that material seem "real," the matter of history. This "affectation" of the historical manner is strongest in Defoe, but it also colors the work of Smollett, Sterne, and Joyce. With their emphasis on linear time and sequence, these fictions of causality stand in polar opposition to the Vichian mode of myth.

For Northrop Frye, every narrative is a form of mythos. In his essay "History and Myth in the Bible," he argues that since there is no boundary line that separates "myth, legend, historical reminiscence, didactic history, or actual history," we have to recognize that the Bible is not a history "but a *mythos*" (7) which is "much closer to poetry than it is to actual history, and should be read as such" (11). Accepting Frye's idea of narrative, Hayden White argues in "The Fictions of Factual Representation" that history "does not therefore stand over against myth as its cognitive antithesis, but represents merely another, and more extreme form of that 'displacement' which Professor Frye has analyzed in his *Anatomy*" (31). Considering that both the novelist and the historian "wish to provide a virtual image of 'reality'" (White "Fictions" 22), White hypothesizes that there is no essential difference in the narrative forms of myth and history—the latter is simply an extreme displaced form of the former. Working from his assumptions that all history is narrative and that the form of narrative derives from myth, White concludes that there is no basic difference in the narratives of history and myth.

Because I, following Cassirer, associate the synchronicity of myth with a past, pre-rational mode of consciousness, I have less trouble than Hayden White or Northrop Frye in accepting a difference in the way myth and history inscribe themselves in narrative. In contrast to the repetitive, timeless, eventless cyclical pattern of the myth I describe, historical narratives accept the irreducible reality of time; their narrative mode is linear, based on a sense of causality, oriented toward the unique, the nonrepetitive, and the "actual" rather than the probable or the prototypical. Although the eighteenth-century novelists whom I consider share a "revolutionary nostalgia" for the synchronicity of myth, their fundamental orientation is historicist rather than mythic. Joyce in *Ulysses* is less "Vichian" than some commentators suggest; in many ways he is like these earlier novelists in their adherence to historical modes. The literary influence works both ways. If we read Joyce's "grandfathers" through Joyce's perspective, we find mythic elements within them that we had not noticed before. If we read Joyce through the grandfathers' eyes, we discover more traditional elements that we had ignored before. Creating his grandfathers, the artist is also created by them.

Joyce and His Grandfathers

Why these grandfathers and not others? Barbara Hardy suggested early in my work that Swift would be an appropriate antecedent to Joyce. Certainly, the number of allusions to his work in *Ulysses* far exceeds that of any of these others; and the idea of myth and history is particularly relevant to Swift's own work. Yet my main interest was to explore the relevance of a tradition of the English *novel* to Joyce's work; the issues I wish to explore are issues with *genre* implications which Swift's work does not address, or addresses very differently. Undoubtedly, Fielding's use of historical materials in his fiction would have resonances for Joyce's *Ulysses*. One thinks, for example, how the intricate plot of *Tom Jones* is coordinated to the historical realities of the Jacobite rebellion in much the same way "Bloomsday" is tied to the concrete events of June 16, 1904. The balanced intricacy of Fielding's plot, in contrast with the fluidity of Joyce's book, is one reason why Joyce would not have conferred grandfatherhood upon this earlier writer. Another is that Fielding's approach to myth is not Vichian but euhemeristic. As Ronald Paulson has perceptively demonstrated, Fielding as a novelist uses the euhemerism of Abbé Banier by "showing the simultaneous construction and explanation of myth, showing how it is produced by poets out of historical events" (180). As for Richardson, while I agree with Elizabeth Deeds Ermarth that *Pamela* is "mythic" (118) in the way I use the term, Richardson's *kind* of novel has more to do with realism than with the fiction Joyce produced.

Joyce remarked to Pound: "I have little or no imagination and work very laboriously, exhausting myself with trifles" (quoted in Ellmann JJ

661). We see what Joyce means. His is not the invention of a Henry James, a Lawrence, a Virginia Woolf; he does not richly fabricate stories from the inner resources of his imagination. Rather, as he remarked to Jacque Mercanton, "Why regret my talent? I haven't any. I write so painfully, so slowly. Chance furnishes me with what I need. I'm like a man who stumbles: my foot strikes something, I look down, and there is exactly what I'm in need of" (Ellmann JJ 661). None of the writers in my tradition is "imaginative" in the Jamesian sense; they all fabricate their stories from what they have stumbled upon. They use their own lives—most overtly in Smollett, most covertly in Defoe. They incorporate real people, real events, real documents, direct historical testimony into their fiction. There is a real sense in which for them, as Joyce, agreeing with Vico, told Frank Budgen, "Imagination is memory" (Ellmann JJ 661).

We find other similarities among these novelists, some of a more superficial character. They all show an interest in low life—not the romance of society or the aristocracy but the ordinariness (even squalor) of everyday life is their concern. They relish a certain degree of crudity, particularly in their scatological humor. They show a fascination with sexuality, especially in its more odd, even febrile manifestations. On a more significant level, we find that they are interested in experimental forms. They do not try to mediate stylistic oppositions, as do Richardson and the realistic tradition; instead of smoothing over differences, they are interested in testing limits, pushing contradictory narrative stances to extremes. This results in a certain roughness of juxtaposition that can create ungainly, unaccommodated fictions. When we think of these writers, we are more apt to think of Hogarth than Gainsborough, of Van Gogh than Renoir.

What, finally, lies behind these external similarities and, in fact, generates them is the way in which their fiction explores the tensions between mythic and historic modes of narration, an exploration provoked by the epistemological crises which produced these writers and their novels. Obviously, all novels work within both synchronic and diachronic axes. What I argue is that these novelists—themselves all liminal artists in relation to the central tradition of realistic fiction—are driven by the idiosyncratic nature of their imaginations to exaggerate these dialectical tensions. Such an emphasis, of course, intensifies the problems of mediation; and they achieve "concord fictions" in odd ways, if at all. If it still seems odd for me to consider such writers together, let me have recourse one final time to Focillon: "Between masters who have never had the slightest personal acquaintance, and whom everything has kept apart—nature, distance, time—the life of forms establishes an intimate relationship. Here, then, is a new refinement upon the doctrine of influences: not only is there never a question of mere passive influence, but we are not obliged to invoke influence at any cost to explain a kinship which *already* exists and which calls for no active contact" (*Life* 52). The affinity I sense is an affinity of form—a form which must be divined as well as deciphered.

Describing first the organizational pattern of my study and then illustrating my method of analysis by recurring to Bloom's ad should make it easier for my reader to "decipher" my sense of the formal affinities between Joyce and his grandfathers. Chapter 2 focuses centrally on the problem of time in Defoe. I describe certain image patterns, narrative choices, uses of emblematic characters, and emphases on liminal situations by means of which Defoe creates the effect of timelessness which Cassirer describes as characteristic of myth. In addition, drawing on Eliade, I discuss how Defoe contrasts this pagan sense of time with the historicity which developed out of the Judaeo-Christian tradition. Mythic and Christian time were important to Defoe because they offered paradigms which helped him to give a coherent shape to reality. The drama of Defoe's career as a novelist occurs when he abandons Christian time and tries to find meaning in secular linear time by infusing it with the power of myth.

Chapter 3 focuses on mythic and historical uses of language in Smollett. Widely thought of as a rationalist, Smollett shows from the earliest stages of his career as a novelist a Vichianlike idea that the most imaginative use of language occurred in primitive societies, among peasants, and frequently, one should add, among women. Most of Smollett's characters use language in rationalist ways; in fact, the failure to find a believable language for his characters is Smollett's most significant flaw as a novelist. As Barfield has argued, language in the age of myth is unitive, filled with emotional force; poetic diction in Barfield's terms attempts to reinfuse modern abstract language with some of that force. Win Jenkins's malapropisms are important, then, not as evidence of Smollett's rationalistic spoofing of philological practices but as evidence of his sense of her mythic role in his novel. At issue is the question why Smollett introduces such mythic language into a fiction which otherwise demonstrates marked tendencies toward history.

With Sterne in chapter 4, the focus is on the relation between historical and mythic narrative and plot and structure. Mythic plots are cyclic, involving characters in repetitive actions. Somewhat paradoxically, though such plots are static, allowing little opportunity for growth or change, they are complete. Thus, a mythic plot has a sense of finished shape, even if it does not allow for that sort of change and growth that we often think essential to fiction. Accepting Hannah Arendt's idea that the thread of historical continuity was "the first substitute for tradition," Kermode calls history so considered "a fictive substitute for authority and tradition, a maker of concords between past, present, and future, a provider of significance to mere chronicity" (Kermode 56). From this perspective, history creates plots which also yield a sense of order while permitting change and growth. Sterne associates plot with history; but for reasons different from Joyce's, he feels the need to escape from the patterns that history imposes. Thus he seeks to mediate between mythic and historical time by creating unclosed closures, endings that do not end. In this way, he anticipates those "concord fictions" which Kermode sees as a characteristic of our modern times and our effort to deal with "mere successiveness" without being "merely successive" (58).

Other issues than time, language, and structure certainly play a significant role in these eighteenth-century texts as well as in *Ulysses*. Nevertheless, the centrality of these particular concerns to Joyce's novel is a further illustration of why he would choose to father, as well as be fathered by, these particular grandfathers. Chapter 5 will demonstrate how *Ulysses* more effectively mediates the tensions generated by synchronic and diachronic narrative than the earlier works had. Joyce follows the example of his grandfathers in grappling with these same issues they dealt with on more rudimentary levels. He creates his grandfathers *for us* through his more sophisticated response to their common difficulty, enabling us to understand more clearly the problems they had more dimly perceived in their efforts to deal with narrative questions at the opening of the novel tradition.

Our key to *Ulysses*'s role in the tradition of the English novel has been Bloom's ad. Returning to it, we can illustrate inductively the method of analysis that will be followed in these pages. As Hynes's inquiry to Bloom in Hades becomes transformed into the reality of the obituary notice whose misspelling nettles "L. Boom" in Eumaeus, we understand that, thanks to Bloom's perseverance, the ad will exist eventually as a historical fact intended to promote the business of one Alexander Keyes. It also contains, as Bloom explains, an allusion to a historical context. "The idea . . . is the house of keys. You know, councillor, the Manx parliament. Innuendo of home rule" (99). Stanley Sultan points out that crossed keys also form a part of the emblem of the Vatican (111), which suggests the Roman Catholic influence on the Ireland of 1904. The word *ad* itself contains two letters which, being capitalized, form the abbreviation for *anno Domini*. Deciphering its horizontal implications, we find in the ad a rich cluster of references to historical acts which unfold themselves in time, implying not only extension but also sequence.

But we must also divine or intuitively apprehend the mythic implications of the ad as well. The major clue here, of course, is Bloom's phrase, "A circle." The circle, on one level, is a symbol of the feminine. We notice that woman here is archetypal, faceless in contrast with the historical specificity of the male—an individualized Alexander Keyes. Molly's anima-function is prefigured in contrast to the role specificity of the male Bloom's search for a satisfactory persona. The circle also represents the pattern of cyclic return, the pattern of life for the pagan world, as Eliade has taught us, just as the irreversibility of history became that for the Judaeo-Christian tradition. Max Schulz has finely articulated the implications of life within archaic societies: "Man lives within a mythic network of divine archetypes whose extrahuman processes he repeats in his own activities, thus giving paradigmatic value to his life. For him there is no past and future, only an ever regenerative present in its repetition of celestial beginnings" (3).

In its end of nourishing life, the ad's horizontal reading suggests the economic and political aspects of historical being. In contrast, the vertical reading continually pulls one back to the reality of death, the reabsorption in the center from which life will emerge again. We need to remember a scene from Hades to digest this point. The first mention of *two* keys together (references to Bloom's key and Stephen's at this point occurring separately) comes in the cemetery as the caretaker, John O'Connell, walks, "puzzling two long keys at his back" (88). Seeing him do so reminds Bloom of final things: "Keys: like Keyes's ad: no fear of anyone getting out. No passout checks. *Habeas corpus.* I must see about that ad after the funeral" (88). Bloom's quick mental movement from thoughts of death to thoughts of the ad mirrors historical man's fear of the archetype. In historical societies, Schulz says, "man lives in time, free to organize his present in ways calculated to affect his future. Such freedom releases him from the tyranny of conformity to archetypal patterns, but it conversely oppresses him with the burden of history and its terrors" (3).

The ad does more, however, than simply suggest irresolvable binary oppositions. The seemingly innocuous description of Alexander Keyes as a "tea, wine and spirit merchant" suggests Joyce's intent. "Tea" is material, historical; "spirit" suggests the metaphysical and the transhistorical. "Wine," with its associations with communion where body and spirit are joined, serves, then, to mediate two modes of reality. The ad becomes, in my reading, a symbol of how Joyce wants us to read his novel. Only by looking both horizontally (historically) and vertically (mythically) will we be able to grasp his "triliteral monoideal symbols" (559). By grasping the myth, the history, and the mediation between them, we will achieve the "triliteral" sense of his "monoideal" meaning; for, as Bloom says, the "infinite possibilities hitherto unexploited of the modern art of advertisement" are not only "to interest" but also "to convince, to decide."

2

Mythic and Historic Time in Defoe

Evidence outside the text of *Ulysses* as to how Joyce would have read Defoe exists in the lectures he gave on Defoe and Blake titled "Verismo ed idealismo nella letteratura inglese." While critics have recognized that the pairing reflects a tension between idealism and realism in Joyce himself, they have generally assumed that Joyce read Defoe as a realist and Blake as an idealist. Even a Vichian critic has argued that Joyce "chose to present Defoe as the embodiment of realism and poetic vision" (Hughes 83). But even in 1911–12 when these lectures were given, it was not Joyce's style to polarize radically his own ambivalences. Joseph Prescott, the editor of Joyce's lecture on Defoe for *Buffalo Studies*, seems more attuned to Joyce's purposes when he maintains that in these lectures "opposites meet as they were to meet increasingly in Joyce's fusion of realism and symbolism" (3).

Opposites meet not merely between the two lectures but within each, for Joyce's tribute to Defoe's realism is oddly conflicted and ambiguous. We need to note, first, his differentiation between Defoe's historical writings and his novels. "On the one hand, we have these writings which hinge upon some occurrence of the day and, on the other, the life-stories, which if they are not true novels in the sense in which we understand the term because they fall short in love plot, psychological analysis, and the studied balance of characters and tendencies, are literary documents in which the soul of the modern realistic novel is glimpsed like the soul that slumbers in an imperfect and amorphous organism" (15). In Defoe's historical writings, like "The Storm," Joyce finds "neither lyricism nor art for arts sake nor social criticism" (17); but "certain passages of *Robinson Crusoe* and *Duncan Campbell* [are] quite suddenly irradiated with a brief, gentle splendor" (18). Joyce does, in fact, see Defoe the historical writer as a realist; his reaction to Defoe the incipient novelist is considerably more complex.

Were Defoe still alive, Joyce speculates that "by his gifts of *exactitude and imagination*, by his farraginous experience, and by his neat prose style" (20, emphasis mine), he would be a famous special correspondent for an American or English newspaper—an Ignatius Gallaher, in fact. Exactitude is an aspect of realism, but imagination suggests something different; and Joyce's essay on Defoe demonstrates his trying to come to terms with exactly what he finds in the earlier writer. Partly, he is determined to dissociate Defoe's "realism" from the "wrathful order of corruption which illumines with pestiferous phosphorescence the sad pages of Huysmans" (23) and other types of modern realism. Joyce senses that beneath Defoe's use of characters from the "lowest dregs of the population" lies a symbolic meaning. "You will find, if anything, beneath the rude exterior an instinct and a prophecy. His women have the indecency and the continence of beasts; his men are strong and silent as trees. English feminism and English imperialism already lurk in these souls which are just emerging from the animal kingdom" (23). Joyce apparently sees Defoe's characters as reaching in two directions, backwards toward their animal origins and forward to their roles as historic prototypes.

It is easy to understand Joyce's sense of Defoe as a realist whose writings reach forward historically to fulfill certain foreshadowings of the English character. Of *Robinson Crusoe* he says: "Whoever rereads this simple, moving book in the light of subsequent history cannot help but fall under its prophetic spell" (25). Nevertheless, the word *prophecy* is paired with the word *instinct* four times within the essay (pp. 23, 24, 25); and Joyce apparently finds part of the power of Defoe in his "revolutionary nostalgia" for the past as well as in his historic thrust toward the future.

The appendix to the *Buffalo Studies* edition of Joyce's lecture includes the conclusion of a draft version which is worth looking at carefully. "The narrative which turns on this simple marvel [Crusoe's discovery of the footprint] is one long harmonious, and consistent national epic, a solemn and triumphant music accompanied by the mournful chant of the savage and artless soul. Our age, which is fond of tracing current phenomena to their sources in order to reassure itself of the truth of its evolutionist doctrine, which teaches that when we were little we were not big, could reread the story of Robinson Crusoe and his man Friday with much profit. It would find many very useful observations there for that international industry of our time, the cheap manufacture of the English imperialist type and its sale at reasonable prices" (27). There are two contradictory impulses behind this passage, which is undoubtedly why it was omitted from the lecture. These contradictions color Joyce's perception of Defoe, however, and need to be noted. Joyce clearly alludes to Vico's idea that early, mythic men existed as giants in his reference to evolutionists' inability to understand that we were "big" (giants) when we were "little" (young). We could, with profit, find this "mournful chant of the savage and artless soul" in the story of Crusoe and Friday. The other thrust of the passage does, however, validate that very evolutionist perspective it mocks; Crusoe does become the prototype of English imperialism.

Joyce's general impulse in the lecture was to show that in Defoe "the star of poetry is conspicuous, as the saying goes, by its absence" (18). Thus this draft conclusion, with its patent ambivalence about what we can find in Defoe, needed to be eliminated. But even within the body of the text we discover that Joyce's "reading" of Defoe is not so simple as we have assumed. He differentiates the "life-stories" or incipient novels from the historical materials; and while he wants to make these novels serve his attack on the English character, he cannot ignore their evocation of instinctual life beneath their "prophetic spell." Nor can he ignore the imagination that underlies their exactitude. Unlike Virginia Woolf's, Joyce's Defoe is not one confined to a "sense of reality."

Since the early work of G. A. Starr and J. Paul Hunter, we too have become accustomed to reading Defoe as more than a realist; indeed, allegorical and symbolic readings are now perhaps the norm rather than the exception. Although myth is too central to Defoe's fiction not to have been addressed by many other critics, only two have looked at Defoe's use of myth from an epistemological rather than an archetypal, etiological, or other mode. As I pointed out in chapter 1, Damrosch associates myth with "God's plot." Where MacCaffrey showed how Milton re-created the Christian myth in his poem, Damrosch suggests the "tangled development of the novel flows directly *from the myth itself*, dramatizing tensions that lie at its very heart" (15). Perceiving less tension, Ermarth parallels MacCaffrey's analysis more closely, suggesting that "Crusoe shifts out of time into a providential universe where ordinary measures, especially temporal ones, are meaningless" (106). Following Eliade's association of myth with pagan time and history with Judaeo-Christian time, I believe we ought to read Defoe's fiction not as caught between nonbelief and Christianity, but as poised between pagan belief in the synchronic nature of reality, the "timeless" world of myth that Cassirer describes, and a diachronic sense of historical being. In other words, we find a different explanation for the tensions that obviously exist in Defoe's fictions and which have caused such diametrically opposed readings of his works. He is not a historicist who is hypocritical about his Christian professions, but a Christian-historicist who has a certain nostalgia for mythic remnants.

Focusing itself primarily in terms of his treatment of time,[1] Defoe's "revolutionary nostalgia" for myth relates as much to technical problems the novel form raised for him as to deeper epistemological uncertainties. Defoe's commitment to retrospective narration inevitably locks him into a historical conception of time; yet, on the simplest level, he recognizes the advantages of immediacy to be found in the present tense. His persistent efforts to counteract the effects of retrospection suggest, on a deeper level, his larger ambiguity about historicism. The other technical problem time raises for Defoe deals with closure. As long as he works within the premises of Christian time, Defoe can effectively "end" his fictions. Once he begins, as did his grandson Joyce, to envision history as a nightmare, he loses that control. His efforts to find solutions for the problems of closure in mythic cyclicity are faltering and problematic, yet they serve as foreshadowings of Joyce's more sophisticated treatment of time in *Ulysses*.

Robinson Crusoe's "Journal" is such a confusing mishmash that one is tempted simply to write it off as another illustration of Defoe's fabled carelessness. Written not as its events occur but about a year and a half later when Crusoe had gotten settled enough to build a table, the journal is itself a retrospective narrative. Thus the described events are subject to editorializing from this later perspective. But, as in the June 16 entry where Crusoe notes that he might have gotten hundreds of turtles on the other side of the island (86), the insight is often that of the sixty-odd-year-old narrator of the main narrative rather than the much younger writer of the journal. Added to these unconscious (perhaps careless) breaks in the authenticity of the journal as a record written only a year and a half after the fact are the extended commentaries on the miracle of the barley and Crusoe's illness which can only have been written by the narrator of the novel, not by the narrator of the journal.

What purpose does the journal serve? One would be tempted to relate it to the Puritan tradition of keeping a journal as a way of enabling one to turn time to productive Christian purposes, but Defoe seems specifically to deny that idea. Earlier, Crusoe describes his notched post by means of which he kept his "Kalander, or weekly, monthly, and yearly reckoning of Time" (64). But in the journal entry of November 7 he tells us, "I soon neglected my keeping Sundays, for omitting my Mark for them on my Post, I forgot which was which" (72). Crusoe will go back to notching his Sundays and will, ultimately, be delighted that his Kalander is only one day off "real" time. But prefigured here is the tension in the novel between the linear time of the retrospective account and the daily cyclicity of the journal, or more immediately lived story.

The purpose of the journal is to counteract the historicity of retrospective narration with some of the immediacy and consequent suspense of the present. Since any journal entry, no matter how immediate, involves past tense verbs, Defoe's most effective achievement of immediacy is in those brief entries that do not use verbs. Crusoe's entries about his sickness (June 19–25), by omitting verbs ("Very ill," "A little better," "Very bad again," etc. [86]), evoke some of the immediacy and suspense that the past tense of retrospection kills. A more significant repression of historical time occurs tellingly in the Christmas season:

> Dec 24. Much Rain all Night and all Day, no stirring out.
> Dec 25. Rain all Day.
> Dec.26. No Rain, and the Earth much cooler than before and pleasanter. (75)

Where we might have expected the date would awaken Crusoe to reflections on the pattern of the Christian year and historical time, we find only an underlining of the immediacy of the present.

Crusoe has two calendars: one is the post to whose marking of the linear and Christian year he is intermittently faithful, and the other is the calendar by means of which he marks the rainy and dry seasons (106). No verbs mark this calendar, for it is purely cyclic; and Defoe recognizes how much of his effort to delineate Crusoe's psychic stability in his twenty-eight-year captivity will depend on his (and the reader's) attunement to the underlying rhythms of natural recurrence rather than to historical time. To think of historical time in Crusoe's situation would drive one mad; to think in terms of the cyclic repetitions of the seasons becomes more manageable. By interweaving the journal and retrospective narration, Defoe tries to loosen his readers from strict commitment to historical time. After analyzing retrospectively how his illness led to his Christian repentance, Crusoe remarks, "But leaving this Part, I return to my Journal" (97). In fact, he does not, and the whole journal device disappears at this point. To return to the journal would be to return to present time rather than to retrospection and to return to nature rather than to Christian repentance. Clearly, both to maintain some suspense for his narrative and to indulge his nostalgia for myth, Defoe wants to qualify as much as he can the historicity of his retrospective narrative stance. By suggesting that the narrative itself has become the journal, he creates such an illusion.

One central image pattern reinforces the effort to achieve the immediacy of a timeless present that we have found in these journal entries. Whether in the baskets he weaves, the pots he makes, the rounds he walks between his various "estates," the enclosures he persistently constructs, Defoe uses the circle to show Robinson Crusoe's commitment to the cyclic. His fort-house is the most interesting of these images. Crusoe details for us the careful placement of his tent against the wall of the cliff and then describes how he hollows out storage places behind it. Fearful of discovery, he plants first one half-circle of trees and then another around the tent until, finally, he must let himself down from the top of the cliff by a ladder which he draws after him whenever he wants to enter or leave his dwelling space. Although the cave may become a womb where Robinson "must recreate himself within that mother" (Erickson 59–60), the metaphysical implications of the image are more important than the psychological. Eliade has shown the importance of the *omphalos,* or world navel, for the archaic sense of cyclic time. These holy places were worshiped as spots from which life emerged only to return and eventually begin anew the physical cycle of human existence (12–17). In this sense, Crusoe lives in a mythic mode where he re-creates himself each time he lets himself down into this "world navel." Responding to the symbolic value of the circle, we see Defoe's "revolutionary nostalgia" for the world of perpetual mythic renewal; and the power that his images have over us bespeaks our own continued attraction to such vision.

Beyond these efforts (through manipulation of retrospective narration and the use of imagery) to create a sense of immediacy lies Defoe's larger effort to use the tensions between mythic and historical time to structure his novel. The pattern for the novel, upon which its successful closure will depend, is found in the cautionary example drawn from Exodus 16:1ff., which the Spanish prisoner uses to warn Crusoe against sending over too quickly for the other shipwrecked sailors: "You know, says he, the Children of *Israel,* though they rejoyc'd at first for their being deliver'd out of *Egypt,* yet rebell'd even against God himself that deliver'd them, when they came to want Bread in the Wilderness" (191). This passage becomes an emblem for Crusoe's own adventures on the island. Like the Hebrews, he will worship at the false altars of cyclicity and repetition. Awakened to the weaknesses of mythic vision, he will reenter Judaeo-Christian historic time. His progress, like that of the Hebrew tribes, will be a dilatory one, with many shiftings back and forth between pagan and redeemed time.[2] Only with the coming of Friday will Crusoe finally enter historical time in a permanent way.[3]

Looking closely at one extended sequence will demonstrate the novel's tensions between mythic and historical time. Crusoe sets out on his effort to sail around his island on the sixth of November, "in the sixth Year of my Reign, or my Captivity, which you please" (137). From the point of view of myth, he reigns as the omnipotent controller of his world where he is perpetually reborn; from the point of view of history, he is a captive, unable to escape the dread chain of circumstances that has ensnared him. At this point, Crusoe creatively balances the two orientations to time; but as happens so frequently, an external catastrophe drives him toward God and historical time. The first occasion had been his illness; this time it is the danger of being swept out to sea. He is, however, saved. "When I was on Shore I fell on my Knees and gave God Thanks for my Deliverance, resolving to lay aside all Thoughts of my Deliverance by my Boat" (141). Besides turning Crusoe toward God, the other consequence of this adventure is to make him miss "Society" (144).

Within a page we are brought to Crusoe's eleventh year (145) without being told how he has passed the time other than his having created a wheel to arrive at "an unexpected Perfection in my Earthen Ware" (144); to have much improved his Wicker Ware (144); to have built "Traps" and "Pit-Falls" for the goats (145); and to have made "Enclosures" to contain them (146). This emphasis on images of containment and circularity suggests a reabsorption in the mythic. Although he quotes Psalm 78:19, "What a Table was here spread for me in a Wilderness" (148), Crusoe's description of himself at table appeals not to our sense of Christian history but to our mythic sense of omnipotence: "It would have made a Stoick smile to have seen, me and my little Family sit down to Dinner; there was my Majesty the Prince and Lord of the whole Island; I had the Lives of all my subjects at my absolute command. I could hang, draw, give Liberty, and take it away, and no Rebels among all my Subjects" (148). If only over dogs, cats, and parrot, Crusoe is king, a "ruler" not a "captive."

The next major event occurs within a few pages: Crusoe discovers the footprint on the beach (153). Where previous crises have reawakened religious feeling, this one occasions a curious waffling in Crusoe which is reflected in an undercutting of the authority of retrospective narration by passages which stress the *now* of the present. First, he declares that "Fear banish'd all my religious Hope; all that former Confidence in God which was founded upon such wonderful Experience as I had had of his Goodness, *now* vanished" (156, my emphasis). The next two pages, however, show him reconciling himself to God's will. We do not learn till later that this reconciliation did not occur until a long time had passed: "And it afforded me a great many curious Speculations afterwards, when I had a little recover'd my first Surprize; I consider'd that this was the Station of Life the infinitely wise and good Providence of God had determin'd for me . . . and that it was my Part to submit to bear his Indignation, because I had sinn'd against him" (156–57). Since Crusoe says this determination led him to go abroad again and to "milk his Flock," we assume it came to him soon after the sighting of the footprint. Yet within a page he tells us, "I did not *now* take due Ways to compose my Mind, by crying to God in my Distress, and resting upon his Providence, as I had done before, for my Defence and Deliverance" (159–60, my emphasis). Like the Hebrews, Crusoe will move back and forth between belief in God's historical time and pagan cyclicity. Defoe's task, awkwardly accomplished here, will be to focus on the immediate absorption in myth while indicating Crusoe's ultimate deliverance.

Leaving vague the details of Crusoe's struggle with religion, Defoe's narrative specifies that one of Crusoe's first actions on the discovery of the footprint and the retreat from religious resolution is to increase his fortifications. "I resolv'd to draw me a second Fortification, in the same Manner of a Semicircle, at a Distance from my Wall just where I had planted a double Row of Trees, about twelve Years before" (161). It is at this time that Crusoe seals up his castle in such a way that it can be entered only by ladder (162), thereby achieving the perfect *omphalos,* from which he emerges and to which he retreats. In other words, his ultimate response to the footprint is to immerse himself more fully in the mythic framework. "I continu'd pensive, and sad, and kept close within my own Circle for almost two Years after this: When I say my own Circle, I mean by it, my three Plantations, *viz.* my Castle, my Country Seat, which I call'd my Bower, and my Enclosure in the Woods" (166).

One of the things that preoccupies Crusoe after he discovers that the savages are cannibals is his plan to destroy them. Only gradually does he talk himself out of this response. Interestingly, the religious motive comes in only last; his first reasons for not doing so are drawn more from secular history. Since volumes 2 and 3 of Defoe's saga about Robinson Crusoe become less mythic and more insistently historical, it is interesting to compare a passage from *Robinson Crusoe*, on the killing by the Spanish of so many millions of native South Americans, with one on a similar theme from the *Serious Reflections* (vol. 3). In the former Crusoe decides that one reason *not* to slaughter the cannibals is that it "would justify the Conduct of the *Spaniards* in all their Barbarities practis'd in *America,* and where they destroy'd Millions of these People, who however they were Idolators and Barbarians, and had several bloody and barbarous Rites in their Customs, such as sacrificing human Bodies to their Idols, were yet, as to the *Spaniards,* very innocent people" (171–72). In "Of the Proportions between the Christian and Pagan World," chapter 6 from the *Serious Reflections*, Crusoe, the nominal narrator, justifies the destruction of "millions" of natives because they followed rites of blood sacrifice. He advocates a war on the pagans: "This is my *cruisado,* and it would be war as justifiable on many accounts as any that was ever undertaken in the world, a war that would bring eternal honour to the conqueror, and an eternal blessing to the people conquer'd" (251). When under the influence of myth on the island, Crusoe is much more tolerant; in the *Serious Reflections*, where he has entered the historical world, he becomes a religious bigot. Eric Voegelin speaks of the "easy toleration" of one society's mode of ordering for that of another during the compact, mythic phase of man's development. Rivalry among competing orders only developed in the differentiated mode when history arose (*Order and History* I 6ff.). Some such idea lies behind Crusoe's different responses here.

Crusoe lives, as many critics have pointed out, much of his island experience in a state of fear. How are we to accommodate these fears to the anxiety-free life archaic man supposedly lived? In the first place, one doubts that the absence of fear, or better, knowledge of death which Eliade sees as the primary benefit of living in cyclic time actually relieved archaic man of all the discomforts and anxieties of his existence. We also notice, however, that Crusoe's response to his fears is to seek ever-deeper centers, as though he could overcome these anxieties if he could penetrate deeply enough into the core. It is, of course, at this point that he discovers his cave, the place where he can cache his powder and his valuables. Likening himself to the Cyclops, he thinks of himself as having at last found a safe haven: "I fancy'd my self now like one of the ancient Giants, which are said to live in Caves, and Holes, in the Rocks, where none could come at them; for I perswaded my self while I was here, if five hundred Savages were to hunt me, they could never find me out; or if they did, they would not venture to attack me here" (179). Here, in Crusoe's twenty-third year of residence on the island, we can most appreciate the romantic, or mythic, readings of the novel. Crusoe reflects that he has become "so naturaliz'd to the Place, and to the Manner of Living" that if he could have only had "Certainty that no Savages would come to the Place to disturb" him, he could "have been content to have capitulated for spending the rest of my Time there, even to the last Moment, till I had laid me down and dy'd, like the old Goat in the Cave" (180). Having penetrated so deeply to the center, Crusoe does find that contentment we nostalgically associate with archaic life. In aligning himself with the old goat he buried in the cave, he sees himself now as a part of the ongoing cycle of life—not merely human life—emerging from and reentering the *omphalos*, life constantly being renewed.[4]

Two events reawaken Crusoe's historic sense. The cannibals come for the first time to his side of the island; and, then, he discovers and subsequently visits the wreck of the Spanish ship. The intensified fear of the cannibals revives the religious sense which has been intermittent throughout the whole island experience; but the wreck awakens in Crusoe a desire for companionship that seems to overwhelm the religious impulse: "All my Calm of Mind in my Resignation to Providence, and waiting the Issue of the Dispositions of Heaven, seem'd to be suspended" (198). The metaphysical and human needs converge, of course, in the coming of Friday; and it is Crusoe's instruction of Friday in religion that completes his own conversion to historical time. He reflects that in teaching Friday about God: "I really inform'd and instructed myself in many Things, that either I did not know, or had not fully consider'd before" (220). At this point, Crusoe feels a different sort of pleasure than that he had felt at his high point of mythic absorption. Now that he sees himself as an agent to save Friday's soul by awakening him to the truths of Christian revelation, he says that "a secret Joy run through every Part of my Soul" (220). He adds that their conversations about religion were such "as made the three Years which we liv'd there together perfectly and compleatly happy, *if any such Thing as compleat Happiness can be form'd in a sublunary State*" (220).[5]

The concluding episodes of the novel extend and comment on the sense of a complete pattern that Friday's conversion gives the novel. Crusoe's masterful retaking of the ship from the mutineers demonstrates that he can not only recognize the value of but that he can become decisively involved in history. While critics have generally dismissed the episode in which Crusoe and his party fight off a pack of wolves in the Pyrenees as an embarrassing blot on the novel—something written to pad out the tale, it provides, as David Blewett has cogently argued, "the final and appropriate demonstration of Crusoe's control in the face of the terrors and dangers of the world" (42). Since the wolves can be read as emblems of the terrors of historical existence, Crusoe's mastery of them symbolizes his final commitment to, and effective manipulation of, his life in historical time. Instead of being a blot on the novel, the episode completes its symbolic pattern. Nevertheless, one cannot help feeling that the novel has gone on too long, that Defoe has effectively "closed" his fiction long before he actually ended it.

Defoe's "revolutionary nostalgia" is for the timeless world of the primitive which Vico was to make so important to James Joyce. It is a world which looks at time as Cassirer has described it for us. At its ultimate (as seen in Crusoe's reflections on the cave and the dead goat), it is a timeless world; on planes of lesser intensity, it is still a world which relates to time in ways different from our rational, scientific one. Time hovers for Crusoe between two different kinds of reality; throughout most of his island experience he lives in a liminal world between the time of myth and that of history.[6]

This concept of liminality is a key motif throughout not just *Robinson Crusoe* but all of Defoe's novels. In *The Ritual Process*, Victor Turner tells us that "liminality is frequently likened to death, to *being in the womb*, to invisibility, to *darkness*, to bisexuality, *to the wilderness*, and to an eclipse of the sun or moon" (95, emphasis mine). It is a threshold state where one lives in a world which is not simply itself but which partakes of another realm. One thinks immediately of Defoe's worlds of pirates, thieves, mistresses, sailors, "gentlemen," and primitive peoples who live on borderline oceans, islands, African deserts, etc. In these worlds and vocations which so fascinated Defoe, people live liminally between law and disorder, civilization and anarchy, culture and nature. Undoubtedly, Defoe sensed that an appeal to darkness would make a good selling point for his fiction; but as my underlinings in the Turner quotation indicate, part of Defoe's genius was to recognize that deeper than the atavistic drive was one toward the peace of the womb. Defoe's next novel,[7] *Captain Singleton*, extends Defoe's interests in the liminal world from the womb and darkness of Crusoe's cave to the wilderness of Africa and the pirate seas.

An earlier version of Captain Bob's story, *The King of the Pirates*, was written in the mode of factual history. In choosing to treat *Captain Singleton* more as a novel than as history, Defoe faces again the problems of retrospective narration and closure. From a novelistic point of view, he offers only non-solutions for these issues, thereby disbalancing his fiction towards myth. Since Bob is consistently associated with the liminal worlds of the mutineer and the pirate, Defoe can free him from any sort of moral concern. After the ship he was sailing on is captured by an Algerine rover, he remarks, "I was not much concerned at the Disaster" (3). When he has been taken as a mutineer, he remarks, "The Manner of his [the captain's] Process I was too young to take Notice of; but the Purser and one of the Gunners were hang'd immediately, and I expected it with the rest. I do not remember any great Concern I was under about it" (10). The same pattern is repeated on Madagascar and even much later on the trip to the African coast, where he remarks, "I had no Anxieties about it; so that we had but a View of reaching some Land or other, I cared not what or where it was to be, having at this time no Views of what was before me, nor much Thought of what might, or might not, befal me" (44). The novel is in fact "surprisingly free from moral comment; the reader tends to lose all sense of right and wrong, and simply to follow Singleton from one piratical success to the next" (Sutherland 147).

Defoe associates this ethical neutrality with an indifference to a Christian sense of time. Bob reflects that "Fate certainly thus directed my Beginning, knowing that I had Work which I had to do in the World, which nothing but one hardened against all Sense of Honesty or Religion could go thro' " (6–7). When his Portuguese master threatens him with the Inquisition, he reflects, "as I knew nothing about Religion, neither *Protestant* from *Papist,* or either of them from a *Mahometan,* I could never be a Heretick" (7–8). Becoming a papist to avoid the Inquisition, Bob has few qualms about joining in a pagan ritual (60–61) with the African natives whom he wants to carry the pirates' equipment across Africa. He is, in fact, a free and pagan personality, as indifferent to his own fate as he is to that of the African natives he leads two thousand miles across Africa, only callously to abandon them. It is not simply that "Singleton is hardly a moral agent at all" (Sutherland 147), but that he lives, literally, without any sense of the historic meaning of his life.

By not allowing Bob any moral growth, Defoe obviates the problem of retrospective narration. Had Bob achieved any real moral insight, his narrative of his past amoral experiences would be conflicted between his present perspective and his past amorality. As it is, Defoe's treatment of Bob obliterates any distinction between past and present, giving Bob a life that has a spatial reality but not one of sequence. As

Alkon astutely notes, Defoe "shifts in *Captain Singleton* from temporal to spatial verisimilitude" (31). Such emphasis on space over time is, of course, one characteristic of myth.

The organization of the novel around two repetitive sequences of event, each taking Bob away from England and then finally back, stresses the idea of repetition and forestalls any effective sense of closure. The central event of the first sequence is the pirates' trek across Africa. Nearing the Atlantic coast, Bob and his men meet a stark naked Englishman living with a remote tribe. As Quaker William will represent an alter ego pushing Bob toward history in the second sequence, the Englishman represents one that would lead Bob deeper into myth.[8] He counsels that they seek out the gold that lies all about them. An obvious manna symbol, the gold tempts the men to stay in pagan nature rather than to return to the civilization that they have been so industriously seeking. Bob says, "the Tongue of our new Acquaintance had a Kind of Charm in it, and used such Arguments, and had so much the Power of Perswasion, that there was no resisting him" (131). They stay for six months, are trapped by the rainy season, and then stay for another three months to capitalize on the gold which has been washed from the hills. Finally, however, they decide to leave for the shore and civilization. Paradoxically, Bob's very lack of historic experiences is the factor that saves him from engulfment in manna worship; he remarks, "I had no Notion of a great deal of Money, or what to do with my self, or what to do with it if I had it" (132).

Having returned to society, Bob has no sense of how to live there and soon squanders and loses his money. Thus he enters the second sequence of his adventures with the same attitude he took in the first: "I did not care where I went, having nothing to lose, and no Body to leave behind me" (138). Soon, Bob is deeply enmeshed in the life of a pirate. In one dramatic episode, Bob and his crew attack a ship and discover a group of Negro slaves who have rebelled and killed or driven off the white sailors who were transporting them. Having no knowledge of sailing or navigation, the Negroes have let the ship wander at its will around the ocean. With no language to communicate with the whites, they cannot easily answer questions. But even beyond that, they lack any historic sense of what has happened to them: "They could give me no Account whereabouts this [place of their rebellion] was, whether near the Coast of *Africk*, or far off, or how long it was before the Ship fell into our Hands; only in general, it was a great while ago, *as they called it,* and by all we could learn, it was within two or three Days after they had set sail from the Coast" (163). The situation of the Negroes represents the extreme expression of mythic existence in the novel. Although there are obvious contrasts, the situation of the pirate crew parallels that of the drifting Negroes. While articulate, the pirates do not really understand their relations to historical reality any better than the Negroes do; they drift about, constantly seeking the manna of wealth but without, as Bob says, any real sense of its meaning.

As the naked Englishman suggested the mythic emphasis of the first sequence, William the Quaker functions as an emblem of history in this second one. Forced to join the pirates because he has medical skills, William really does so willingly since he is a "very merry Fellow" (143). Having prudentially insisted upon Bob's signing a certificate saying he was impressed against his will so that if captured he will not be automatically hanged, William thus gains relatively safe entree into the free and irresponsible world of the pirates. In return, he brings education, a moral sense, and a historical perspective to Bob. When the pirates capture the Negro ship, they prepare to torture the Negroes because they will not answer their questions. William logically points out something that seems never to have occurred to the pirates: the Negroes do not know the language of the questioners and cannot therefore understand them (160–61). Bob quickly grasps the lesson even if his second lieutenant has great difficulty in doing so. After the pirates hear that some Europeans have been stranded in Japan, William tries to convince the crew that it is their moral duty to save these men from pagan idolaters as a way of "making amends for the Mischiefs [they] had done in the World" (203). In this instance, he finds that his words have very little weight with men who are as idolatrous as the Japanese. Bob says: "we, that had no Concern upon us for the Mischiefs we had done, had much less about any Satisfaction to be made for it; so he found that kind of Discourse would weigh very little with us" (203). Quaker William's presence is not forceful enough to make the second sequence of events anything other than a repetition of the first.

Although William convinces Bob to leave off trade and to repent, the novel offers no satisfactory sense of closure. Instead of achieving a linear development leading to a convincing reversal, *Captain Singleton*'s plot is essentially a mythic one, circling back upon itself. While the naked Englishman and Quaker William attest to Defoe's sense of the tension between myth and history, neither exerts a strong enough influence to enable Defoe to reach a satisfactory way of ending his fiction.

Defoe's return in *Moll Flanders* to a more serious consideration of the relations between myth and Christian history intensifies the problem of retrospective narration. Since Captain Bob underwent no appreciable conversion experience, his gusto in recounting his experiences raises none of the charges of hypocrisy that have been so frequently aimed at Moll. Being converted to the true view, Moll ought not take such pleasure in her adventures. We note, however, that Moll's "gusto" is more sharply evident during her thieving years than at other points in the novel. Moll's experiences as a thief form the mythic core of her novel just as his island adventures did for Robinson Crusoe, and Defoe underlines Moll's feelings of gusto and primacy as a way of suggesting their mythic character. The gusto gives a sense of immediacy that effectively characterizes the experiences but which works oddly within the larger context of retrospective analysis.

By framing Moll's experiences in the liminal world of thievery on one end by her discovery of her real mother in Virginia and on the other by her reconciliation with her son, Defoe differentiates his mythic picture from the historical recounting. Within this frame, Moll abandons those family relationships that tie her to history and assumes those proper to synchronic reality. In spite of Moll's misgivings that parting with her child by Jemy means to let him be murdered by uncaring nurses, the governess convinces Moll that she can and must do it: "As I was very free with my Governness, who I had now learn'd to call Mother; I represented to her all the dark Thoughts which I had upon me about it, and told her what distress I was in. She seem'd graver by much at this Part than at the other; but as she was harden'd in these things beyond all possibility of being touch'd with the Religious part, and the Scruples about the Murther; so she was equally impenetrable in that Part, which related to Affection" (174). Consistently associated with the mythic mode in the novel, the word "harden'd" signifies Moll's ability to free herself from those family ties that restrict freedom. Rejecting her historical role as mother, the fifty-year-old Moll is free to play "child" to her "Mother Midnight."

This relationship is "a parody of the natural relationship of mother and child" (Blewett 78) only as it underlines how the mythic mode frees Moll from the reality of time. Eternally repeating her acts of theft, she here lives in a way that precludes development into adulthood and creates her as a permanent "child." Ironically, Moll becomes trapped in the pattern of repetition. She castigates the drunken man whom she has taken to bed: "Thus you see having committed a Crime once, is a sad Handle to the committing of it again; whereas all the Regret, and Reflections wear off when the Temptation renews itself" (236–37). But this passage perfectly describes Moll's own career as a thief. Although early in the process she wants to stop thieving, her governess/mother influences her to continue. Soon, she says, "I had not so much as the least inclination to leave off" (221). Finally, as the governess tries to convince her to stop, she says: "I was as backward to it now as she was when I propos'd it to her before, and so in an ill Hour we gave over the Thoughts of it for the present, and, in a Word, I grew more hardn'd and audacious than ever, and the Success I had, made my Name as famous as any Thief of my sort ever had been" (262).

The disruptions of chronological sequence in the thievery sections provide Defoe another means of introducing a kind of mythic presentness into the larger pattern of historical retrospection. Time as we know it historically is irrelevant to Moll's life as a thief because that life is not dependent on sequence. Thus, immediately after having committed her first robbery of a watch, Moll comments: "My new Partner in Wickedness *and I* went on together so long, without being ever detected, that we not only grew Bold, but we grew Rich, and we had at one time One and Twenty Gold Watches in our Hands" (202–3). From a strictly historicist view, such comment seems a narrative mistake: it reduces suspense, takes away surprise, deprives the story of climax, interferes with the development of character. Yet, that is Defoe's point: as thief, Moll *is* free from the ordinary confines of temporality. She lives in a repetitive rather than a sequential world.

Moll becomes conscious at one point of the difficulties that life defined by repetitive acts makes for ordinary narration. She tells the story of how she disguised herself as a man, joined forces with a young lad, and was nearly brought down after he was caught. She then recites her adventures in the country while she waited for the trail to cool; and then she describes a similar instance where she worked with another woman who was caught carrying goods Moll had stolen. Breathing a sigh of relief when the woman is transported, she remarks: "The Disaster of this Woman was some Months before that of the last recited Story, and was indeed partly the Occasion of my Governess proposing to Dress me up in Men's Clothes, that I might go about unobserv'd" (223). In historical narrative, such inversion of event would be confusing, but in a world of repetitive action the failure of sequence does not matter. The shape of the narrative comes from repetition, not from cause and effect.

The reintroduction of Jemy, Moll's Lancashire husband, becomes another means to keep the presentness of myth vivid despite retrospective narration. Since he had been a highwayman "full five and twenty Year, and had never been taken" (304), his life, Moll enviously says, "would have made a much more pleasing History, than this of mine" (304). What is interesting is that Jemy's story, unlike Moll's, persistently refuses to lend itself to history. Although an otherwise unexplained "great Person" (305) has arranged for Jemy to be transported rather than hanged, he refuses to submit to transportation because "Servitude and hard Labour were things Gentlemen could never stoop to . . . it was but the way to force them to be their own Executioners" (301–2). The religious allegory is obvious; God requires Jemy to submit to His service and to work by the sweat of his brow. Were Jemy to undergo a conversion, his story would indeed become a "history" parallel to Moll's.

But Jemy's mythic idea of himself as a gentleman never permits him to attune himself to Christian history. Convinced by Moll to submit to circumstances, he is much mortified to have been brought on board ship as a prisoner "since it was first told him he should Transport himself, and so that he might go as a Gentleman at liberty" (311). Indeed, Moll can only note that "he was as much at a loss as a Child what to do with himself, or with what he had, but by Directions" (311). Living in jail "as he did in a Figure like a Gentleman" (311), Jemy has wasted much of his "stock" and depends largely upon Moll for both personal and financial direction. Nor does he prove much more helpful in Virginia: "The Case was plain, he was bred a Gentleman, and by Consequence was not only unacquainted, but indolent, and when we did Settle, would much rather go into the Woods with his Gun, which they call there Hunting, and which is the ordinary work of the *Indians*, and which they do as servants; I say he would much rather do that, than attend the natural Business of his Plantation" (328). The identification between the "gentleman" and the "Indians" here is telling, suggesting that Defoe saw similar archaisms in both.

In refusing conversion and thus closure, Jemy's story parallels Moll's experiences as a thief. The pattern of such mythic sequences arises from repetition rather than resolution. Although Moll remains attracted to the world of repetition (she lays out her final £250 of stock to make Jemy "appear, as he really was, a very fine Gentleman" [340]), her retrospective narrative is a truer "history" than Jemy's and needs to be resolved. *Moll Flanders* marks Defoe's last real effort to try to achieve closure by appeal to the conversion experience. One suspects that concern for narrative strategy played more of a role than desire to illustrate the value of belief in Defoe's decision in this text. There is even a suggestion in the narrative that history per se begins to take precedence over Christian history.

Moll's reentry into historical time is said to begin on Christmas Day, though the theft for which she is imprisoned does not take place till three days later. "It was," she says, "on the *Christmas-day* following in the Evening, that to finish a long Train of Wickedness, I went Abroad to see what might offer in my way" (269). What offers is an empty silversmith's shop where Moll is apprehended before she actually steals anything and manages to brazen her way out of being taken before a judge. Why did Defoe not simply have Moll imprisoned for this attempted theft rather than letting her talk her way out of it only to be apprehended and sent to Newgate three days later? While he wants ultimately to show that her salvation will come through her Christian repentance (which would appropriately begin on Christmas Day, a time for spiritual rebirth), he apparently wants first to show that she must reenter historical time. She cannot move immediately from the synchronic view of pagan myth to Christianity; first, she must attune herself to the realities of life in history.

In Newgate Moll's life will begin for a second time. She will make "the discovery of her identity" (Blewett 80) there; but it will be a complex pattern that evolves from a humanist perception of diachronic truth to the Christian revelation where transcendent vision arises out of history.[9] In these terms, the free, mythic self becomes oppressed by the forces of history to the point that it loses all sense of autonomy and surrenders to external reality. Moll's initial description of Newgate supports such a reading as does her initial response to the environment: "I was carried to *Newgate;* that horrid Place! my very Blood chills at the mention of its Name; the Place, where so many of my Comrades had been lock'd up, and from whence they went to the fatal Tree; the Place where my Mother suffered so deeply, where I was brought into the World, and from whence I expected no Redemption, but by an infamous Death: To conclude, the Place that had so long expected me, and which with so much Art and Success I had so long avoided" (273). This is a powerful, evocative passage; yet we note that only the image of the "fatal tree" and the word "redemption" evoke Christian repentance. Otherwise, as John J. Richetti notes, the picture is one of "compulsive circumstance" (133) where Moll can no longer live in the warm world of myth but must endure historical existence leading not to repetition but to final death.

Moll's awakening to religion forms a complex pattern; at first she insists that her repentance is an unsatisfying one: "I was a Penitent as I thought, not that I had sinn'd, but that I was to suffer, and this took away all the Comfort, and even the hope of my Repentance in my own Thoughts" (274). Later, she pinpoints her failure more explicitly: "And now I was ingulph'd in the misery of Punishment, and had an infamous Death Just at the Door, and yet I had no Sense of my Condition, no Thought of Heaven or Hell at least, that went any farther than a bare flying Touch . . . I neither had a Heart to ask God's Mercy or indeed to think of it, and in this I think I have given a brief Description of the compleatest Misery on Earth" (279). Like Stephen Dedalus (who has similarly tried to find comfort in a mythic perception), Moll has to face the "nightmare of history."

Joyce posited no easy Christian solution for Stephen, and commentators have argued for years over whether we can take Defoe's solution for Moll seriously. I would argue that there is much narrative reason to do so (this does not mean that Defoe himself believes in the Christian answer). Having once shaken Moll out of her pattern of repetition, Defoe carries her convincingly through, first, a recognition of the terror of history, and, second, an awakening to Christian revelation. Having awakened Moll to a sense of the other in circumstance, Defoe then awakens her to a personal other. Lingering in Newgate, unable to achieve repentance, Moll discovers that Jemy has been taken prisoner. Her response is dramatic (some would say incredible): "I Was overwhelm'd with grief for him; my own Case gave me no disturbance compar'd to this, and I loaded my self with Reproaches on his Account; I bewail'd his Misfortunes, and the ruin he was now come to, at such a Rate, that I relish'd nothing now, as I did before, and the first Reflections I made upon the horrid life I had liv'd, began to return upon me, and as these things return'd, my abhorrance of the Place I was in, and of the way of living in it, return'd also; in a word, I was perfectly chang'd, and become another Body" (281). Although some critics have made much of the fact that Jemy was always Moll's favorite husband, I think we have to recognize that from the psychological view it matters relatively little which of Moll's husbands she might have met in Newgate. (From a thematic view, it matters more; Jemy has been the husband most involved like Moll in mythic action.) Whoever the husband, he is primarily the *occasion* for Moll's recognition of a personal other which can draw her out of the solipsistic world of myth.

A further withdrawal from the mythic state occurs when Moll begins, as she says, "to think, and to think is one real Advance from Hell to Heaven; all that Hellish harden'd state and temper of Soul, which I have said so much of before, is but a deprivation of Thought; he that is restor'd to his Power of thinking, is restor'd to himself" (281). Having begun to think, Moll begins to think about God. When her governess/mother, herself now a penitent, sends a minister to her, his talk so impresses Moll that she says, "I thought I cou'd freely have gone out that Minute to Execution, without any uneasiness at all, casting my Soul entirely into the Arms of infinite Mercy as a Penitent" (289). The submerged religious imagery that has been associated with Moll's incarceration in Newgate (that is, imagery of death, the "fatal tree," and redemption) is finally brought to the surface as Moll opens herself to Christ in repentance.

Critics have found Moll's response, after she has been transported, to the son from her incestuous marriage as unconvincing as her religious conversion. After the callous way she has treated her other children, why should she feel anything for this particular son unless she thought to gain some financial benefit from him? Her reaction on first seeing him must, they argue, be hypocritical: "It was a wretch'd thing for a Mother thus to see her own Son, a handsome comely young Gentleman in flourishing Circumstances, and durst not make herself known to him, and durst not take any notice of him; let any Mother of Children that reads this, consider it, and but think with what anguish of Mind I restrain'd myself; what yearnings of Soul I had in me to embrace him, and weep over him; and how I thought all my Entrails turn'd within me, that my very Bowels mov'd, and I knew not what to do; as I now know not how to express those Agonies" (322). Although it is remarkably convenient that Humphry turns out to be wealthy and affectionate, my reading alleviates some of the onus of hypocrisy on Moll's part. Reattuning herself to historical time after a long period of submergence in the repetitive world of thievery, she appropriately shows concern for her son and those ties of family feeling she had denied in her mythic life. At the beginning of the theft sequence, she allows her archetypal "Mother Midnight" to persuade her out of her feeling for her son by Jemy; at its end, having made her final farewell to her governess, she renews her relationship with Humphry. Read from the point of view of modern psychology, Moll's relations with her children are crude and inexplicable. Read as an allegory of Defoe's ambivalent attitude toward mythic time, they become more understandable. At this point Moll "began secretly now to wish that I had not brought my *Lancashire* Husband from *England* at all" (335). What seems Moll's sheer expediency can be her wish to disencumber herself from the mythic.

As Starr's analysis has shown, *Moll Flanders* and *Robinson Crusoe* are Defoe's two novels most susceptible to analysis along the lines of spiritual autobiography. This fact should be interpreted in light of Defoe's search for narrative pattern as much as in terms of his attitude toward belief. During those five extraordinary years of foment and creativity in which he was writing novels, Defoe was searching for some sort of pattern by means of which he could structure time within his fictions. In *Robinson Crusoe* Christianity, giving shape to history, provided that pattern. In *Singleton* repetition seems more significant than resolution. *Moll Flanders* returns to the providential pattern, but in a way that places religion in the context of history (rather than vice versa).

Abandoning the conversion experience as a way of achieving closure for his fictions, Defoe explores other ways of relating time and structure. Often placed in the same category as such historical works as "The Storm," *The Journal of the Plague Year* might seem an unlikely candidate for relevance to Joyce's *Ulysses*. Yet if we assume the narrator H.F. refers to Defoe's uncle Henry Foe (Burgess 15), we can understand Defoe to be fathering his own "father" in the manner of Joyce. And analysis of the *Journal* reveals, even more explicitly than in Defoe's novels, his preoccupation with the tensions between mythic and historic time. Although several critics think of the *Journal* as a novel, I shall not, since, in Joyce's own words, it "fall[s] short in love plot [and] psychological analysis" (*Daniel Defoe* 15). Perhaps because it is more history than novel, the *Journal* offers us a more successful mediation between synchronic and diachronic narration than any of Defoe's novels.

Where Crusoe's "journal" had the form of a real journal with a series of dated entries, Defoe's *Journal*, as Paul Alkon has pointed out, departs from the "available genres by avoiding the day-by-day pattern of a journal, by avoiding the shapes of spiritual autobiography . . . and by conspicuously avoiding the appearance of a conventional history" (183–84). Alkon believes that the *Journal* creates its unique form by carefully balancing two different kinds of time. The first of these is chronological time as revealed, for example, in H.F.'s encounter with the waterman or in his story of the three men who escape from London to avoid the plague. In such narrative the chronological order of the events is carefully observed, and there is a "predominantly one-to-one relation between events and their narration" (Alkon 215). The effect of such narrative, from Alkon's point of view, is a rapid increase in the pace of the narrative. The conception of time here is the one consistently developed in such historical writings as "The Storm" and *The Memoirs of a Cavalier*.

Alkon believes, however, that H.F.'s narration "bears least resemblance to the conventional literary forms by which the past is ordered and thus brought under some measure of control" (183). Primarily, the *Journal* only infrequently follows the chronological order of the narrated events. The episode with the three men is, for example, a rare one, and even it is used primarily for a sense of contrast. The text does not "facilitate a clear understanding of mere chronology, how the plague spread from week to week" (183). If H.F. generally does not provide a chronological link, neither does he "provide a topical organization following throughout any logic of necessary progression from topic to topic" (183). What we generally get instead is a different time-frame, one which follows the "sequence of H.F.'s memories instead of the chronological progression of the plague" (95). The characteristics of this time sequence are disruptions of chronology, frequent repetitions, reversal of cause-effect sequence, and emphasis on slowness of pace. It is a subjective conception of time whose only pattern is the arbitrary one dictated by H.F.'s train of thought.

Alkon suggests that Defoe uses such subjective time almost as a form of *la durée*, to cause the reader to experience the same kind of duration the Londoners experienced during the plague itself (230). He also suggests that such time is more widely used "for didactic purposes to create the effects of spatial form that are a significant part of Defoe's emblematic method" (167). Joseph Frank associated spatial form with myth; and I think we can parallel Defoe's use of subjective time in the *Journal* with that found in the idea of myth that I have been developing. Looking at the text through Vichian eyes, I would emphasize more than Alkon does the dialectical interplay of mythic and historic time. Defoe's work does not resolve itself in one direction or the other so much as it energizes itself from the interaction of both.

A central symbolic pattern reinforces this idea of dialectic. As Zimmerman points out, H.F. "refers to the shutting up of houses obsessively and although generally against it, is unable to rest on any conclusion" (115). To imprison all the uninfected inhabitants of a house that has been visited by the plague seems to H.F. at times unfair, indeed almost an act of murder. But, at other times, he recognizes that such practice may indeed help to contain the disease. Depending on whether H.F. perceives the situation from the subjectivity of self or the objective view of society, he takes radically contradictory attitudes toward the issue. Complicating matters is his recognition that one of the ways he might survive the plague since he has chosen to stay in London would be to shut himself up in his house. Indeed, for an extended period he does just that. The house symbolism in the *Journal* can be related to similar symbols in Defoe's fiction. There is a compulsive use of imagery of containment, along with a very deep ambivalence about containment. I have been interpreting this imagery not psychologically but philosophically, seeing it as a reflection of Defoe's ambivalence toward the isolation of myth. For H.F. the house stands as a safe retreat, but only if he is willing to forswear involvement in history. For a time, he does so, only to return to the observation of society. The force of Defoe's work really arises from H.F.'s commitment to both diachronic and synchronic time.

Carefully attuning the subjectivity of mythic time to that of objective time, Defoe is able to achieve an effective closure to his text, one that can recognize "mere successiveness" without being "merely successive" (Kermode 38). When he tries to apply this lesson of the *Journal* to his last two novels, he is less successful. Neither effectively mediates myth and history, and neither achieves a successful sense of closure. The admonition of Colonel Jack's unknown father to remember that he is a gentleman colors Jack's life, setting him apart from circumstances in his Gatsby-like platonic conception of himself. Although we can thus identify Jack as a "crypto-trickster figure, a magically privileged hero" (Richetti 152), depiction of his hero's mythic resonances does not seem to be Defoe's central concern in this novel.[10] Instead, the novel raises persistent problems of structure as Defoe struggles with the questions secular history raises for closure. Near the middle of the book, after Jack has been able to transform the misfortune of being transported as an indentured servant into the triumph of becoming an overseer on a large plantation and the holder of property and slaves of his own, he meets the felon whom he calls his "tutor." In addition to teaching Jack Latin and history, the tutor awakens in him an interest in Christianity. What is interesting, however, is the almost clinical interest Jack takes in the phenomenon of religion. He says: "tho' I was now in a kind of search after Religion, it was a meer looking, *as it were,* into the World to see what kind of thing, or Place it was, and what had been done in it" (168). Defoe allots an extended number of pages to this discussion of Christianity only to have Jack conclude: "As to commencing Penitent, as this Man had done, I cannot say, I had any Convictions upon me, sufficient to bring it on, nor had I a Fund of religious Knowledge to support me in it; so it wore off again Gradually, as such things generally do, where the first Impressions are not deep enough" (171). Although one could argue that Defoe simply could not let Jack be converted half way through the novel, we are still left with the question of why he introduced the religious material so extensively here and gave only a cursory lip-service treatment to it at the end of the novel. While the reason could be pure carelessness, I think that Defoe meant Jack to reject a commitment to Christian historical time.

Jack's rejection of Christianity in the middle of the novel is less a rejection of history per se than a rejection of providential history. Unlike his tutor (or Robinson Crusoe), who finds the Bible his door to repentance, Jack prefers secular histories such as those Defoe himself loved and relied upon extensively in his writings.[11] In fact, not biblical exhortations but history readings cause Jack to change his life. His tutor "read History to me, and where Books were wanting, he gave me Ideas of those things which had not been Recorded by our Modern Histories" (171). This information makes Virginia seem such a backwater to Jack that he determines to travel to those places where history is made. The secularization of historical process which had begun in the second sequence of events in *Captain Singleton* is carried even further in *Colonel Jack*, where history becomes something not to dominate but to respond to.

Thus the book carries on with an odd mélange of events and styles. Jack leaves for England, but gets captured by the French. Freed, he goes off to Ghent to observe the war. Later, he marries in England only to divorce his wife when she betrays him. Jack then describes his experience with Dillon's Irish regiment in Italy (where the style switches to that of the *Memoirs of a Cavalier*: Jack himself apologizes after a dozen pages by saying, "I hasten on to my own History, for I am not writing a Journal of the Wars" [215]). He marries again, but is again betrayed. He goes to England, meets a widow whom he marries; but their initial happiness is destroyed by her dependence on alcohol. He marries a lower class woman, hoping to find stability if not love in marriage. Against his wife's advice, he rides off in the Jacobite cause though, fortunately, briefly and anonymously. When his fourth wife dies, he returns to America after twenty-four years of wandering abroad. There he finds his first wife one of his indentured slaves. They marry, but Jack cannot settle down because fellow Jacobites have been sent to Virginia as indentured slaves and he fears being recognized. He travels to Antigua for his "health" and is later taken by the Spanish authorities in Cuba. After purchasing his freedom from the government, he sets up a profitable smuggling trade with Spanish merchants, but is stranded in Cuba where spare time and a head-clearing fit of the gout lead to repentance and acceptance of the Christianity he neglected at the middle of the book. He is now free to return to England, where his wife comes to meet him and their adventures end.

This sketchy summary of the last half of the book illustrates one point: the trouble that Defoe had in giving a shape to his novel once he turned his eyes away from the providential patterning of history to a secular patterning. In *Ulysses*, Stephen Dedalus thinks secular history has no meaning; therefore, no structure or pattern of events can be seemingly generated from it. *Colonel Jack* becomes a chaotic book in its second part; this manifests itself primarily in the book's inability to end, to achieve closure. Jack's adventures become increasingly random (and tedious) as the novel proceeds. His need to sail to Antigua has, in fact, been prepared for by the story of his involvement with the Royalists at Preston, though that story is inconveniently told *after* the death of "Moggy," his fourth wife; but why need Jack's ship have been driven into Cuban waters, leading to his being taken prisoner by the Spanish and to another whole sequence of very unbelievable events, including those that happened to his ship's crew as they were chased across the peninsula to the Mississippi by a Spanish ship while Jack was stranded in Cuba?

What makes the latter part of *Colonel Jack* so unreadable is that the synchronic impulses that usually meliorate the effect of diachronic narrative do not operate. In mythic terms, the very quality of repetition gives some shape to Moll's experiences as a thief. She steals, she steals again; and she could go on stealing for hundreds of pages. But the act of repetition itself insures that the reader senses a *pattern* behind her actions. The sheer diversity of Jack's actions in the latter half of his novel militates against that sense of pattern. He is a farmer, a merchant, a soldier, a husband, a royalist, a smuggler, a prisoner, etc. Apart from the repetition involved in his four attempts at marriage, his career is simply too historic to offer much sense of mythic coherence. Had Jack repented in the middle of the book under the aegis of his tutor, his story would have been in essence identical to Moll's: a person deeply enmeshed in mythic repetition would have moved into a sense of Christian time and purpose. Instead, Jack became deeply enmeshed in diachronic experience. Having shared with him the randomness and purposelessness of secular history, the reader finds it too difficult to accept Jack's perfunctory conversion to the Christian sense of *telos* at the end. Instead of offering a sense of closure, the novel simply seems to stop, abruptly, inconclusively, but none too soon. Suspended tenuously between mythic and secular time without convincing recourse to the consolations of Christian revelation, Jack thus becomes a more convincing prototype for Stephen Dedalus and Leopold Bloom than either Robinson Crusoe or Moll Flanders.

And *Roxana* articulates even more precisely the problem of time which will bedevil Joyce's characters. Even further alienated from the pattern of Christian history than Colonel Jack, Roxana will alternate between mythic and historical time in her search for meaning.[12] Since Roxana is the most intensely guilty of any of Defoe's heroes or heroines, the problem of retrospective narration becomes acute in this novel. How is the guilty, retrospective narrator to convey any of the sense of amoral pleasure she took in moments of mythic freedom? Although it raised the charge of hypocrisy, Moll's zest did convey some sense of what thievery meant for her. Roxana's guilt makes it difficult for Defoe to suggest what her periods as a "quintessential courtesan" symbolized. One of the ways Defoe compensates for this problem is in the creation of Amy, the servant who functions as a projection of Roxana's more mythic personality.[13] Like the true shadow, Amy feels no shame because she recognizes none. She also fairly easily lures Roxana into this mythic world where the amorality of repetition presides. In her retrospective narrative, Roxana calls Amy a "Viper and Engine of the Devil" (38) for counseling her to take the jeweler as her lover. Her moral language differentiates Roxana from Amy, suggesting a greater commitment to diachronic reality. Even within the present (rather than narrated) time of the scene, Roxana insists, "I am a Whore, *Amy,* neither better nor worse, I assure you" (40). Nevertheless, Defoe makes clear that Roxana can and does subscribe to Amy's mythic amorality. In trying to convince Roxana to sleep with the jeweler, Amy has told her that like Rachael she should put her maid to bed with him (39). Later, after she has begun her affair, Roxana does in fact put Amy to bed with her lover, all the while standing by and watching. Although this scene has outraged critics, I take it as Defoe's effort to demonstrate that Roxana, in the mythic time of the action rather than in the historic time of the narration, enters the amoral world of the undifferentiated self.

Roxana's indifference to the children of her affairs (she says she is glad the child she and the prince had in Italy died because it would have been a nuisance to their traveling [104]) is, like Moll's, a key to the mythic nature of her adventures. Toward the end of her years as courtesan, Roxana takes, disastrously, a rekindled interest in the children of her legal marriage—the children, that is, who occupy for her a place in real history. In this sequence of events, the doubling relationship with Amy takes on a grim significance. Critics have wondered, first, why Defoe should picture the daughter Susan as such a nemesis insistent upon gaining recognition from her mother and, second, why Roxana and Amy are so terrified by the danger of exposure.[14] To recognize Susan is to commit herself totally to the historical world, and that Roxana is not prepared to do. Torn between Susan as a symbol of the real world and Amy as a symbol of the mythic,[15] Roxana remains paralyzed, unable to choose between them. When Amy murders Susan, it is an act Roxana both abhors *and* desires: "But, *as I said, Amy* effected all afterwards, without my Knowledge, for which I gave her my hearty Curse, tho' I cou'd do little more; for to have fall'n upon *Amy,* had been to have murther'd myself" (302). Unlike her shadow Amy, Roxana cannot live fully in the timeless world of myth. Her filiations with diachronic existence, symbolized primarily in her marriages and her children, result in a partially differentiated, time-centered self that contrasts sharply with Amy's absence of self-analysis.

Only by distinguishing between what being a mistress and what being married signify in the novel can we understand fully why Susan represents such a threat to Roxana. One would hardly assume from reading *Roxana* that being a mistress was much fun. Each time she takes up with a new lover, she shuts herself away from society for a period of years. With the jeweller, she lives retired within her house after sending her children off to her husband's family. For the prince she lives confined within her house for three years; pleasure in sex (she enjoys recalling that for one fortnight "he stay'd wholly with me, and never went out of my Door" [68]) and in dressing up in fabulous clothes for him apparently compensates her for the loss of society. Her affair with the king is again imaged as a period of retreat: "For three Years and about a Month, *Roxana* liv'd retir'd, having been oblig'd to make an Excursion, in a Manner, and with a Person, which Duty, and Private Vows, oblige her not to reveal, at least, not yet" (181). Roxana is not afraid that her last lover, who has a key giving him private access to her bedroom, will ever find her abed with anyone, "for, in a word, I convers'd with no-body at-all" (186). Even when the attentions of her "old lewd Favourite" (207) finally drive her out of her profession, she cannot escape the instinct to retreat. Dropping all connection with her past life, she takes up lodgings with a Quaker woman, where she frequently wears Quaker garb as a disguise (211). Like Moll Flanders's life as a thief, Roxana's years as a courtesan are devoted to repetition—a repetition that, like Moll's, takes her out of historical time.

Although Roxana marries for little other reason than that her husband danced well (7), theirs is nevertheless a legal, Christian marriage. Undeceived by her mythic self (Amy), she enters into her first adulterous relationship with a real sense of her religious sin. Unhappily married, the jeweler convinces himself that their affair is a "marriage"; but Roxana reflects that the "hardness of Crime I was now arriv'd to . . . was owing to the Conviction that was from the beginning, upon me, that I was a Whore, not a Wife; nor cou'd I ever frame my Mouth to call him Husband, when I was speaking of him" (45). By the time she meets the Dutch merchant who saves her from the Jew in Paris, Roxana's position on marriage has "hardened" even further. Now she offers what some scholars have taken as a proto-feminist position on marriage: "That the very Nature of the Marriage-Contract was, in short, nothing but giving up Liberty, Estate, Authority, and everything, to the Man, and the Woman was indeed, a meer Woman ever after, that is to say, a Slave" (148). The merchant accuses her of being radically ahistorical, telling her that marriage "was the ordinary Method that the World was guided by; that he had Reason to expect I shou'd be content with that which all the World was contented with" (149). When he discovers that Roxana is pregnant, he appeals to her in more explicitly Christian terms: "As you are a Christian, and a Mother, not to let the innocent Lamb you go with, be ruin'd before it is born, and leave it to curse and reproach us hereafter" (156). Although Roxana's retrospective narrative voice says, "If I had not been one of the foolishest, as well as wickedest Creatures upon Earth, I cou'd never have acted thus" (158), her mythic self remains obdurate. Only at the very end of this extended sequence do we learn the real, mythic motivation that has lain behind her refusal: "Having already been ador'd by Princes, I thought of nothing less than of being Mistress to the King himself" (161).

In the earlier part of the novel, then, marriage becomes symbolic of one's commitment to Christian historical time. As Roxana tells us, for "six and twenty years of wickedness, without the least Signals of Remorse; without any Signs of Repentance" (188), she has defied marriage for the life of a courtesan. Having retired from that life to the Quaker's, she discovers that her mind runs on her "ridiculous Conduct" in refusing her Dutch merchant. And she flatters herself "that if I cou'd but see him, I cou'd yet Master him, and . . . he wou'd forget all that had pass'd, that might be thought unkind" (214). What is prefigured here is Roxana's effort to master history in purely secular terms. Continuing unrepentant, she nevertheless wishes to move back into diachronic reality—to escape from the mythic world in which she has lived so long. Since, like Stephen Dedalus, she has rejected Christianity, the only way she can try to give meaning to secular history is to mythicize it. To some extent she succeeds, but her past life in the figure of Susan, symbolizing all the inassimilable contingency of linear history, finally destroys her.

Defoe underlines these tensions in the strange, seemingly careless way he organizes the novel's final sequences. Having agreed to marry her Dutch merchant, Roxana hears from Amy that the prince wishes to find her in order to marry her. She becomes strangely elated, "and the Prince, or the *Spirit of him,* had such a Possession of me, that I spent most of this Time in the realizing all the Great Things of a *Life with the Prince*" (234). Roxana wonders retrospectively that her anxiety whether to pursue the bird in the bush or the one in the hand "did not make me Mad" (235). Of course, when the prince is wounded while hunting, turns repentant, and declines to pursue Roxana any further, she is happy to have retained the rudely treated merchant. Still, she is nearly made ill by her loss of her prince: "For in losing him, I forever lost the Prospect of all the Gayety and Glory, that had made such an impression upon my Imagination" (236). History seems flat to Roxana without the color of romance; but Defoe gives her another opportunity. Her merchant tells her that he will make her both a lady (in England) and a countess too (in Holland). Roxana thinks "that this Proposal would make me some Amends for the Loss of the Title that had so tickl'd my Imagination another-way" (240). She seems well on the way to coordinating historical contingency with the powers of mythic vision.

At this point Defoe gives his novel two different closing sequences. In the first, Roxana marries the merchant, they disclose their fabulous wealth to one another (though Roxana keeps some of hers reserved), and they buy their titles both in England and Holland. Roxana reflects that she has brought all the glories of romance into touch at last with the actualities of diachronic existence: "I was now in the height of my Glory and Prosperity, and I was call'd the *Countess de———*; for I had obtain'd that unlook'd for, which I secretly aim'd at, and was really the main Reason of my coming Abroad: I took now more Servants; liv'd in a kind of Magnificence that I had not been acquainted with; was call'd *Your Honour* at every word, and had a *Coronet* behind my Coach; tho' at the same time I knew little or nothing of my new Pedigree" (261–62). As Roxana's earlier mythic revelations had come without the benefit of clergy, this realization of Paradise Now comes without benefit of submission to Christian revelation. "I was not," she reflects, "come to that Repentance that is rais'd from a Sence of Heaven's Goodness; I repented of the Crime, but it was of another and lower kind of Repentance, and rather mov'd by my Fears of Vengeance, than from a Sense of being spar'd from being punish'd, and landed Safe after a Storm" (261). Having brought Roxana to this secular bliss, Defoe suddenly claps an unhappy close upon this sequence in which Roxana's reflections on her former actions "eat into all my pleasant things; made bitter every Sweet, and mix'd my Sighs with every Smile" (264).

The second ending sequence goes back to cover the same time period but from a totally different perspective. During this narrative, Roxana describes her daughter Susan's relentless pursuit of acknowledgment from her mother and Amy's murder of Susan. No mere psychological explanation seems adequate to explain this chilling sequence of events. Susan's determination against all reason and self-interest to make a claim on her mother; Amy's ferocious and repeated insistence upon the need to murder Susan (270, 272, 298, 302, 311, 322); Roxana's ambivalence and crippling anxiety: all demand a more symbolic reading. Ultimately, Amy the unrepentant mythic self (265) kills Susan to try to preserve the secular paradise Roxana has achieved. Ironically, in doing so Amy makes historic being intolerable for Roxana by introducing the burden of guilt. In purely novelistic terms, all those critics who have attacked the infamous non-ending of the novel are right; it does leave the situation in limbo:

> I can say no more now, but that, *as above,* being arriv'd in *Holland,* with my Spouse and his Son, *formerly mention'd,* I appear'd there with all the Splendor and Equipage suitable to our new Prospect, *as I have already observ'd.*
>
> Here, after some few Years of flourishing, and outwardly happy Circumstances, I fell into a dreadful Course of Calamities, and *Amy* also; the very Reverse of our former Good Days; the Blast of Heaven seem'd to follow the Injury done the poor Girl, by us both; and I was brought so low again, that my Repentance seem'd to be only the Consequence of my Misery, as my Misery was of my Crime. (329–30)

Narratively and psychologically inadequate, these final two paragraphs do have a symbolic coherence; they juxtapose the purely secular earthly paradise Roxana has tried to create with an image of the emptiness of existence without the blessing of a divine will.

Since Eric Voegelin has told us that the key disorder of the modern post-Renaissance world is its desire to create earthly paradises ("Post-script: On Paradise and Revolution" 31 et passim), we can only admire the perspicuity of Defoe's mind in recognizing, and dramatizing, both the impulse to create such visionary worlds and their insufficiency. *Robinson Crusoe* and *Moll Flanders* work more fully within the traditional framework of spiritual autobiography; Crusoe and Moll leave their pagan, mythic Edens to enter a historical world of time which can be redeemed only by a larger transcendent power. With *Colonel Jack* and *Roxana*, Defoe comes closer to the modern, humanistic sensibility. Unable to remain in the comforting world of myth, Jack moves into a random, purposeless historical world. Similarly compelled into historical existence, Roxana tries to give it a mythic meaning through the very force of her imagination. The remorseful but relentless ending of her novel suggests how acutely Defoe sensed both the limitations of a purely human effort to resolve metaphysical problems in a post-mythic world and the narrative complications such efforts posed.

Many critics have raised the question of the sincerity of the religious professions within Defoe's novels. But the question of what he believed is less important than the way Defoe was able to use the idea of belief as a way to give shape and coherence to his novels. Deeply involved with mythical remnants at the same time that he was actively engaged in writing modern history, Defoe found the central creative thrust for his fiction in the tension between diachronic and synchronic vision. Deeply attracted to the sense of shape found in mythic repetition, Defoe nevertheless was too much a modernist not to give priority to history. In the Judaeo-Christian conception of time, he had a tradition that allowed him to bring together linearity with some of the same sense of form found in myth. As the Christian *telos* gave shape to history, so repentance could give form to fiction. Both *Robinson Crusoe* and *Moll Flanders* illustrate Defoe's use of the Christian paradigm to give coherence to their stories; *Captain Singleton* operates, contrarily, in the world of myth. In *Colonel Jack* and particularly in *Roxana* Defoe no longer tried to energize a religious alternative to the synchronic structure of myth. Instead, Roxana tries to order secular history by imposing her own mythic shape on it. Whatever Defoe's religious beliefs, he was too clear-sighted not to recognize, along with Stephen Dedalus, that linear history without a sense of transcendental purpose was a nightmare. Unlike Joyce, Defoe could not achieve a containing form to structure that insight. Once he brings Roxana to that vision, his career as a novelist ends:

> Not all the Affluence of a plentiful Fortune; not a hundred Thousand Pounds Estate; (for between us we had little less) not Honour and Titles, Attendants and Equipages; *in a word,* not all the things we call Pleasure, cou'd give me any relish, or sweeten the Taste of things to me; *at least,* not so much, but I grew sad, heavy, pensive, and melancholly; slept little, and eat little; dream'd continually of the most frightful and terrible things imaginable: Nothing but Apparitions of Devils and Monsters; falling into Gulphs, and off from steep and high Precipices, *and the like;* so that in the Morning, when I shou'd rise, and be refresh'd with the Blessing of Rest, I was *Hag-ridden* with Frights, and terrible things, form'd meerly in the Imagination; and was either tir'd, and wanted Sleep, or overrun with Vapours, and not fit for conversing with my Family, or any-one else. (264)

3

Mythic and Historic Language in Smollett

In *The Dialogic Imagination*, M. M. Bakhtin describes how the novel incorporates various genres both artistic and extra-artistic which, "as they enter the novel, bring into it their own languages, and therefore stratify the linguistic unity of the novel and further intensify its speech diversity in fresh ways" (321). He concludes that the consequent "novelistic hybrid is an *artistically organized system for bringing different languages in contact with one another*, a system having as its goal the illumination of one language by means of another, the carving-out of a living image of another language" (361). In this chapter I will explore some of the different languages we can find in Smollett's work; in this way I shall follow Bakhtin's injunction that the real task of stylistic analysis lies in "uncovering all the available orchestrating languages in the composition of the novel, grasping the precise degree of distancing that separates each language from its most immediate semantic instantiation in the work as a whole" (416).

Since Bakhtin theorizes this condition of multiple languages for *all* novels, readers may believe that undercuts my hypothesis of a special kinship between the novels I am studying. Bakhtin, however, recognizes within the broader genre different kinds of development where we can differentiate uses of language. For example, he argues that although "we find the same parodic stylization of various levels and genres of literary language" in Fielding, Smollett, and Sterne, the "distance between these levels and genres is greater than it is in Dickens and the exaggeration is stronger" (308). Although Bakhtin recognizes that a "sharp opposition between two stylistic lines of the novel comes to an end" toward the beginning of the nineteenth century, he does allow for their continued development "off to the side of the mainstream of the modern novel" (414). In this way, he corroborates my idea that we can find a line of descent from Defoe, Smollett, and Sterne to Joyce's *Ulysses* "off to the side" from the realist tradition.

The tensions within Smollett's work, and particularly in his use of language,[1] are tensions between what Bakhtin calls "unitary" language and heteroglossia (by which he does not mean polysemousness, as many modern critics seem to believe). For Bakhtin, unitary language "constitutes the theoretical expression of the historical processes of linguistic unification and centralization." Always posited rather than something given, it makes its "real presence felt as a force for overcoming this heteroglossia, imposing specific limits to it, guaranteeing a certain maximum of mutual understanding and crystallizing it into a real, although still relative, unity—the unity of the reigning conversational (everyday) and literary language, 'correct language' " (270). One way of describing the parameters of Smollett's career would be to say that he moves from being a writer who overvalues unitary language to become a novelist who "welcomes the heteroglossia and language diversity of the literary and extraliterary language into his own work not only not weakening them but even intensifying them" (Bakhtin 298).

Unlike Joyce, whose pre-*Ulysses* experiments with the diachronic and synchronic tensions in narration are all intrinsically valuable, Smollett did not achieve a finished fiction in any of his earlier writings. Nevertheless, several of these novels interestingly reflect the struggles with language and voice he was finally able to resolve in *Humphry Clinker*. There, he achieved a sophisticated sense of the value of illuminating the language of history by juxtaposing it against a mythic voice. While Smollett only sporadically attempts in his first novel the mythic language he uses so effectively later, he does use a historical mode as a means to stabilize both the rather frenetic voices of the satirist and of the narrator Roderick. Roderick Random is involved in a world dense with historical references.[2] Beyond this background of historical detail, we find extended sequences which Smollett takes both from his own personal experiences and from the history of his time. These lengthy episodes find Roderick playing different roles; sometimes he is merely their reporter, and other times he participates as a fictional character within episodes which are based more or less directly on history.

For example, in the episodes dealing with the expedition to Carthagena, Smollett draws upon his own experience and his interpretation of historical event. This heading for chapter 33 will suggest economically how Smollett chose to incorporate these materials into his novel.

> A breach being made in the walls, our soldiers give the assault, take the place without opposition—our sailors at the same time become masters of all the other strengths near Bocca Chica, and take possession of the harbour—the good consequence of this success—we move nearer the town—find two forts deserted, and the channel blocked up with sunk vessels; which however, we find means to clear—land our soldiers at La Quinta—repulse a body of militia—attack the castle of St. Lazar, and are forced to retreat with great loss—the remains of our army are re-imbarked—an effort of the admiral to take the Town—the oeconomy of our expedition described. (184)

In this particular chapter Roderick figures less as a character within a fiction than as a spokesman for Smollett's interest in writing history.

But in other instances in the series of chapters dealing with the Carthagena campaign (31–34), Roderick plays much more the role of a fictive character participating in a fiction loosely based on historical reality. For example, he describes how his ship is assigned to batter the port of Bocca Chica. During this encounter Dr. Macshane, the surgeon who has been Roderick's enemy throughout his sea career, prostrates himself on the deck in terror while Roderick is scarcely able to refrain from doing so. Roderick then remarks:

> And that the reader may know, it was not a common occasion that alarmed us thus, I must inform him of the particulars of this dreadful din that astonished us. The fire of the Spaniards proceeded from Bocca Chica mounting eighty-four great guns, besides a mortar and small arms; from fort St. Joseph, mounting thirty-six; from two faschine batteries, mounting twenty; and from four men of war, mounting sixty-four guns each.—This was answered by us, from our land battery, mounting twenty-one cannon; our bomb

> battery, mounting two mortars, and twenty-four cohorns, and five men of war, two of eighty, and three of seventy guns, which fired without intermission. (181)

Whether this is actual history or not, it certainly introduces the language of historical realism into a fictional scene. After this brief synopsis, we are switched back directly to a fictional episode as Roderick amputates the wounded hand of his friend Jack Rattlin.[3]

Smollett frequently uses this historical voice to stabilize a more frantic narrative voice. For example, the following brief paragraph covers six months of Roderick's life in only six lines, but it does so in a way that seems historically real to the reader: "In less than a fortnight after, we made the land of Guinea, near the mouth of the river Gambia, and trading along the coast as far to the southward of the Line as Angola and Bengula, in less than six months disposed of the greatest part of our cargo, and purchased four hundred negroes, my adventure having been laid out chiefly in gold dust" (409–10). In contrast with those passages describing Roderick's "adventures" which cram as much action into every moment as they can, this passage suggests a more historical sense of the way time actually seems to unfold. Smollett thus at times introduces the manner of history into his novel proper.

As analysis of "The *History* of Miss Williams" (my emphasis) will show, Smollett uses what Bakhtin calls "unitary" language—a "correct literary language attuned to the speech of everyday"—to present not just his historical material but also that fictional material that aims at being taken as history. Miss Williams is a woman Roderick becomes engaged to in his fortune-hunting days, only to discard when he finds her in bed with another man. Later he finds Miss Williams, destitute and pox-ridden, deathly ill; then he saves her by feeding her and curing her pox. He also listens to her story. This "history," as Smollett labels it, is spread out over two chapters, interrupted in the second by a "scene" in which Miss Williams is falsely arrested and collects a guinea in damages which enables her and Roderick to move to more comfortable quarters before she finishes her story. This story itself has a number of narrative features which set it apart from the main narrative. For one thing, the story is linear, not cyclical. Miss Williams, proud of her intellectual powers, nevertheless foolishly allows herself to be seduced, becomes pregnant, and leaves home. Her path afterward is the downward one from courtesan to street-walker until Roderick saves her from dying of starvation. Thereafter, she will become a maid (Narcissa's in the main story), permanently losing her social class and making no return to her place of origin. There is, for her, no mythic return. Related to this is her "growth" or change as a character. Intellectually proud, vain of her beauty, she learns from experience and accepts the humble role of lady's maid as the most she can hope for. While myth frequently involves its characters in marriage and the family romance, more historic narrative emphasizes the unique story of the individual. Within her own history Miss Williams does not marry; it is only when she is absorbed into the main narrative that she does (and even then only to Strap, who is much beneath her previous social level).

Linguistically, the most interesting thing in this history is its univocal quality, the monotone of its narrative. Whereas the main narrative has linguistic variety acquired from the use of anecdote, caricature of characters, romantic interchanges, and satiric interludes, Miss Williams's story is all told in one color; it aims for what Ian Watt would call a "realism of presentation." Moreover, while the novel as a whole is written in the past tense, an interplay of time sequences is achieved between the past-tense of the story and the present-tense of the chapter headings (e.g., chapter 50 heading: "I long to be revenged on Melinda, apply to Banter . . . He contrives . . . I make . . . grow melancholy" etc.). The heading of chapter 22 is simply "The History of Miss Williams"; there is no juxtapositioning to an ongoing present. Finally, the language itself is invariably abstract: "After this mutual declaration, we contrived to meet more frequently in private interviews, where we enjoy'd the conversation of one another, in all the elevation of fancy and impatience of hope, that reciprocal adoration can inspire" (120). Although all parts of the novel are touched by this stiffly correct style, it is only in Miss Williams's story that it is so consistently maintained. (The one linguistic concession to mythic usage is the name of her first seducer, "Lothario.")

Perhaps the most significant feature of her history is its total lack of humor. Deeply attracted to the writing of history,[4] Smollett must have understood that the reality of events of his time left little room for comedy. John H. Burke, Jr., has argued that Fielding refused to yield to "historical pessimism" and abandon the comic mode. Rather, he "filtered history out of his prose fictions" (60–63). By deemphasizing historic reality, Fielding kept open for himself the possibility of comedy. Unlike Fielding, or at least the Fielding of *Joseph Andrews* and *Tom Jones,* Smollett was not willing to abandon diachronic history. Nor was he willing, in the novel proper, to abandon comedy. But, in the section of the novel that comes closest to history in its narrative method and language, he eschews comedy; Miss Williams's story is baldly serious. (The introduction of the comic scene of Miss Williams's being falsely accused and taken to jail occurs within Roderick's narrative and not in her "story." It suggests that Smollett felt the need for some comic relief even within this relatively short history.)

Were I concerned with the intrinsic merits of *Roderick Random* rather than its foreshadowings of later, more successful accomplishment in *Humphry Clinker*, I would want to demonstrate its language of satire and also the dynamic voice of the irascible, rather than romantic, side of its narrator. Along with the historic voice, these languages work in more fruitful conjunction than in any other of Smollett's early fictions. For my purposes, however, it is more important to concentrate on peripheral and even implicit language patterns than on these more central ones. And, after all, these other voices have been carefully explored before: see particularly the work of Ronald Paulson and Damion Grant. My own essay on Smollett's development as a novelist also considers these language patterns. If G. S. Rousseau's notion that there is a "dearth of incisive critical writing about Smollett's works" (68) remains true, perhaps an approach that emphasizes seemingly tangential aspects of *Roderick Random* rather than reworking often discussed material can be justified as an effort to articulate a coherent overview of Smollett's career that can explain how he came in *Humphry Clinker* to achieve a worthy predecessor to Joyce's *Ulysses.*

In the preface to *Roderick Random,* Smollett writes that romance "owes its origin to ignorance, vanity, and superstition" (xxxiii). The twenty-six-year-old Smollett's early position on myth is euhemeristic, not Vichian. The "heathen mythology . . . is no other than a collection of extravagant Romances" (xxxiii) by means of which the family and adherents of famous men magnified their virtues and, imposing on the gullibility of the vulgar, deified them. With the advancement of learning and taste in the classical period, tragedy and epic replaced mythology and romance. Reborn in the dark ages of religious superstition, romances "filled their performances with the most monstrous hyperboles" (xxxiv) until Cervantes "reformed the taste of mankind, . . . converting romance to purposes far more useful and entertaining, by making it assume the sock, and point out the follies of ordinary life" (xxxiv).

The word "converting" is ambiguous; does he mean altering the purpose but maintaining the form of romance, or does he mean eliminating it altogether? The militant rationalism both toward the "superstition" of the ancient myths and the "imposition of priest-craft" (xxxiv) in medieval times would suggest that Smollett meant to eliminate romance (and myth) altogether. Yet, since his novels follow the pattern of romance,[5] it seems more likely that he wants to maintain the form of romance but within a more rationalistic frame. What I shall be arguing is that Smollett wants to keep the form of romance as a way of giving minimal shape to what would otherwise be formless satiric panoramas. What he discovers, however, is that romance demands its own language. As long as he adheres to the euhemerist view of myth, he is unable to find that language. Only as he, perhaps as the result of exposure to "Vichian" ideas of myth, widens his concept of mythic language does he finally resolve this problem in his last novel. A certain susceptibility to the ideas I have been exploring is hinted even in this rather cockily rationalist preface when Smollett gives as one reason for making his hero a Scotsman the idea that he "could represent simplicity of manners in a remote part of the kingdom, with more propriety, than in any place near the capital" (xxxv). Alongside the neoclassic concern for propriety, we discover the nostalgia for the primitive—a kind of capsulization of the tensions I see in Smollett.

Narcissa's romance, which is the antithesis of Miss Williams's history, can serve as a model of Smollett's early interest in, if not myth as I have been defining it, romance archetypes that operate in a way different from his historical voice. Disguised as a footman, Roderick introduces her by remarking that he saw her aunt approach, "accompanied with the young lady, whose name for the present shall be Narcissa" (219). Since the name is never changed, this remark seems rather peculiar. Perhaps Smollett meant to give her a more fully rounded characterization and consequently to alter her name to something less archetypal—like Melinda, the name of the woman Roderick courts for her fortune and who later marries Narcissa's brother. Instead, as the story proceeds, he actually emphasizes more fully her archetypal nature. Narcissa might seem an unfortunate archetype to evoke for a heroine—and very inappropriate to the bland, unself-centered woman Smollett portrays; but I think Smollett really intends us to see her as a kind of anima-figure of Roderick himself. *He* is the Narcissus, and through identification with her he enters her mythic world. Miss Williams similarly tries to draw Roderick into her historic world by making him a "double" of her seducer, Lothario: "He was the exact resemblance of you, and, if I had not been well acquainted with his family and pedigree, I should have made no scruple of concluding him your brother" (119).

The main feature of Narcissa's world is that it is cyclic, not linear. Although at the end of the novel she lives in Scotland rather than in England, nothing has changed in her life; she is in the same social class, economic bracket, and emotional state. She has achieved no insight to mark her experience as linear; even her passion is marked by stasis rather than growth and condemns her, as Robert Caserio says such passion must (236), to perpetual childhood rather than the life of an adult. Her pregnancy, which might mark entry into mature life, is treated in a mythic way to emphasize the synchronicity of family romance rather than the individual development on which historical narration is based: "My dear angel has been qualmish of late, and begins to grow remarkably round in the waist; so that I cannot leave her in such an interesting situation, which I hope will produce something to crown my felicity" (435). Miss Williams's pregnancy and miscarriage marked clear stages in her development as an individual; pregnancy simply marks the mythic "return" Narcissa and Roderick have made at the end of the novel.

Narcissa remains, then, not a character but simply a type of the romantic heroine, featureless throughout. What interests one is why she, and the romance pattern she signifies, figure as largely as they do in the book, and why Smollett was so unsuccessful at energizing them. The answer to the first question is that the "romance" she embodies offered Smollett a means by which to achieve a pattern for his fiction. Much as Defoe used providential time, Smollett relies on archetypal patterns of return to structure what could otherwise become miscellaneous satiric gatherings. The answer to the second question is made clear to us by Roderick himself; he has no language to signify his meaning: "But, alas! expression wrongs my love! I am inspired with conceptions that no language can convey!" (351). He remarks, in describing his secret garden meeting with Narcissa before beginning his last sea journey to the new world, "Because my words are incapable of doing justice to this affecting circumstance, I am obliged to draw a veil over it" (406). And when he returns from that voyage and remeets Narcissa, he exclaims: "Heavens! what was my situation! I am tempted to commit my paper to the flames and to renounce my pen for ever, because its most ardent and lucky expression so poorly describes the emotions of my soul" (425). Since this is the first time that the narrator has made the reader conscious of him as someone actually using a pen and paper, we can only wonder whether Smollett articulates his own frustration here.

Certainly, the language Smollett uses when forced to describe Roderick's passion rings very hollow: "Good heaven! what were the thrillings of my soul at that instant! my reflection was overwhelmed with a torrent of agitation! my heart throbbed with surprizing violence! a sudden mist overspread my eyes! my ears were invaded with a dreadful sound! I panted for want of breath, and in short, was for some moments intranced!" (337). Although there is some suggestion of mythic response here as Roderick's feelings become translated into actual physical responses, there is none of the linguistic skill used to make Win Jenkins's prose credible. In contrast, Roderick's language in responding to Miss Williams (now Narcissa's maid) may not convey any more realistic sense of character, but at least it is not so silly as his romantic speeches. "The sentiments of this sensible young woman on this, as well as on almost every other subject, perfectly agreed with mine; I thanked her for the care she took of my interests, and promising to behave myself according to her direction, we parted" (342). The slight note of the Machiavel in this speech suits, in fact, our sense of Roderick as a dynamo—as "random" as his culture is, according to James H. Bunn (469). Unfortunately, Smollett is unable to achieve any language to catch Roderick in his static role as lover. Awakening from their first night of connubial bliss, Roderick writes: "I was distracted with joy! I could not believe the evidence of my senses, and looked upon all that had happened as the fictions of a dream!" (430). *We* cannot believe his language.

While Smollett is far from mastering a synchronic language, there are clear indications, even in this first novel, that he is searching for one. Roderick's early master, Mr. Lavement, has a French accent that challenges the correctness of unitary language: "Ah! mon pauvre Roderique! you ave more of de veracité dan of de prudence—bot mine vife and dater be diablement sage, and Mons. le Capitaine un fanfaron, pardieu!" (111). Compare the credibility of this voice with Roderick's own more correct one a page later: "Sir, appearances, I own, condemn me, but you are imposed upon as much as I am abused—I have fallen a sacrifice to the rancour of that scoundrel . . . who has found means to convey your goods hither, that the detection of them might blast my reputation, and accomplish my destruction" (113). In his speech to Roderick's dying grandfather, Captain Bowling (Roderick's uncle) also shows Smollett's experiments with accent and dialect to attain greater credibility: "What! he's not a weigh? How fare ye—how fare ye, old gentleman?—Lord have mercy upon your poor sinful soul. . . . Here's poor Rory come to see you before you die and receive your blessing.—What, man! don't despair—you have been a great sinner, 'tis true,—what then? There's a righteous judge above, isn't there?—He minds me no more than a porpuss.—Yes, yes, he's a going—the land crabs will have him, I see that;—his anchor's a peak, i'faith!" (12). The speech clearly points to Trunnion's great death scene in *Peregrine Pickle*, where an effect of mythic language is achieved.

In conception Smollett's most coherent novel,[6] *Peregrine Pickle* is in fact almost unreadable for the modern taste. Very damaging is the inclusion of so much adventitious satire in Peregrine's own story. The stale pranks of the foreign tour and the absurd machinations with Cadwallader Crabtree at Bath and in London create an unbridgeable gap between Perry as satirist and as character in a romantic story. Moreover, the long interpolated histories of Lady Vane and MacKercher's relation to the Annesley claimant work against the unity of the story. It is not just that they are interpolated stories—one could skip them—but that the language they introduce into the novel works against the idea of peripety and moral growth that is voiced in the more central plot.

There has been much speculation about Smollett's relationship with Lady Vane, about why he included her memoirs in *Peregrine Pickle*, and about whether he had a hand in their writing. Most critics agree that Smollett probably smoothed out the memoir if he did not actually write it—perhaps at Lady Vane's dictation.[7] I would argue that Smollett, possibly unconsciously, uses Lady Vane's story to qualify Peregrine's fictive one. Smollett "creates" the story of Peregrine's pride and its consequences. He develops it quite carefully, in much fuller detail than anything else in his fiction, to show that his hero must learn to curb his false pride and develop a true one if he is to achieve full maturity. As a consequence for doing so, he is rewarded with a restored fortune and Emilia. But Smollett then includes the "history" of Lady Vane to give a diachronic version of the same theme. Married first for love, the lady is soon widowed. At the advice of her friends, she then marries Lord Vane, who can fill neither her emotional nor her sexual needs. Thus begin her "adventures" (real rather than imagined, however) as she moves from one lover to another, trying both to escape the persecutions of her husband and to find the romantic attachment her heart desires. Her search for this ideal love offers a parallel to Peregrine's passion for Emilia. Like Perry, she makes the point of not being bound by historical necessity; but, of course, her memoirs show that she must continually submit to her sicknesses, her lack of money, her loss of lovers, her family, and her husband's demands. At the end of her story, she has not integrated her mythic world and the world of reality. Instead, she has returned to her mad husband and is trying to make the best of her situation. Her story historicizes the idea Smollett wants to develop. If Lady Vane has "learned" anything from her experiences, it is not a character-reversing revelation—perhaps more appropriate to fiction than to real life—but rather the need to accommodate her wishes to reality as best she can. In that way, her "history" offers a corrective mirror to Peregrine's adventures, much as Miss Williams's history does to Roderick's earlier adventures. Linguistically, Lady Vane's story works in the same monochromatic way as that of Miss Williams, offering a further undercutting to the tonal variety of Peregrine's fable of moral development.

Another illustration of the historicist impulse in *Peregrine Pickle* is the inclusion of the long story of MacKercher and the Annesley case. Lewis M. Knapp and Lillian de la Torre have shown that Smollett closely modeled this material on a manuscript copy of the Annesley *Case* and that he probably got from MacKercher himself the details of his life (30–32). In other words, he directly imported historical materials into his novels. Why? Since the Annesley material describes a famous historical instance where a son has been unjustly debarred from his rightful inheritance by a cruel parental figure, its relation to Peregrine's case seems obvious. In the beginning of the novel, Peregrine's mother takes an unnatural dislike to her son and forces her henpecked husband to disown him. But Peregrine's father has neglected to make a will, and at his death Peregrine inherits the family estate, which seems a just reward for the moral growth he has achieved.

The Annesley claimant does not fare so well. The alienation between his mother (and her family) and his father makes the young boy totally dependent on his dissolute father. Upon his death, the boy's uncle, playing Peregrine's mother's role, plots to have his nephew killed, gives out the story that he has died, and takes over the estate. Spared death, the boy is sent as an indentured slave to America. After years of struggling to become a free man, he turns up as a sailor in the Carthagenean campaign, where the rumors of his claim begin to surface. (Undoubtedly Smollett heard them at that time.) Befriended by MacKercher—who plays a role parallel to Trunnion's in Peregrine's story, he returns to England and enters a suit against his uncle. Though he wins a judgment against the uncle, the latter is able to use the law to delay the carrying out of the court decision. In Smollett's version, MacKercher and his protégé are jailed after the former's fortune has been expended trying to achieve justice for the claimant. In life, the latter died before any final decision that would have reinvested him in his rightful position was reached.

The differences between Smollett's historical and his fictional treatment of this theme of the wrongfully disinherited son are instructive. There is no happy ending in the Annesley case; the villains of the piece (apparently one of the few additions Smollett made to the *Case* was to underline the blackness of one of these [Knapp and de la Torre 31]) are not defeated; the hero does not win out. A generally pessimistic tone prevails as history seems to reveal little other truth than that entrenched might will prevail. Peregrine's story, however credibly, incorporates a mythic pattern. Having largely squandered one fortune and having behaved unpleasantly throughout, he, in fact, seems undeserving of a happy ending. Yet Smollett's "myth" demands that the cyclic pattern be completed, and he restores the same fortune to Perry that he had given Roderick. The one concession to historic reality seems to be that Peregrine has achieved more genuine self-insight and knowledge of his flaws than Roderick ever attained. One wonders whether Smollett has not included the story of the Annesley case to placate his sense of historical reality. This kind of narration, he tells the reader, can be trusted, for it tells things as they really are. Again, the language of the Annesley case is a rigorously "correct" one which eschews the tonal variety of Peregrine's fictive story. Language is also made to mirror things as they are.

The MacKercher-Annesley material is interesting on another level, too. Knapp and de la Torre have shown that MacKercher was a close friend of Smollett, and the inclusion of the material clearly was meant to puff MacKercher's generous behavior as well as to publicize the claimant's case. But, at least unconsciously, Smollett is involved in the projection of certain anxieties of authorship. As author, he guides Peregrine through certain experiences, uses him to express satiric views of many different sorts, creates many humorous, even farcical scenes around him, involves him in romantic and sexual scenes, and crowns it all by having his hero undergo a growth experience that justifies his being rewarded with a beautiful wife and large fortune. As an eighteenth-century intellectual aware of the process of historicization in his century, Smollett could not have been very comfortable with this fictional representation of experience; and he projects that discomfort in the figure of MacKercher. A self-made man like Smollett himself, a figure of force and power as Smollett undoubtedly thought himself after the success of *Roderick Random*, MacKercher is, nevertheless, totally impotent before historical necessity. All his efforts to guide his protégé are foiled. He expends all his powers—money, influence, social stature—in vain. The life that he is trying to make for the claimant cannot be made; the entrenched powers of reality are simply too strong to be overcome. A tribute to his friend, Smollett's picture of MacKercher also projects a recognition of the impotence of the imagination before historical forces.

One way out of this impasse for the creative writer would be to revive archaic forms of knowing which had been subsumed by historical modes. These could give larger play to imaginative truth. Smollett does, in fact, give voice to a nostalgia for the mythic in *Peregrine Pickle*'s extended emphasis on family romance. Although his earlier criticism stressed Smollett's satire, Ronald Paulson has recently, quite brilliantly, commented on this mythic aspect of *Peregrine Pickle*. Studying the way the earlier chapters of *Peregrine* and *Tom Jones* give an extensive prehistory of their heroes, he concludes that they generate a "myth" in which they describe their heroes' withdrawal (or expulsion) from Eden. In Defoe the son as rebel had defied the father and left, but in this version of the mythos, the parents are seen as the original fallen Adam and Eve figures who visit their sins upon their son, who, "having inherited his original sin (unlike Crusoe, who created it himself), reenacts the parents' fall" (Paulson 72). While archetypal patterns operate in the background of all Smollett's fiction, Paulson seems right to find the first part of *Peregrine Pickle* to be structured more explicitly around a version of the family romance. This concentration on the family leads, Paulson feels, to better writing on Smollett's part. "Though his reputation is first and foremost as a writer of the episodic picaresque narration, Smollett always becomes a tighter, more intense, and more interesting writer when he gets to a small hierarchical group" (65).

The use of myth does, then, intensify the synchronic effect of the tighter plot. Why does Smollett abandon it less than a quarter of the way through the novel? We have to recognize that this sort of synchronic vision was not Smollett's congenial material. Smollett does achieve in the family scenes at the opening of this novel a Richardsonian blending of historicism and myth, a muting of the extreme needs of both that permits the emergence of the realist school. Unlike Richardson, Smollett could not work continuously within the framework of a small family group which gave him the opportunity to explore the mythic dimensions of character. He needed myth; but he also needed history. His effort to write a coherent novel of the realist sort in *Peregrine Pickle* did not suit his talents. Even within the earlier, more tightly knit part, other kinds of narrative impulses intrude on the story. Perry's pranks as a child are meant to illustrate the growth of his pride; nevertheless, they are excessive in number and often more indicative of Smollett's propensity to satire than to characterization. And, as I have illustrated, within the larger framework of the novel, we find Smollett more attuned to historicity than to myth.

The basic problem again is that of language. Smollett clearly has an interest in myth and synchronic vision, but he has not yet found a way to express it. As in *Roderick Random*, there are a few hints of what will come in Win and Tabby's letters. Deborah Hornbeck's letter to invite Perry to an assignation foreshadows Win Jenkins's later efforts: "Heaving the playsure of meating with you at the ofspital of anvil-heads, I take this lubbertea of latin you know, that I lotch at the *hottail de May cong dangle rouy Doghouseten*" (219). Smollett's second attempt at comic polysemy, this letter is a great improvement over the one "Clayrender" wrote Roderick. There the whore's literary pretensions, seen in her classical allusions, were undercut by her comic misspellings; here, Deborah has no pretensions. Her language simply shows an inevitable interweaving of the physical with the abstract.

As many critics have pointed out, the single most effective passage in the novel is the great scene of Trunnion's death, and its power derives largely from Smollett's language:

> Swab the spray from your bowsprit, my good lad, and coil up your spirits. You must not let the top-lifts of your heart give way, because you see me ready to go down at these years; many a better man has foundered before he has made half my way; thof I trust, by the mercy of God, I shall be sure in port in a very few glasses, and fast moored in a most blessed riding: for my good friend Jolter hath overhauled the journal of my sins; and by the observation he hath taken of the state of my soul, I hope I shall happily conclude my voyage, and be brought up in the lattitude of heaven. (392)

The first thing we note about this passage is the near absence of any abstracting or generalizing language. Except for "the mercy of God" and "the state of my soul," all of Trunnion's speech is cast in concrete naval terms. Yet it is a concreteness that accommodates a dimension of feeling as well. The phrase to keep your heart up had become an empty cliché. Trunnion's revivification of the metaphor in his injunction to Perry not to "let the top-lifts of your heart give way" not only renews the metaphor but also makes the emotion credible. The rich specificity of his language opens up the spiritual dimension of his death as well. We see this effect in the wonderful phrase "fast moored in a most blessed riding," as well as in "lattitude of heaven," where what might be empty clichés are wonderfully revivified by Trunnion's language. That language is concretely specific, yet brilliantly inclusive, enabling the reader to respond to his death on a number of levels. We see, first, the death of the man who has been so deeply fixated on his professional life; yet Trunnion convincingly enacts the death of Everyman, as well as that of the Christian. Smollett achieves this effect by stressing the synchronic aspect of language, its ability to hold many dimensions in suspension at the same time.[8] The hostess's speech describing Falstaff's death does the same thing; critics have frequently noted the similar effect of the two death scenes. Since Smollett's larger purposes in *Peregrine Pickle* are more realistic and historicist, he puts much less emphasis on verbal ingenuity in Trunnion's speech than in the Hornbeck letter; thus he keeps Trunnion within the framework of his action yet also stresses his archetypal significance.

Richardson, of course, achieves the ultimate accommodation of myth and realism in Clarissa's death scene. His task was easier than Smollett's since he did not have to deal with the stylizations of comedy as well as those of myth. The synchronic emphases in Smollett's scene press beyond the limits of realistic fiction. Trunnion is simply too much larger than life to fit into the tradition of comic realism established later by Austen and Trollope. Dickens creates similar figures; but he uses sentiment to integrate their archetypal reverberations into his realistic frame. One remarkable feature of Smollett's scene is how free it is of any overtone of sentimentality.

In one sense, we could simply say that Smollett's use of language in this death scene is "poetic" in contrast to the historic language we have largely been tracing in his earlier fiction. Vico, of course, found the distinguishing feature of early societies to be their innately poetic quality. We cannot conclude that Smollett had renounced his early euhemeristic view of myth for something like a Vichian one on the solitary example offered by Trunnion's death scene. Nevertheless, *Peregrine Pickle* illustrates Smollett's problems in trying to create a language suitable to the romance forms he uses to structure his fiction.

This difficulty continues in *Ferdinand, Count Fathom* and *Sir Launcelot Greaves*. In both these later novels, Smollett can effectively add a historic voice to the perpetual voice of satire; but whether he follows the Gothic or the Cervantic pattern, he cannot discover a consistently adequate language for elements which demand an extra-rational, intuitive understanding. Since I in no way challenge the general critical view that these are Smollett's weaker achievements, one example will be enough to illustrate my point. Following an unknown woman in order to return her lost purse, the love-maddened Sir Launcelot is surprised to find that she is his beloved Aurelia. During the course of an interview, he learns that she did not intentionally send him a letter of rejection and that she still loves him. The scene reaches an incredible climax:

> So saying, he approached this amiable mourner, this fragrant flower of beauty, glittering with the dew-drops of the morning; this sweetest, and gentlest, loveliest ornament of human nature. He

> gazed upon her with looks of love ineffable; he sat down by her; he pressed her soft hand in his; he began to fear that all he saw was the flattering vision of a distempered brain; he looked and sighed, and, turning up his eyes to heaven, breathed, in broken murmurs, the chaste raptures of his soul. (168)

The language here is not ironic, just turgid; and Smollett's novel suffers from his inability to give his hero a credible romantic voice.

An affinity between *Ulysses* and *The Expedition of Humphry Clinker*, besides their interest in the mythic dimension of language, is their use of their authors' lives. Smollett appropriates his own historical experiences, his autobiography, for the basis of his fiction as freely as Joyce does. The novel is not a simple rewrite of Smollett's historical journey to Scotland from May to August 1766. It is a novel, fiction, but fiction that has a basis in the reality of place and person. Although Jery's story of Tim Cropdale's tricking Birkin out of a new pair of riding boots may be a fabrication, the garden and house where the joke occurred were as real as 7 Eccles Street is in Joyce's Dublin. Jery's letter of June 10 is, in fact, Smollett's sly joke as his fictional character describes a visit to the home of his creator, the historical Smollett. The actual antics of the hack writers who sponge off S——t (as he is referred to in the novel) and then abuse him behind his back may be "fictional," but undoubtedly the scene reflects Smollett's historical attitude toward his peers. In a similar way, the Mr. Smollett whom the characters in the novel visit during their tour of Scotland is James Smollett, the novelist's cousin, who had inherited the family estate at Bonhill. The Bramble party actually stays at Cameron House rather than the older family home, just as Smollett and his wife did in 1766. While Bramble calls James Smollett's home a "Scottish paradise" (244), he does not return to a mythic center as Roderick and Perry do, but he visits a concrete, historical spot—a diachronic rather than a synchronic place.

Perhaps Smollett's most interesting use of himself in the novel occurs during Bramble's meeting with Mr. Serle. The fictional story of Serle's aid to Paunceford and the latter's ungenerous treatment of his benefactor after he acquires great wealth had its origin, as Lewis M. Knapp has shown (290–92), in a real incident in which Smollett experienced the ingratitude of one Alexander Campbell. Here we have the very Joycean situation where real characters serve as the basis for a fictional episode. Interestingly, the story is followed just a few pages later by Jery's story of Tom Eastgate and George Prankley. Eastgate, wishing a living in Prankley's power to give, has long suffered the latter's rudeness till he is informed that the position will be given to someone else. Although a cleric, he challenges Prankley to a duel and frightens him into giving him the living. The story, entirely fictional as far as one can tell, offers a rich counterpoint to the fiction based on historical truth. An act of ingratitude is not suffered mildly but gets its comeuppance; justice wins out. We note how this episode reverses the effect of Miss Williams's story in *Roderick Random*: her "history" qualified the romance of fiction; Eastgate's fiction alleviates the grimness of history.

Like Joyce, Smollett uses other historical figures besides himself in his fiction. Sometimes he does so in a much more flatly historicist way than Joyce ever does. In Matt Bramble's letter of May 19 from Bath, he speaks of the landscape painting of Mr. T—— (John Taylor), which he admires greatly. In a slightly more novelistic way, he recounts in his July 4 letter from Scarborough the story of his old acquaintance H——t (William Hewett) and his eccentric voyages. At points like this, the fiction is very close to historical anecdote. More Joycean is Smollett's treatment of the actor James Quin. Satirized in both *Roderick Random* and *Peregrine Pickle*, Quin is treated more evenhandedly here. Jery's letter from Bath of April 30 begins with a realistic description of Quin's personality and habits, but then quickly transforms the historical figure into an actor within the drama of the book. He first draws Quin into an opinion about one of the novel's central themes, the effects of democracy on society; involves him in an anecdote about watching women competing for favors at a tea party; and creates a humorous interchange between Quin and Tabitha over whether he is a descendant of Nell Gwynn. Progressively, Quin moves from being a real person into being a real person observing a fiction, and finally into a real person involved as a character in a fiction.[9]

The larger affinity between *The Expedition of Humphry Clinker* and *Ulysses* is, of course, their use of language. Recognizing Smollett as Joyce's linguistic grandparent will help to establish a context for his experiments; but perhaps more importantly, looking at Smollett through Joyce's eyes can make us aware how Vichian his interests had become in his last novel. Smollett here addresses his language theme both abstractly and dramatically. The abstract articulation of the theme summarizes the idea of language as a mode of historical recording which we have been addressing in Smollett's earlier novels. The dramatic projection embodies an idea of language as myth which has been a slowly gathering ground swell throughout his fiction. The spokesman for the historical attitude toward language within the novel is Lismahago, whose perspective is even more conservative than that of Samuel Johnson. In arguing with Jery whether English is spoken with more propriety at Edinburgh or London, Lismahago asserts that "the Scottish dialect was, in fact, true, genuine old English, with a mixture of some French terms and idioms, adopted in a long intercourse betwixt the French and Scotch nations; that the modern English, from affectation and false refinement, had weakened, and even corrupted their language, by throwing out the guttural sounds, altering the pronunciation and the quantity, and disusing many words and terms of great significance" (194). Johnson regretfully accepted the inevitability of change in language; Lismahago apparently believes the Scots have resisted and can resist the "affectations and false refinement" which corrupt language. As he demonstrates, an ambiguity has grown up in England about the word *gentle*. Does it mean mild and meek or noble and high-minded? The Scots, however, do not have trouble with the word because they have retained its original, true meaning (194).

Inevitably, such discursive passages reveal a good deal about Smollett's own sense of language.[10] And we recognize throughout much of the novel that one of the pressures on the letter writers is to use language in a way consistent with this essentially conservative position. That is, they are to use a "correct" language which permits them to represent, as unequivocally as possible, a historical reality. In doing so, they often turn language into a very abstract, emotionless instrument. Even Lydia, whom Smollett tries without much success to characterize as a sentimental girl, expresses herself in emptily abstract terms: "Unexperienced as I am in the commerce of life, I have seen enough to give me a disgust to the generality of those who carry it on—There is such malice, treachery, and dissimulation, even among professed friends and intimate companions, as cannot fail to strike a virtuous mind with horror; and when Vice quits the stage for a moment, her place is immediately occupied by Folly, which is often too serious to excite anything but compassion" (296). Although such language is colorless in emotional terms, it does have the advantage of being clear and unambiguous. Liddy expresses herself with a great deal of confidence that she can say exactly what she means. It is in response to such linguistic usage that generations of critics have built up "historicist" readings of *Humphry Clinker*. Language in the novel often reflects reality in such a way as to suggest to us that a true "history" is being given.

This conception, of course, reflects the high value that Smollett's age placed on the post-mythic, logical world of diachronic history. History, says an essay which has been attributed (probably wrongly) to Smollett, "is the inexhaustible source from which [the poet] will derive his most useful knowledge respecting the progress of the human mind, the constitution of government, the rise and decline of empires, the revolution of arts, the variety of character, and the vicissitudes of fortune" (Cunningham III 299).[11] Much of Smollett's work does reflect an effort to record the processes of actual life in what Bakhtin calls unitary language. Still, as the writer of this essay concluded, it is "not that the poet or painter ought to be restrained to the letter of historical truth" (Cunningham III 299). And another aspect of Smollett's fiction is his exploration of a mythic mode of expression. A historicist, Smollett nevertheless felt a "revolutionary nostalgia" for the intuitive language of myth.

This theme is dramatized, not developed discursively, in the letters of Win Jenkins and Tabitha Bramble.[12] As we see when we look closely at Win's and Tabby's letters, their language is not abstract but intensely concrete. It evokes not the age of consciousness with its emphasis on logic and rationality but an earlier stage which, as Barfield says, did not postulate but simply assumed a reality in which there was no differentiation between spirit and body. Smollett's "nostalgia" for myth parallels Barfield's idea of poetic diction; it is an effort to *re*use language in such a way as to recapture its lost emotional overtones and meanings. A letter of Win's dated April 26 begins: "Heaving got a frank, I now return your fever" (41). Both misspellings suggest the inevitable attachment of mind to body. The abstract "favor" becomes a physical "fever"; and an indefinite "having" becomes a concrete "heaving." The misspellings undoubtedly show Win's sexual nature; but it would be reductive, I think, to suggest that was their only purpose. And her reference to "handsome Christians, without a hair upon their sin," shows that her mind also works the other way, elevating the physical "chin" to the spiritual idea of sin.

While we regard the idea that Smollett is trying to create an ideolect for Win as naive, we would be more likely to accept the notion that he is trying to mirror in written form the sound of her Welsh dialect. Actually, Smollett's purposes are more complex because they depend as much on how we *see* the words as how we *hear* them. The effect of inscription is synchronic; writing is a configuration in space that allows us to perceive multiple meanings. We visually perceive "sin" and think of what that spelling means in our own pronunciation; then we have to figure out by context what Win means. Were we to hear the passage read to us, there would not be the ambiguity. Speech, in fact, is more diachronic than writing. Pronunciation and intonation, for example, limit ambiguity. In speech, meaning is sequentially determined, for each new word affects and limits the possibilities of meaning in the following words. Smollett is not just trying to make us *hear* the passage the way Win would speak it in her dialect; rather, his primary emphasis is on the *visual* aspect of the words which awakens the reader to their multiple overtones. The Welsh might pronounce *favor* as *fever;* but Smollett clearly wants us to think first of the meaning of *fever* and then understand how, for Win, the abstract *favor* still echoes with the physical implications language had in earlier, mythic times. Consistently, by making us both *see* and hear Win and Tabby's language, Smollett evokes in their letters the lost unity between matter and spirit.

A longer passage from this letter reveals the brilliance of Smollett's imagining:

> Dear girl, I have seen all the fine shews of Bath; the Prades, the Squires, and the Circlis, the Crashit, the Hottogon, and Bloody Buildings, and Harry King's row; and I have been twice in the Bath with mistress, and na'r a smoak upon our backs, hussy——The first time I was mortally afraid, and flustered all day; and afterwards made believe that I had got the heddick; but mistress said, if I didn't go, I should take a dose of bum-taffy; and so remembring how it worked Mrs. Gwyllim a pennorth, I chose rather to go again with her into the Bath, and then I met with an axident. I dropt my petticoat, and could not get it up from the bottom—But

> what did that signify? they mought laff, but they could see nothing; for I was up to the sin in water. To be sure, it threw me into such a gumbustion, that I know not what I said, nor what I did, nor how they got me out, and rapt me in a blanket—Mrs. Tabitha scoulded a little when we got home; but she knows as I know what's what—Ah Laud help you!—There is Sir Yury Micligut, of Balnaclinch, in the cunty of Kalloway—I took down the name from his gentleman, Mr. O Frizzle, and he has got an estate of fifteen hundred a year—I am sure he is both rich and generous——But you nose, Molly, I was always famous for keeping secrets; and so he was very safe in trusting me with his flegm for mistress; which, to be sure, is very honourable; for Mr. O Frizzle assures me, he values not her portion a brass varthing—And, indeed, what's poor ten thousand pounds to a Baron Knight of his fortune? and, truly, I told Mr. O Frizzle, that was all she had to trust to—As for John Thomas, he's a morass fellor—I vow, I thought he would a fit with Mr. O Frizzle, because he axed me to dance with him at Spring garden—But God he knows I have no thought eyther of wan or t'other. (42)

In the diachronic world of the travel book, we would have the Circus, the Crescent, the Octogon, the Bladud Buildings, and Harlequin's Row of eighteenth-century Bath. But Win's language probes beneath the historic scene to a more synchronic reality where flesh and spirit intertwine in a more universal way. This is, perhaps, most obvious in "Crashit" for "Crescent." Once a living symbol both for virginity (Diana) and religion, the word *crescent* had become what Barfield calls a "dead metaphor." The deliberate emphasis on the excremental in Win's naming is a poetic evocation of a former mythic unity—perhaps the only way centuries of abstraction can be purged from the word.[13] Similarly, "Bloody Buildings" suggests a more archetypal physical presence than does Bladud, as well as evoking a vaguely sexual tone. "Circlis" also has sexual overtones, suggesting "clitoris." In naming Harlequin's Row "Harry King's row," Win shows the tendency of myth toward the particular and concrete rather than the abstract; and calling squares "Squires" demonstrates the tendency of myth to anthropomorphize.

This tendency toward mythopoeia is persistent throughout the passage. Win has spelled the word *know* correctly three times in her letter;

nevertheless, she says, "But you nose, Molly . . ." In mythic time one does "know" with other organs than the intellect; knowing is a matter of the senses rather than an abstraction, not unrelated to the way dogs "nose" one another and, perhaps for that reason, used only in relation to her fellow servant and not her social superiors. "Sin" for chin is repeated; Win thinks she describes only her physical state when she says, "I was up to the sin in water," but of course she evokes her spiritual condition as well. She transforms the Divinity in "Ah Laud help you!" The abstract "Lord" becomes the concrete lauds of the prayers, suggesting the physical direction Win's spiritual yearnings will take later in the book.

John Thomas is a "morass fellor" rather than a morose fellow, reflecting Win's inarticulate sexual impulse. That impulse also motivates her transformation of Sir Ulic Mackilligut into "Sir Yury Micligut, of Balnaclinch, in the cunty of Kalloway." This mythic vision of the knight evokes venality on both the sensual ("Bal," "cunt") and economic ("gut," "clinch") levels as does Win's later description of his "flegm" for her mistress. The synchronic vision can sometimes yield, Smollett suggests, a truer sense of things than the historical perspective.

We could examine the mythic implications of many other words (for example, "smoak," "heddick," "bum-taffy," "gumbustion") in this passage; but it will be more productive to pass on to another letter written as Win is about to set off in a "cox and four for Yorkshire." The coach appears prominently in the diachronic travel narrative: it breaks down and needs to be repaired by Humphry Clinker; it overturns in midstream and nearly kills Matt Bramble, etc. Win's journey, as the pun on *cock* reveals, concerns itself with the more synchronic reality of sex and family romance. (Smollett gives her four "stud" too: Humphry, Dutton, John Thomas, and Archy M'Alpin—called Machappy by Win.) Win goes on to describe how Humphry has been wrongly imprisoned: "The 'squire did all in his power, but could not prevent his being put in chains, and confined among common manufactors, where he stud like an innocent sheep in the midst of wolves and tygers.—Lord knows, what mought have happened to this pyehouse young man, if master had not applied to Apias Korkus, who lives with the ould baliff, and is, they say, five hundred years ould, (God bless us!) and a congeror" (152). In her synchronic way, Win concretizes the writ of habeas corpus into a mythological figure of a five-hundred-year-old conjurer. The biblical expression "sheep among wolves" had become a cliché by this time; but we note how Win renews its mythic potentiality by using the word "stud" (to say nothing of "common manufactors"!), thereby re-introducing the physical and sexual into what had become a spiritual banality.

The letter concludes with a wonderful conflation of religious and sexual meanings:

> Mr. Clinker . . . is, indeed, a very powerfull labourer in the Lord's vineyard. I do no more than yuse the words of my good lady, who has got the infectual calling; and, I trust, that even myself, though unworthy, shall find grease to be excepted.——Miss Liddy has been touch'd to the quick, but is a little timorsome: howsomever, I make no doubt, but she, and all of us, will be brought, by the endeavours of Mr. Clinker, to produce blessed fruit of generation and repentance.——As for master and the young 'squire, they have as yet had narro glimpse of the new light.——I doubt as how their harts are hardened by worldly wisdom, which, as the pyebill saith, is foolishness in the sight of God.
>
> O Mary Jones, pray without seizing for grease to prepare you for the operations of this wonderful instrument, which, I hope, will be exorcised this winter upon you and others at Brambleton-hall. (152)

From a strictly historicist position, I suppose we could say that Win's malapropisms satirically "express the reality behind the spiritual concerns of Methodism" (Rothstein *Systems* 127). Certainly, Tabby's "infectual" calling suggests Methodism as a kind of fever while Win's expectation of "grease" from Humphry's "instrument" suggests that it is merely a sublimation of sexual drives. But Smollett's purposes are more inclusive. "Quick," as in "the quick and the dead," has been reduced to its abstract meaning of "life," but clearly the quick to which Liddy has been touched is much more concrete. And it will, at the end of the novel, "produce blessed fruit of generation." Smollett here revivifies the mythic meaning of the word, and does not, I think, so much satirize the spiritual as ask us to recognize its foundation in the concrete. The spiritual reality of the Bible can withstand being called the "pyebill"; in fact, like the metaphor quick, it is revivified by being brought back into contact with its mythic origin. Jery and Matt's insistent rationalism, on the other hand, is undercut by the word "hart," which demonstrates that it, too, has a basis in the animal.

My argument is not to deny particular satire, but to suggest that Smollett's ultimate purposes are more inclusively to place historical reality in relation to myth, to juxtapose the diachronic and synchronic realities of words. In a marvelous phrase, Win tells Mary Jones to "pray without seizing for grease." Clearly, Win wants no one else touching Humphry's wonderful instrument, however much she wants them to be spiritually moved by it. Here the historical thrust, so to speak, perfectly balances the mythic one. "As for me," Win remarks in a later letter, "I put my trust in the Lord; and I have got a slice of witch elm sowed in the gathers of my under petticoat" (295). Christian revelation *and* pagan superstition: both together allow Win to "deify the devil and all his works" in "the new light of grease" (295).

Often skewing toward the scatological as Win's have toward the sexual, Tabitha's letters also demonstrate a rich use of language. She writes to Mrs. Gwyllim, housekeeper of Brambleton-hall: "I hope you keep accunt of Roger's purseeding in reverence to the butter-milk. I expect my dew when I come huom, without baiting an ass, I'll assure you.—As you must have layed a great many more eggs than would be eaten, I do suppose there is a power of turks, chickings, and guzzling about the house; and a brave kergo of cheese ready for market; and that the owl has been sent to Crickhowel, saving what the maids spun in the family" (264). "Accunt" is one of Tabby's favorite words, conflating as it does her interests in economy and sexuality. "Purseeding" is more subtle since "purse" underlines her meanness in money matters while "seeding" shows her interest in matrimony ("mattermoney," as Win calls it [337]) and procreation. Tabby's gross materialism is revealed in her "reverence to" (reference to) the buttermilk as a source of income; but the word "dew" for due has some of the same effect as seeding. It evokes an innocence and a timeless cyclicity that work against Tabby's mean-spirited commitment to the present. Similarly, "baiting an ass" for bating an ace suggests a concrete sexual impulse beneath Tabitha's principles of accounting. That alliance with the synchronicity of myth comes out in her pursuit of a husband, which despite Matt's and Jery's sneers, reflects strongly her sexual rather than her economic appetite.

Tabby's economic drives, aligned with diachronic historical impulses, may seem to have mastery over her; but her language always knows better. In her first letter to Mrs. Gwyllim, she writes: "The gardnir and the hind may lie below in the landry, to partake the house, with the blunderbuss and the great dog" (8). And, of course, "partake" is what they do, as on her instinctive level she too feels is her "dew." In the passage we have been analyzing, she consciously speaks about her poultry when she says, "I do suppose there is a power of turks, chickings, and guzzling about the house." Her language evokes, however, an image of Falstaffian excess, one that accords not incongruously with Tabby's own libidinal drives.

As Lismahago becomes the overt spokesman for the conservative view of language within the novel, Win dramatizes the counter view of mythic language in some of her letters. Unlike Liddy, who tries to say what she means, Win says more than she means because her language regains some of the vibrancy of myth:

> I pray of all love, you will mind your vriting and your spilling; for, craving your pardon, Molly, it made me suet to disseyffer your last scrabble, which was delivered by the hind at Bath—O, voman! voman! if thou had'st but the least consumption of what pleasure we scullers have, when we can cunster the crabbidst buck off hand, and spell the ethnitch vords without lucking at the primmer. As for Mr. Klinker, he is qualified to be clerk to a parish—But I'll say no more—Remember me to Saul—poor sole! it goes to my hart to think she don't yet know her letters—But all in God's good time—It shall go hard, but I will bring her the A B C in ginger-bread; and that, you nose, will be learning to her taste. (106)

Win thinks Humphry's command of language qualifies him to be clerk of the parish; we may think hers entitles her to be the clerk's wife. Her first sentence seems entirely carnal as she cautions Mary to be careful of her "spilling," with obvious sexual overtones. But this phrase, "I pray of all love," sets up a nice tension between body and spirit that climaxes with the sentence, "Remember me to Saul—poor sole!" Sal, the fellow servant girl, is, of course, a poor soul, a spiritual abstraction. But through the power of Win's language, she is "Matthew-murpheyed" into Saul, the New Testament saint, who has become, paradoxically, a physical body—a sole. And when we remember that the fish was a symbol for Christ who incarnated the spirit in the flesh, our admiration for the unifying aspect of Win's—and Smollett's—language increases.

Deconstructive critics, who seem to exult in the condition of the fall, can certainly point to the slipperiness of a language where "consumption" contends with conception and "sculler" spars with scholar. Win, however, knows in her "hart" that "all in God's good time" Sal/Saul, the poor soul/sole, will know her letters: "It shall go hard, but I will bring her the A B C in ginger-bread; and that, you nose, will be learning to her taste." Mythic language, the A B C in gingerbread, allows for the recovery of lost unities; it also, Smollett discovered, allows for the creation of credible voices for his characters. Win's and Tabby's language, to speak only of that one aspect of characterization, is the most convincing that Smollett gave to any of his characters.

While a deconstructive reading of the comic play on words in these letters can be made,[14] it seems more reasonable to conclude that Smollett had come to share Vico's and Boulanger's feeling that "words bore with them a set of emotive tones which were clues to the true temper of antiquity" (Manuel 218). A passage from Tabby's first letter speaks to this idea: "let none of the men have excess to the strong bear" (8). Pointing to the confusion between "excess" and "access," we could argue that language is unstable, a purely arbitrary and undependable system of signifiers. But we could also argue that the play on "excess"/"access" is a perfect illustration of the power of mythic language to reflect deeper unity rather than perpetual disunity. What Tabby's language really shows is her desire not for deprivation but for fulfillment (and particularly on an animal level, as in "bear" for beer).

As we saw, the archetypal "return" of Roderick Random was quite unconvincing because of Smollett's failure to find an adequate language. Only in *Humphry Clinker* does Smollett achieve a fruitful orchestration of different languages that leads to a convincing closure where myth is integrated with history.[15] Closure is focused in this last novel more around the achievement of an ideal mode of life than around the weddings which resolve its ostensible marriage plot. Always present in Matt's testy sense of the inadequacies of modern society, the idea of an ideal state gets its first extensive development as the characters travel in Scotland. In his letter marked Cameron, Sept. 6, Matt Bramble speaks of a "Scottish paradise" (244). He describes the marvelous foods they eat, the scenery they can view, the company with whom they visit, and he gives a brief history of the clan system. His is the point of view of the historian as he describes enthusiastically the world around him. Indeed, the idea that the Scottish material strays too far from novelistic convention has become a commonplace in Smollett criticism, where it is assumed that his enthusiasm for his native country caused him to lose sight of his novel as a novel (letters from Tabby and Win are nearly submerged in Matt and Jery's more reportorial letters).

As Smollett prepares to modulate from his satiric attack on the ills of society to his picture of its ideal realization, this emphasis on historical language is, however, necessary. By establishing the credibility of a good society on this realistic level, he readies his readers to accept a larger vision which includes a mythic dimension. Two letters by Matt and Jery as they cross back from Scotland to England further this process of modulation. Jery's letter marked Carlisle, Sept. 12, describes, first of all, the episode of the return of one Brown, a captain in the East Indies, who returns home to discover his ancient father at work paving a street. Having been security for his landlord and lost the money Brown had sent him, the old man is reduced to penury, another son having gone to jail for his debts. While Brown, unrecognized, talks to his father, the other son calls out from the prison window that his brother William has returned. His mother, hearing the cry, calls out, "Where is my bairn? where is my dear Willy?" (255). As if the scene were not sufficiently melodramatic and incredible already, Jery remarks that Bramble "was as much moved as any one of the parties concerned in this pathetic recognition.—He sobbed, and wept, and clapped his hands, and hollowed, and finally ran down into the street" (255). What is interesting to us is that this seemingly incredible story had a basis in historical fact. According to Robert Anderson, Smollett changed only the name of the real hero, which was White, into Brown (XI, 415, quoted in Parreaux, xxi). Clearly, Smollett here takes the material of history and turns it not into factual story but into a myth of return and reconciliation.

The second event Jery deals with is the "death" and "rebirth" of Lismahago. Traveling along the dangerous Solway sands, the group perceives Lismahago's dead horse and presumes he has been drowned. He is discovered alive at Carlisle, however; and it is at this point that Jery and Matt decide to encourage him to wed Tabby. Having seen the failure of his ideal vision of his native Scotland, Lismahago will have to embrace history in the vinegary arms of Tabitha. His story is the reverse of Brown's mythicization of history.

Matt's letter on crossing into England describes two "supernatural" events. In one, a story is recounted about how a man has received visionary foreshadowings of a visit from a group of friends (260–61); the other describes how a pragmatic Scotsman has been severely whipped by the ghost of his long dead grandfather (261–63). We soon discover that the latter "ghost" was Lismahago, who was mistaken for his dead father as he beat his nephew for desecrating the family home to commercial ends. A "historical" explanation for this supposed visionary scene is given; yet the other episode is left unexplained. Smollett here interweaves the mysterious and the rational as a part of the general orchestration of event and language that marks the end of the novel.

In the closing pages of the novel, the search for an ideal mode of life is explored in visits to four different country houses. The visit to Lord Oxmington's, which culminates in near strife as Bramble takes umbrage at the lord's condescension, symbolizes all that is wrong in a historical England which has perverted tradition and class standards. We are given a view of how the aristocracy has betrayed its historic social role, as well as of Bramble's quixotic defiance of that betrayal. The visit with Baynard and his wife describes how the lower gentry have also betrayed the ideal of the good life by aping the manners of those above them. Only the timely death of the wife saves Baynard from the bad end her extravagance has made otherwise certain. Under Bramble's guidance, Baynard is able to save himself from the spiritual and monetary bankruptcy Smollett sees as endemic in certain strata of contemporary English society.

The episode at Sir Thomas Bullford's offers a comic interlude which modulates history into myth. "Sir Tummas Ballfart," as Win calls him (295), is a Falstaffian lord of misrule who leads us from the everyday world of historical contingency into the holiday of comic release. The episode in which he figures properly comes, then, just before the climactic recognition scene. His main joke is on Lismahago, who is forced, through Sir Thomas's trickery, to expose himself in a scanty nightshirt at the top of a ladder. In parting, he tells Tabby that she should "remember him in the distribution of the brides's favours, as he had taken so much pains to put the captain's parts and mettle to the proof" (294). The pun on metal/mettle/and sexual organ is evidence that we are entering a freer linguistic world; and Win's reentry into the novel after a long absence confirms that the ideal state offered at the end of the novel will be presented in a wider spectrum of voices and language than that used to describe the "Scottish paradise."

The overturning of the coach in a river between the Bullford and the Dennison scenes plays an obvious archetypal role. During this symbolic death/rebirth sequence, not only is Humphry Clinker revealed as the natural son of Matt; but Bramble's own regeneration as a freer, more flexible person is confirmed. Metamorphosis, as applied to change in places and customs as well as in character, is as persistent a theme in *Humphry Clinker* as the idea of metempsychosis is in Joyce's *Ulysses*. Humphry first "metamorphosed" (81) his bare posteriors with a suit of clothes, making him acceptable to Tabby's virgin eyes. He is "metamorphosed into Matthew Lloyd" (306) when it is discovered he is Bramble's natural son. Lydia describes how her lover Wilson has been "metamorphosed into George Dennison" (321); and Win also comments on how Wilson has been "matthewmurphy'd" (323) into a fine young gentleman. Concerned as they were with change, both Smollett and Joyce were fascinated with the possibility of transforming history into myth—and also with the possibility that such transformations might be "murphy" tricks, as in Joyce's use of the seaman W. B. Murphy in the Eumaeus chapter of *Ulysses*.

The Dennison estate reflects Smollett's image of the ideal society. Dennison has achieved, Bramble says, "that pitch of rural felicity, at which I have been aspiring these twenty years in vain" (307). Byron Gassman points out that "the disappearance of precise geographical notation here helps remove the novel's final vision of England from historical and geographical particularity. The effect is as if the travellers were still in England, but not the England bound by the historical latitude and longitude of George III's precarious kingdom" (*Criticism* 107). The estate and what it represents thus take on mythic proportions. Much of the description is in Dennison's own voice; the language is more concrete and specific than Bramble's ordinarily more abstract and analytical style. The effect of distancing—Dennison being quoted by Bramble who in turn is separated from Smollett—lends an authority and resonance to this voice not always found in Smollett's fictions.

While Smollett thus introduces some of the synchronic effect of Win's and Tabby's letters into his picture of the Dennison estate, his purpose is not to substitute mythic understanding for rational knowledge. His "revolutionary" nostalgia is not for a simple return to intuitive modes of being. In fact, in Jery's letter that narrates Tabby's response to discovering the truth about Humphry, her myth is turned to history. Here, instead of *seeing* Tabby's own inscribed language with its synchronic effect, we *hear* her through Jery's ears: " 'Brother, you have been very wicked: but I hope you'll live to see the folly of your ways—I am very sorry to say the young man whom you have this day acknowledged, has more grace and religion, by the gift of God, than you with all your profane learning, and repeated opportunity—I do think he has got the trick of the eye, and the tip of the nose of my uncle Loyd of Flluydwellyn; and as for the long chin, it is the very moral of the governor's—Brother, as you have changed his name pray change his dress also; that livery doth not become any person that hath got our blood in his veins' " (306). The effect here is to historicize Tabby, to make her a much more conventional character than her own letters do. Since we inevitably bring echoes of the synchronic energies of those letters to our reading of Jery's transcription of her voice, Tabby retains much of her buoyancy as a character; yet her language has been remarkably flattened.

Thus, while Smollett maintains a variety of languages at the end of the novel, we do notice how each has taken on some of the color of the others. This idea is most triumphantly illustrated in Win's last words, the last of the book itself: "Present my compliments to Mrs. Gwyllim, and I hope she and I will live upon dissent terms of civility.—Being, by God's blessing, removed to a higher spear, you'll excuse my being familiar with the lower sarvents of the family; but, as I trust you'll behave respectful, and keep a proper distance, you may always depend upon the good will and purtection of Yours, W. Loyd" (337). We hear Win assuming the voice of the establishment in this passage, removing herself from the free play of democracy to the privilege of class (the reverse of Matt's own journey). Yet we also note how brilliantly Smollett reveals in the phrase "higher spear" all the emotion and sexuality that counters pure economic abstraction. Win's sexual energies will always be warring on her abstract sense of place, humanizing her. This idea is brought out most tellingly in the phrase "dissent terms of civility," which not only summarizes the dichotomy between the changing (history) and the unchanging (the mythic) which we have been tracing but also suggests how they must ultimately coexist.

Humphry Clinker is not "torn between" its mythic and historic visions, but rather exploits them in individual and effective manipulations of form, structure, and especially language. Understanding what Joyce has done in a nonrealistic form helps us to look back and better understand Smollett's similar achievement. Joyce took his own chance encounter with a Mr. Alfred Hunter and transformed it into the adventures of a modern Ulysses occurring within a single archetypal day. Smollett took his own trip to his native Scotland from May till August 1766 and fashioned it into a symbolic journey from spring to the rebirth of the Christmas dinner promised in Matt Bramble's last letter. Joyce's novel demonstrates both the historical world of Dublin 1904—drawing upon actual events, places, persons, and things—and the mythic world of Bloom's family romance. Smollett's five letter writers undertake a trip through a historical England and Scotland filled with real persons (including the author himself!) and events; but they also enact their family romance, moving from an initial estrangement to an ultimate harmony with one another.

The central point of comparison between the two novels lies in their use of language; but we find similarities also in the reconciliation of sons and fathers, the growth of the hero into a wiser perception of his relation to life, the emphasis both novels place on human excretions and the scatological, etc. What seems to lie behind all of these is their authors' persistent interest in the relation between what is ever renewed and what is perpetually changing. When Joyce violates the standards of realism to exploit the incompatibilities as well as the harmonies of synchronic and diachronic vision, we consider that he has written a masterpiece. Perhaps we owe *Humphry Clinker* a similar consideration. One modern critic has said that *Humphry Clinker* "is too much a 'gossiping novel,' too much of a pleasant potpourri of events, persons, data, observations, criticism, and moralizing ever to submit to the kind of analysis that discovers a single underlying principle dictating form and content to a work of fiction" (Gassman *Bicentennial Essays* 168). Not a novel in the realist tradition, neither is it a mere potpourri. It is a deeply original exploration of the relation between myth and history.

4

Mythic and Historic Plotting in Sterne

In "The Origin of Plot in the Light of Typology," Jurij M. Lotman analyzes the origin of plot from a typological rather than historical perspective. From this angle, mythic texts "are not, in our sense of the word, plot-texts and, in general, could only be described with great difficulty by means of our usual categories" (161). Speculating about the nature of these myths which antedate "those novelistic pseudo-myths which first come to mind at the mention of mythology" (164), Lotman emphasizes that their "first characteristic is the absence of the categories of beginning and end: the text is thought of as a mechanism which constantly repeats itself, synchronized with the processes of nature" (161). In myth, human life is "regarded not as a linear segment enclosed between birth and death, but as a constantly recurrent cycle" (Lotman 161–62). While myth verified the primordial order, historical plot-narration developed from the "fixing of unique and chance events"; and the "modern plot-text is the fruit of the interaction and reciprocal influence of these two typologically age-old types of texts" (Lotman 163). In addition to myth's cyclic structure—its absence of beginning and end—we discover its "tendency to make different characters unconditionally identical" (162); or, as Lotman says, "the more noticeably the world of characters is reduced to singularity (one hero, one obstacle), the nearer it is to the primordial mythological type of structural organization of the text" (168).

Sterne's plots demonstrate the "interaction and reciprocal influence" of myth and history, but as his career advances the ratios of influence shift. Early in *Tristram Shandy*, the emphasis is more on linear development, while in the later volumes the cyclical receives larger emphasis. In *A Sentimental Journey*, the movement is more pronouncedly toward myth. The *ab ovo* plan of the earlier novel suggests, of course, the straight line of history as we follow Tristram from conception to maturity and (eventual) death. But, as many critics have pointed out, the digressions create the effect of synchronicity, pulling us more and more into depth rather than extension. Nevertheless, as Tristram's diagrams of the plots of his volumes at the end of volume 6 (II 570–71) indicate, in spite of the digressions, the stories are linear. And, as he says, they become more decorously so as he proceeds in the novel till, in the pursuit of Toby's amours, he hopes to proceed in a straight (really flat) line with no digressions at all. The irony of this straight line, of course, is that it leads us in a circle, ending the novel well before it began. We see, at the end, that we have been caught up in a cyclical action rather than a linear one.

Such may have been Sterne's intention from the beginning; but in this chapter I want to explore how, belatedly and perhaps inadvertently in *Tristram Shandy* and more consciously in *A Sentimental Journey*, Sterne turned away from more traditional conceptions of linear plot to the primordial cyclic view of myth. Lotman has given us an excellent account of how linear plots help us to form coherent pictures of life:

> Plot represents a powerful means of making sense of life. Only as a result of the emergence of narrative forms of art did man learn to distinguish the plot aspect of reality, that is, to break down the nondiscrete flow of events into discrete units, to connect them to certain meanings (that is, to interpret them semantically) and to organize them into regulated chains (to interpret them syntagmatically). It is the isolating of events—discrete plot units—and the allotting to them, on the one hand, of a particular meaning, and, on the other, a particular temporal, cause-result or other regulatedness that makes up the essence of plot. (183)

Sterne wrote at a time before a breakdown of belief in the coherence of history began to erode this view of plot. Yet the pattern of his fiction, as we shall see, is to move away from this sense of purposive, revelatory plot. In this matter he reminds us more of Joyce than of Fielding, Richardson, or even Smollett. Yet we must recognize that Sterne's turn from linear plotting does not represent, as Robert Caserio has shown it did for many nineteenth-century novelists, a loss of confidence in plot's ability to mirror a coherent reality; rather, under the duress of his protracted ill-health, he comes to wish to turn away from historical process itself. That is, he does not mistrust linear plot's ability to shape reality; rather, he becomes imbued with nostalgia for another sort of reality, the deep vision of mythic repetition. While Joyce was clearly influenced by Sterne's use of cyclic plot (most fully in *Finnegans Wake*), his attraction to myth had undoubtedly more to do with an attenuation of his faith that linear plots could reflect reality.[1]

Lotman's thesis that mythic plot reduces the world of characters to singularity while linear plots emphasize differentiation provides another instructive way to look at Joyce and Sterne. Both writers distribute narrative authority among their characters in complex ways. For both this has much to do with how they project themselves into their various characters. Joyce makes complex use of his family and other historically real figures as models for his characters. He "projects" himself in Stephen just as he does his real father John Joyce in his portrait of Simon Dedalus. More complexly, he portrays himself as a father in his picture of Leopold Bloom, modeled on the real-life Alfred Hunter. Although Sterne does not use actual life-models for his projections as Joyce does, there is a sense—noticed by many critics (e.g., Stovel 124 and Brissenden 206–7)—that his characters seem "real" rather than literary constructs. In part, this has to do with the same sort of self-projection into his characters that we find in Joyce. Sterne projects himself into Tristram; and in a complex way he "fathers" a double parent in Father Shandy and Uncle Toby. Though having no historical prototype as Simon Dedalus did, they undoubtedly project certain psychological realities for Sterne.

In the case of Yorick, the issue is even more complex. John Hay was one of the first to notice the discrepancy between the time of Tristram's apparent conception and his delivery—only eight months had passed. Recognizing the "latent suggestion that Walter is not Tristram's father" (84), he nevertheless held that Sterne clarified the issue at the very end of the novel when Dr. Slop suggested Obadiah's child was premature (89–90). Sterne had teased the reader with the possibility of infidelity only to demonstrate that Tristram's was really a case of premature birth. Writing later, Lila Graves argued that Walter was "probably a cuckold" (262); and Richard Macksey has suggested that we must see Yorick as the best candidate for Tristram's real father (1010). The text of the novel makes so clear Mrs. Shandy's total lack of sensuality (II 736) that it is hard to credit any real infidelity. Why, then, has Sterne strewn such deceptive clues through the work? Not, I think, just to tease the reader but rather to suggest the complex symbolic possibilities of fatherhood for the artist and his creation. In the simplest sense, we can accept Yorick as Sterne's own self-projection; the publication of the *Sermons* under Yorick's name amplifies that identification. In this case, Sterne shows through the hint of Yorick's being Tristram's father that he—the author—fathers the son—the art construct. In a more complex way, however, Tristram as a son "fathers" Yorick, creating him much the same way he creates My Father and Uncle Toby. The son fathers not only his "father-figures" but the indefinably more real "father" who, paradoxically, is himself.

Stephen's theory, in the library scene of *Ulysses*, of the artist becoming not only his father but his father's father would seem to owe something to the complexities of self-projection that we find in Sterne's *Tristram Shandy*. Behind Stephen's theory and Sterne's practice lie both the unitive aspect of mythic plot and the differentiation of linear plot. From the point of view of history, My Father Shandy, Uncle Toby, Yorick, and Tristram himself all enact separate roles; but from the point of view of myth all embody the same character who represents a complex representation of Sterne himself. And, as we shall see, the mythic action at the end of the novel reduces differentiation among the different projections. In *Ulysses* the theory is Stephen's rather than Joyce's; and although he allows Bloom and Stephen to grow toward one another as the end of *Ulysses* looms, Joyce never lets his plot slip as far into myth as Sterne does.

"Myth always speaks about me," Lotman says; but "'News,' an anecdote, speaks about *somebody else*. The first organizes the hearer's world, the second adds interesting details to his knowledge of this world" (163). Focusing on the end of *Tristram Shandy*, I have been treating Sterne as though he were all "me"; but, in fact, much of this novel is concerned with "news," or knowledge of our world. It is time to stand back from theory and generalization and look more specifically at Sterne's texts. What I want to do first is to show the extent to which he accommodates historical reality to his linear plots. Although Sterne did make the satire of his novel more general than that of his trial run *A Political Romance*, it has a strong historical base.[2] Dr. Slop, for example, is a satirical picture of Dr. John Burton (Cash I 179). And Stovel argues that "the real-life experience of gossip" is the basis for Sterne's art (123), while Rogers contends that he "makes fiction aspire to the condition of journalism" (142). Perhaps of more interest to us than the sources in actuality of much of Sterne's material is his use of historical documents in his fiction. As Cash points out, he incorporated his own sermon "The Abuses of Conscience," preached on Sunday, 29 July 1750, into *Tristram Shandy* (I 234). Admired by some, the sermon is dismissed by Byrd as padding introduced into the volume "by a nervous first novelist" (100). One can admire the cleverness with which Sterne adapts the reading of the sermon to the tension between Slop's Catholicism, Toby's bland Anglicanism, and Walter's scientific curiosity without being much taken with the document itself.

Other major historical documents introduced into *Tristram Shandy* are the "Memoire presenté à Messieurs les Docteurs de Sorbonne" and "Ernulphus's Curse." The patent absurdity of the first text clearly appealed to Sterne's sense of the ridiculous; as the editors of the Florida edition point out, the fact that it is *not* fiction but a historical record "is surely the very essence of Sterne's satirical point" (II 940). The comedy of Sterne's suggestion that pre-consummation baptism could be achieved "*par le moyen d'une* petite canulle, and, *sans faire aucun tort a le pere*" (I 70) has perhaps never been so adequately clarified as in this edition (II 943). The Florida editors have also described Sterne's sources for the excommunication document and have suggested the likely source of the English translation in the *Gentleman's Magazine* (II 952–57). As cleverly as Sterne stitches the curse into the dramatic context of his fiction, one can only believe he stretches the limits of how much historical documentation a fictional plot can accept.

In addition to historical documentation, *Tristram Shandy* is strewn with pseudo-documents—materials either made up entirely or in part but passed off as documents by Sterne. The chief of these, of course, is the pretended translation of Slawkenbergius's Tale. The Florida editors "see no reason to believe that a source exists for his 'Fabella.' Indeed, it seems likely that Sterne wrote the English version and then translated it into Latin" (III 279). The Fragment, "Upon Whiskers," is a somewhat more complex case where Sterne may be following one or more of the numerous scandalous accounts of Margaret of Valois's court (III 341). What is interesting here is simply the impulse to give the appearance of history to material which obviously is not.

We ought also to note that Tristram frequently refers to himself as a historian. He speaks of sitting down "to write a history" (I 41); again refers to his work as a "history" (I 75); talks of the "history" of Toby's campaigns (I 113); remarks that all that concerns him "as an historian, is to represent the matter of fact, and render it credible to the reader" (I 381), etc. In a discussion of Locke's *Essay on the Human Understanding*, Tristram tells his reader that it is "a history-book, Sir . . . of what passes in a man's own mind" (I 98). Building around this passage, many critics have suggested that *Tristram Shandy* is, in fact, an illustration of what history becomes in a post-Lockean (or post-Humean) world where communal life is replaced by the isolation and estrangement of individualism.

Although these historical materials primarily appear in the earlier volumes, there is a resurgence of them in volume 7, which one critic has said "could be read as a preliminary draft for the later travelogue" (Hamlin 212). While it is possible that the disparate materials in this volume do result from Sterne's efforts to eke out another volume,[3] we might also interpret them as reflecting the tensions Sterne felt over plotting his work. The three roads from Calais to Paris which confront Yorick could symbolize Sterne's three narrative options as he was coming to understand them.[4] First, there is "the road by Lisle and Arras, which is the most about—but most interesting and instructing" (II 579). This might be conceived as the plot of the "travel-writer" (II 579) Sterne refers to in chapter 4. Such a writer, observing history, would give useful and pleasing information to his readers. A chapter illustrating this mode of "plotting" would be chapter 5, Sterne's extended comment on Calais, its churches, convents, square, town hall, etc. That this purely historical style might not be Sterne's most congenial is suggested in the notes to the Florida edition, which indicate that the chapter is "a parodic rewriting of Piganiol's entry on Calais, *Nouveau Voyage*" (III 450).

The second route is "that by Amiens, which you may go, if you would see Chantilly" (II 579). Perhaps the chapter on Janatone can serve as a gloss on this plot option. Rather than satisfy "your worships" as to the "length, breadth, and perpendicular height of the great parish church, or a drawing of the fascade of the abbey of Saint Austerberte which has been transported from Artois hither" (II 589), this more novelistic mode will focus on telling stories about the human form: "he who measures thee, Janatone, must do it now—thou carriest the principles of change within thy frame, and considering the chances of a transitory life, I would not answer for thee a moment; e'er twice twelve months are pass'd and gone, thou mayest grow out like a pumpkin and lose thy shapes—or, thou mayest go off like a flower, and lose thy beauty—nay thou mayst go off like a hussy—and lose thyself.—I would not answer for my aunt Dinah, was she alive—'faith, scarce for her picture—were it but painted by Reynolds" (II 589–90). The imagery of impregnation, as well as the allusion to Aunt Dinah, suggests a plot about a human "fall" so common as scarcely to be recordable in a significant way unless ("were it but") by the master realist Sterne considers Reynolds.

The third route is "that by Beauvais, which you may go, if you will. For this reason a great many chuse to go by Beauvais" (II 579). Caught between the ephemera of stories of the banality of human passions and the factuality of history, Tristram seeks, even "wills,"[5] to find a third mode of plotting. Clearly, that mode would be mythic; but Sterne enacts a curious pattern here, setting up mythic or synchronic situations and then either demonstrating that they do not work or having Tristram run away from them.

I shall limit my discussion of this point to two episodes, only one involving Tristram. In one of the few stories included in this volume, Sterne describes how the Abbess of Andouillets and the novice Margarita become involved in an imbroglio. Afflicted with a "wicked stiff joint" (II 611), the abbess decided to try the hot baths of Bourbon, taking with her the novice Margarita, who has got "a whitloe in her middle finger, by sticking it constantly into the abbess's cast poultices, &. . ." (II 607). Their muleteer, who believes that the nun has got a "white swelling by her devotions" (II 609), drives the mules faithfully till his wine runs out and he deserts for an inn. Halfway up the mountain, the mules stop; and the nuns fear ravishment. Unwilling to pollute their lips with the curses needed to get the animals moving, they agree to divide the words between them:

Abbess Bou ___ bou ___ bou ___
Margarita ___ ger, ___ ger, ___ ger
Margarita Fou ___ fou ___ fou ___
Abbess ___ ter, ___ ter, ___ ter. (II 614)

I have rather grossly underlined the imagery to whose sexual implications a number of critics have pointed. I believe the innuendoes are more subtle than those of a smutty story, however. We have a little scenario here of the tension between mythic and historic response. If we look at the nuns' words vertically—or synchronically—as they hope the mules will hear them, they are involving themselves in a realm of myth and sexuality that gives an impure reading to the earlier description of them. If, however, we look at their words horizontally—or diachronically, they are being faithful to their religious calling, keeping sinful words from their lips and also keeping their bodies free from sex. Ironically, the nuns are put in a situation where they have to risk mythic contamination to preserve their historical dignity. Even more ironically, their risk does not pay off. "They [the mules] do not understand us, cried Margarita—But the Devil does, said the Abbess of Andouillets" (II 614).

When the lady reader in the next chapter tells him that it is a strange story, Tristram agrees: "Had I thought of writing it upon the purer abstractions of the soul, and that food of wisdom, and holiness, and contemplation, upon which the spirit of man (when separated from the body) is to subsist forever—You would have come with a better appetite from it . . . I wish I never had wrote it" (II 615). Even allowing for an ironic tone here, I think we can feel the Anglican clergyman's persistent ambiguity about the propriety of involving the nuns in a mythic as opposed to Christian and historic narration.

Such ambiguity also underlies the last episode I want to look at, though the situation is made more complex by Tristram's self-admitted sexual incapacitation. Although other travelers might find a great plain boring, Tristram and his mule delight in it, seizing "every handle, of what size or shape soever" to turn a "*plain* into a *city*" (II 648). The crowning episode is the "ring of pleasure" (II 649) which the peasants make of their dance. Invited to join them, Tristram does so joyously though he keeps reflecting on the slit in Nannette's petticoat (II 650): "Why could I not live and end my days thus? Just disposer of our joys and sorrows, cried I, why could not a man sit down in the lap of content here—and dance, and sing, and say his prayers, and go to heaven with this nut brown maid? capriciously did she bend her head to one side, and dance up insidious—Then 'tis time to dance off, quoth I" (II 651). Again, we have a situation where Tristram veers very close to a mythic plot,[6] only to pull back from it to historical time. Working from Tristram's admission of his impotence (II 624), we can take a purely naturalistic view of this whole scene: the recurring anxiety about

Nannette's slit clearly can mark a fear of sexual testing.[7] We can also interpret the scene as reflecting Tristram's anxiety about plot. As in the anecdote about the Abbess of Andouillets, I think we must see Christian and historical plots winning out over pagan cyclicity.[8] Although the option of mythic plotting is raised in volume 7, in his first working through of this material Sterne clearly rejected the full implications of synchronicity that he would later accept in *A Sentimental Journey*. If the slit in Nannette's skirt symbolizes Tristram's fear of sexual adequacy on the naturalistic level, on a more metaphysical plane it can suggest Sterne's anxiety about a fall out of Christian time.

We can further illustrate the often creative tensions between mythic and linear plot in *Tristram Shandy* by comparing Sterne's telling of "Slawkenbergius' Tale" in volume 4 with his later treatment of Uncle Toby's amours with the Widow Wadman at the end of the novel. Whereas in the earlier tale we have a "myth" which is told in a linear historical mode, in the amours we have a "history" that is given a synchronic, mythic dimension to close out the novel. While "Slawkenbergius' Tale" comically and hilariously illustrates Walter Shandy's interest in "noses," on a level of deep content it shows Sterne's concern about the dangers of living in mythic absorption rather than historically. Since the tale really involves two different sets of characters, the problem is explored on two levels. The first group includes Diego, the possessor of the glorious nose, Julia, and her brother Fernandez. Having doubted Diego's nose, Julia has forbidden him to court her. Quickly repentant, she and her brother set off to find Diego after he has taken her at her word. Diego has meanwhile gone to the "promontory of Noses" to make up for his insufficiencies. After having passed through Strasburg and promised to return in a month, Diego meets Fernandez at a small inn, reads Julia's letter of repentance, and, forgetting his promise to the Strasburgers, travels back to Valadolid with Julia and Fernandez. The other group of characters is the Strasburgers—nuns, priests, ministers, innkeepers, trumpeters, and trumpeters' wives. Since he has refused to allow anyone to touch it, their only connection with Diego is through either the sight or report of his enormous nose. Having collectively suffered pangs of desire, lust, regret, curiosity, and anxiety for twenty-eight days, the Strasburgers en masse travel out to the road Diego is to take on his return. While they are away, the French occupy their city.

Having adopted the *form* of romance for his inset story (much as Cervantes had for his), Sterne insists that it adhere to the precepts of classical tragedy as far as its meaning goes.

> Haste we now towards the catastrophe of my tale—I say *Catastrophe* (cries *Slawkenbergius*) inasmuch as a tale, with parts rightly disposed, not only rejoiceth (*gaudet*) in the *Catastrophe* and *Peripeitia* of a *DRAMA*, but rejoiceth moreover in all the essential and integrant parts of it—it has its *Protasis, Epitasis, Catastasis,* its *Catastrophe* or *Peripeitia* growing one out of the other in it, in the order *Aristotle* first planted them—without which a tale had better never be told at all, says *Slawkenbergius,* but be kept to a man's self. (I 316–17)

Peripety is, of course, associated with linear rather than with cyclical plot; and in insisting on this Aristotelian element Sterne is associating his *fabella,* however tenuously, with history, not with myth. Sterne (or Slawkenbergius) insists that Diego achieves such peripety, bringing him "out of a state of agitation (as Aristotle calls it) to a state of rest and quietness" (I 317). Diego, of course, is a vestigial character, hardly developed at all; yet several things associate him with the reality of history. Accused of inadequacy, he promptly acquires the proper goods to prevent Julia's "dying *un*——" (I 321). He will not live in a perpetuity of romantic longing but will achieve a realistic climax to his romance. Sterne underlines this idea by describing how, as he waited for his mule to be harnessed, Diego "eased his mind against the wall" (I 222) by writing an ode to Julia on it. The Florida editors quote Partridge to suggest that "easing oneself was used euphemistically for *ejaculation*" and they suggest that "the text of the verse might support that usage" (III 297).

As his confusing Diego with the Strasburgers as the hero of his story in the breakdown of the plot into its different Aristotelian components suggests (I 317), Sterne is really more concerned with the Strasburgers' catastrophe than with Diego's. In hilarious satirical detail Sterne describes how the preoccupation with Diego's nose involves everyone from the trumpeter's wife to the abbess of *Quedlinburg* to, ultimately, the faculties of the popish and the Lutheran universities. These faculties had previously been involved in a dispute over Martin Luther (which Sterne took from Bayle's *Dictionary* [III 290]), which adumbrates the

Nosarian controversy that Diego stirs up. The "Popish doctors" have proved by his horoscope that Luther must be unavoidably damned for his doctrines; but the Lutheran doctors prove by the name Martin (taken from Martinmas day) that the Catholics have mistaken Luther's birthday. Historical reality undercuts myth. But even the doctors become caught up in the Nosarian controversy, and they all march out of town to observe Diego on his supposed return. This is the catastrophe/peripety Sterne really wants to underscore. By becoming absorbed in the mythic tale (as learned divines become absorbed in the "gulph of school-divinity" [I 315]), the Strasburgers lose sight of historical reality and allow the French to occupy their city. The Florida editors believe that Sterne took the particular account of the fall of Strasburg from Gilbert Burnet (III 298); but, of course, the reason he offers—the Strasburgers' absorption in the nose—is his own. I suggest that we see that reason not simply as a device in the allegory of the fall of the city but as symbolizing Sterne's sense of *why* they fell. That is, their absorption in the synchronic "reality" of the nose blinded them to historical contingency. Beginning as a fabella (albeit a satiric one), "Slawkenbergius' Tale" eventually involves all its characters in a linear plot leading toward peripety—as befits the more satirical first half of *Tristram Shandy*.

The most obvious link between the "Tale" and Toby's amours is the crimson breeches both men wear. The first paragraph of the Tale describes "a crimson pair of breeches" (I 289) in Diego's bag; and after he arrives in Strasburg he changes into them and parades about (I 295). The issue of whether Toby will wear his "thin scarlet breeches" or his "red plush" ones becomes much debated (II 714). Since the thin ones, which Trim thinks would be less "clumsy," have already been turned, Toby is fated to sally forth in the red plush (II 739). Another link occurs in the mention of Slawkenbergius after the blank chapters which obscure Toby's proposal to the Widow. Sterne signals a connection between these two episodes to the alert reader. Beyond these surface links, we have deeper structural similarities. Julia's anxiety about Diego's nose (read penis) causes him to undertake a hero's quest. Donning his red breeches at strategic moments, Diego raises the interest of the Strasburgers in his quest. Whereas Diego as hero successfully completes his quest, the Strasburgers allow it to distract them from historical reality and they "fall" to the French. The widow's anxiety over Toby's wound parallels Julia's over Diego's nose. Though Toby has the red trousers, he is not prepared to complete the hero's journey. His "non-quest" rouses the interest of the family; and its failure marks not only his but their fall. As I shall indicate as I expand this analysis of Toby's amours, he becomes trapped in mythic vision, unable to accept mature sexuality or history.

Toby's bowling green has, in fact, symbolized the myth/history paradoxes he is involved in. Derived from history, an effort to illustrate, not explain, historical battles, the bowling green paradoxically becomes an escapist retreat from historical contingency. W. B. Carnochan has compared it to Gulliver's stables and Crusoe's island, a "paradise of covertly innocent sexuality regained" where Toby "finds a place to hide" (53). Much has been written of the "games" that Toby and Trim play there; perhaps I can focus on a story that does not get told in the bowling green. Seeking to divert Toby, Trim has undertaken to tell him the story of the King of Bohemia, the only one of his stories not taken from his own life. Although Toby insists no date is needed, Trim feels one would give the story a better "face." Unfortunately, the year he chooses, 1712, is bad on two grounds: it is the year that the Duke of Ormond broke up the siege of Quesnoy (III 509), a reminder to Toby of the Peace of Utrecht, and it makes Trim's inclusion of a giant in his story untenable. Agreeing to leave the date out, Trim and Toby get distracted to a discussion of the difference between chronology and geography. Agreeing that chronology is of little importance to a soldier, Toby insists nevertheless on the vital importance of geography. This valuing of space over time is, of course, one of the aspects of myth.[9] Toby's resistance to the telling of the story, in fact, becomes a resistance to time. "Ultimately," Holtz argues, "the strategy of not telling a story is a figure of staying alive, of transcending change" (142).

In contrast with "Slawkenbergius' Tale," which began as a myth but ended having serious historical import, the story of Toby's romance is broached almost as a "history." Toby, Walter, Mrs. Shandy, and Yorick all have status as being more "real" than Diego and Julia. Tristram is, albeit unwillingly, Toby's "historian" in these amours; and the story would focus on a reversal whereby Toby could recognize the folly of his former ways and open himself up not just to the Widow Wadman but to the reality of life and death her name signifies. (*Widow* connotes death; *man* implies life, as *wad* sexually puns on the ejaculate that creates it.)

Toby shows his potentiality for such a growth in understanding when Walter asks him whether his love for Widow Wadman is that of the brain or the liver. Toby replies, "What signifies it, brother Shandy . . . which of the two it is, provided it will but make a man marry, and love his wife, and get a few children" (II 718). This attitude shows a commitment to process, and its compatibility with Christian historicism is affirmed by Yorick's commendation of it. Indeed, Toby's romance with the widow offers him a chance to live in "real" time. But such a "history" is not to be written in the changed ethos of volume 9. As the pervasive historical impulse of the novel's beginning undermined the myth of the "Tale," so the predisposition toward synchronic reality will undercut the historical veneer of the ending.

A subtle masturbation theme foreshadows Toby's inability to accept his own definition of love. Here we discover another link with Joyce's *Ulysses*, where masturbation serves a function similar to the one I describe here.[10] Pipe smoking has been persistently associated with Toby throughout the novel, but a subtle coloration is given it later in the book. To please Toby, Trim has created a set of two batteries which he makes simulate firing guns by smoking ivory and ebony turkish pipes which his brother Tom has given him. Toby, needless to say, is pleased at the effect and yearns to create it. Finally, he does ask Trim for the ivory pipe and retreats with it into his sentry box. Tristram cries out: "Dear uncle *Toby*! don't go into the sentry-box with the pipe,—there's no trusting a man's self with such a thing in such a corner" (II 549). In the description of Widow Wadman's earlier advances on Toby in volume 8, she feigns an interest in his fortifications and squeezes into the sentry box with him. One of the first things she does is "to take my uncle Toby's tobacco-pipe out of his hand as soon as she possibly could" (II 676). Having gotten rid of the masturbatory symbol, she is free to attack both his hands and his legs so that, as Tristram asks, "was it a wonder, if now and then, it put his centre into disorder?" (II 678). The widow's technique lacks finesse; but with someone whose "centre" is as slow to move as Toby's one cannot blame her. Tristram had described how, when the trumpet of war fell out of his hands, Toby had taken up the symbol of love, "the lute, sweet instrument! of all others the most delicate! the most difficult!—how wilt thou touch it, my dear uncle *Toby*?" (II 562). Accustomed to his pipe playing, Toby will touch the lute only very lightly.

Whereas Yorick in *A Sentimental Journey* will hold hands unselectively with lady or grisette, Toby is much more discriminating. Although the widow may attack his hand with hers, Toby reserves his hand holding for Walter. After Walter recovers himself from Toby's definition of love and wishes him many children, "My uncle Toby stole his hand unperceived behind his chair, to give my father's a squeeze" (II 719). If Toby is able to break out of the solipsism symbolized by masturbation, it is only to a fraternal relationship with his brother Walter. Married love, signifying a commitment to historical experience, is beyond him. The chapter of his *eclaircissment* about Widow Wadman's concern for his wound is framed with references to his pipe. At the beginning he has laid his pipe down on the table to count over to himself "upon his finger ends (beginning at his thumb) all Mrs. Wadman's perfections one by one" (II 801). After this encouraging beginning, he learns from Trim that the widow is really concerned about the status of his sexual apparatus. When he does so, "My uncle Toby laid down his pipe as gently upon the fender, as if it had been spun from the unravellings of a spider's web—. / —Let us go to my brother Shandy's, said he" (II 803). Thus, I believe, Sterne signals to us the effectual end of Toby's sexual life and of his involvement in history. Unlike Diego, who responds to Julia's doubts about his sufficiencies by visiting the promontory of noses, Toby can only lay aside his symbol of manhood and retreat to the world of myth.

Toby consequently fails to undergo peripety in his amours. Having been offered the possibility of genuine growth through an encounter with the reality of sexuality, Toby's modesty forces him to continue in his obsession. One result of that obsession, as the inverted time sequence of the novel has revealed, is Trim's taking the weights from the nursery window, ultimately causing Tristram's circumcision and hinted impotence. In fact, as this identity between the fates of Toby and Tristram suggests, one of the centrally mythic aspects about the last volume of *Tristram Shandy* is, in Lotman's terms, the reduction of the characters to singularity. That is, they do not tend toward the differentiation of characters involved in historical plot but to the unitive quality of characters found in texts whose structural organization is primarily mythic. Another example would be Widow Wadman, whose archetypal role is made clear when she is identified as a "daughter of Eve," which, Tristram says "'tis all the character I intend to give of her—" 'That she was a perfect woman' " (II 664). We have, moreover, explicit doubling of paired character relations that further reduce differentiation. Toby's relation with the widow in the parlor is paired with Trim and Bridget's in the kitchen. Paralleling these is Father Shandy's unsatisfactory relation with his wife. The inadequacy of all these relations on either a physical or a spiritual basis underlines the way they are projections of Tristram's own unsatisfactory relation with Jenny. Indeed, in the "Cock and Bull" ending capped on the novel by Yorick, we can see embodied not just the parish bull's and Toby's impotence but that of My Father Shandy, Yorick, and Tristram as well. Instead of remaining individual characters, each of whom offers "news" of an individual, separate fate, the characters at the end speak of the "me" that Lotman says lies behind myth.

In *Reflexivity in Tristram Shandy* (1977), James Swearingen offers a similar reading of the novel. Recognizing that fiction "usually reveals character through diachronic or horizontal presentation of the character's engagement with his world" (94), he argues that in this novel "the strategy is a synchronic or vertical presentation of the structures of Tristram's being" (94–95). Or as he capsulizes his idea, "The analysis is of a being whose existence is process, but the method is the reflexive explication of the synchronic structures of that being" (100). Metaphorically identifying the diachronic method with the "journey" and the synchronic with the "picture," Swearingen recognizes that they "come into irreconcilable conflict" (117–18). Nevertheless, he suggests that by plunging into a synchronic effort to "interpret" his relations to his family, Tristram purifies his "picture" of his tradition. "The form of that purification is the retrieval of a much older and wiser stratum of his tradition represented by Yorick" (15). Although I agree that the novel *ends* on a "picture" of the family, I have seen more emphasis throughout the novel on the idea of linear development or the "journey" of Tristram and his family. The stasis of Toby's amours and the cock and bull ending modifies the more developmental aspect of earlier parts of the novel, such as "Slawkenbergius' Tale." Moreover, while I respect Swearingen's effort to assess the tone of the novel,[11] I find it difficult to separate Yorick's role from that of the others at the end of the novel. All seem to share in the impotence of the bull, making it difficult to believe that any one character represents Sterne's moral position.

The novel has not worked toward the differentiation of character through which we could assess moral development and attitude. Instead, it harmonizes characters, taking them back in time before one, Tristram, was even conceived. In this way, the ending of *Tristram Shandy* goes even further into myth than does Joyce's *Ulysses*. Stephen and Bloom do achieve a coming together, yet they remain separate. Their mythic uniting is only partial, thus permitting a growth in understanding for both. Similarly, Molly's recalling at the end of her soliloquy the seed cake passage which Bloom had earlier remembered shows the symbolic oneness she achieves with her husband; yet both remain individuated characters capable of achieving insight based on peripety, even if joined at some mythic level.

The other major issue raised by the mythic character of volume 9 is the question of ending. I would certainly not argue with Wayne Booth's contention that Sterne had "completed" *Tristram Shandy*. A more relevant question is whether he had "ended" the novel in the sense that we think linear plots do end. Here, Malcolm Bradbury seems correct in arguing that we are left "without that sense of an ending, that drift toward apocalyptic conclusiveness that gives most novels their air of performing integrally as opposed to accidentally" (36). (Bradbury quite rightly recognizes that such an "accidental view of fiction" leaves Sterne's "art open to superb serendipities" [36].) In Frank Kermode's terms, the sense of an ending we would be looking for would be a "concord fiction," something that would draw together our two different senses of plot, the linear one leading to growth and change and the cyclic one leading to attunement. Unlike Joyce, who in *Ulysses* does achieve such a harmonious resolution of plot, Sterne in this novel does not. That particular serendipity will be found in *A Sentimental Journey*, where Sterne works more freely and comfortably with the interaction of history and myth.

As Sterne's frequent commentary throughout the novel makes clear, he had trouble knowing exactly what kind of story he wanted to tell. When Sterne is in high stride, his admonitions on the difficulty of plotting have a high comic flavor—as in the passage on the cow that "broke in (tomorrow morning) to my uncle *Toby*'s fortifications" (I 278). When he speaks, at the opening of volume 7, of never being "more at a loss to make ends meet, and torture the chapter I had been writing, to the service of the chapter following it" (II 663), we sense a real problem. In fact, Tristram enumerates real difficulties: debt, unsold copies of the fifth and sixth volumes of his book, asthma, and hemorrhaging (II 663). One suspects, however, that the deeper problem is more like Walter's as he struggles with whether to spend Aunt Dinah's legacy to enclose the great Ox-moor or to send Bobby on his foreign travels. "No body but he who has felt it can conceive what a plaguing thing it is to have a man's mind torn asunder by two projects of equal strength, both obstinately pulling in a contrary direction at the same time" (I 399). As the complications of the last three volumes suggest, Sterne was undecided which way to turn: to the "history" he developed in volume 7 or to the myth of Toby's romance which he somewhat reluctantly circles around in volumes 8 and 9. Focused on Sterne's own foreign travels, volume 7 emerges fairly coherently; but with much of 8 and 9 we may feel that Tristram's analysis of Trim's problems in telling the "Tale of the King of Bohemia" is an exercise in self-analysis: "For by the many sudden transitions all along, from one kind and cordial passion to another, in getting thus far on his way, he had lost the sportable key of his voice which gave sense and spirit to his tale" (II 748).

One of the most blatant patterns of imagery in the novel suggests Sterne's irresolution. This is a pattern of mediation of oppositions that permeates the book. Yorick, for example, considers "that brisk trotting and slow argumentation, like wit and judgment, were two incompatible movements—But that, upon his steed—he could unite and reconcile everything" (I 20–21). Early in his text Tristram announces that his work is "of a species by itself; two contrary motions are introduced into it, and reconciled, which are thought to be at variance with each other. In a word, my work is digressive, and it is progressive too,—and at the same time" (I 80–81). Walter Shandy is much taken with Bacon's notion of balancing internal spirit with external air (I 474); and his "beds of justice" (II 522–24), as he calls his habit of taking counsel before and after fulfilling his monthly duties to his wife, offer the wisdom of mediation: "For from the two different counsels taken in these two different humours, a middle one was generally found out" (II 524).

But there are other occasions in the novel when the motif of mediation is disputed. As the narrator of "Slawkenbergius' Tale" tells us, "Truth (for once) is found in the middle" (I 323). That parenthesis, "for once," suggests a qualification of the principle of mediation. And, indeed, as in the case of the contention between radical heat and radical moisture (I 471), there seems no resolution. Similarly, the failure of "good understanding" (I 326) between the brain and the heart is one reason the continuation of the tale of Diego and Julia does not get told. In other cases, resolution to oppositions is achieved, but only by strokes of fate that simplify choices. Bobby's death relieves Walter's indecision between the tour and the Ox-moor. Similarly, Walter's ambivalence between the systems of Prignitz and Scroderus about noses is ended when Ambrose Pareus overthrows both (I 276).

Largely, however, the imagery of the book supports the idea of mediation. When Didius thinks he has trapped Yorick on the horns of a dilemma, the latter's good nature allows him to reconcile opposites (I 376). And Walter's comment, "Every thing in this world . . . is big with jest,—and has wit in it, and instruction too,—if we can but find it out" (I 470), seems symbolic of the novel's effort to seek mediation of opposites. The marble page, "motley emblem of my work!" (I 268), can also be seen as mediating between the black one which symbolizes Yorick's death and the blank one which awaits the widow's picture. In his letter to Toby about love, Walter offers advice directly apropos the need to mediate: "Let not thy breeches be too tight, or hang too loose about thy thighs, like the trunk-hose of our ancestors. . . . —A just medium prevents all conclusions" (II 726). But the "total inactivity in my uncle Toby's life" for a "period of fifteen or sixteen years" (II 739) has made his ceremonial attire so tight that he might as well be attacking the widow "in armour" (II 739). No mediation here, rather the rigidity of myth.

Of course Sterne's plot, already completed by this point in this backwardly written novel, commits him to a static, unmarried Toby. However Sterne came upon this conception—whether accidentally, gradually, intentionally, even unconsciously—it suggests the power mythic remnants held for him. While the pattern of mediation suggests how Sterne might have combined this interest in myth with the historical concerns which dominated the earlier volumes, how he might have joined his "revolutionary nostalgia" for myth with his sense of the ongoingness of history, the ending of *Tristram Shandy* does not so adequately reconcile synchronic and diachronic vision as does that of *A Sentimental Journey*. Like Joyce, Sterne will have to become his own father (i.e., the Yorick of *A Sentimental Journey*) before he can assimilate the mythic impulse to historical vision.

That process by which Sterne transformed himself from Tristram to Yorick is made clearer for us because *A Sentimental Journey* is tied closely both to volume 7 of *Tristram Shandy* and to the *Journal to Eliza*. Kept by Sterne after Eliza Draper's departure for India, apparently (though scholars disagree on this) not meant for publication, the *Journal* was only luckily saved from complete obliteration (Cash II 284). More a "document" than a literary work, it offers a historical counterpoint to the *Journey*, with which it was (at least in part) being concurrently written. Volume 7 of *Tristram Shandy* explores the same, or very similar, material as the *Journey* but does so in a very different mode. I will begin my analysis of the synchronic aspect of *Journey* by a comparison with the *Journal* and conclude it by focusing on its difference from volume 7.

Sterne's "obsession" with Eliza Draper resulted in the creation of the *Journal to Eliza* (Cash II 304). Begun after Mrs. Draper had sailed to India to rejoin her husband, it was to be a day-to-day recording for her of Sterne's thoughts and feelings, as her corresponding diary was to record hers for him. Sterne envisioned various "endings" for these records; one was that they would read each other's journals after Mrs. Draper had obtained her husband's permission to return to England. Thus the journals (we have no record whether Eliza, in fact, kept one) were to be "histories," true records of personal feelings. The standard view is that the *Journal*, "maudlin" (Stedmond 163) though it is, provides the inspiration for the *Journey* (Brissenden 225). I argue for a considerably more complex relationship between the two works than this usual view suggests. Primarily a historical work, the *Journal to Eliza* does serve a therapeutic purpose for the lonely, desperately sick Sterne. But in order to create the fictional *A Sentimental Journey*, Sterne needs to divest himself both of the real presence of Eliza and the historical mode he has used to address her. He can create his novel only when he has succeeded in mythologizing his experience.

I will demonstrate this point by comparing the role plot plays in each work. Since life is often said to be random, one would not associate the journal form with plot. Yet plotting permeates Sterne's work both in language and in actions. In the June 6 entry, he notes, "I sit down upon the first Hillock solitary as a sequester'd Bramin—I wake from my delusion to a thousand Disquietudes, which many talk of—my Eliza!—

but few feel—then weary my Spirit with thinking, plotting, & projecting—& when I've brought my System to my mind—am only Doubly miserable, That I cannot execute it" (241). Although Sterne uses the word *plot* only this once, he uses the cognate word *plan* frequently (e.g., 243, 244, 254, 257). In a related pattern, he twice thinks of his situation as a play complete in setting and plot and lacking only Eliza: "I have this and a thousand little parties of pleasure—& systems of living out of the common high road of Life, hourly working in my fancy for you—there wants only the *Dramatis Personae* for the performance—the play is wrote—the Scenes are painted—& the Curtain ready to be drawn up.—the whole Piece waits for thee, my Eliza" (250—theater image repeated 258). The image of the theater—where dramatic events lead to peripety—suggests Sterne's association of plot with history in the *Journal*. These are plots that will lead to change, if only in the fantasy of the lonely man.

Some of these plots are negative fantasies. He dreams that Eliza, a widow, has married someone else (251); or he creates the scenario whereby Draper wins Eliza's pity and sways her from her plans to leave him (253). Other plots, perhaps equally "Castles" (254)—presumably from the phrase "castles in the air"—lead to concrete actions: he tells her of weeding the path he often walks in preparation for her coming (245), and he describes how he has renovated his house to make her a sitting room and bed chamber (252). Offered (he says) a living in Surrey, he writes, "I cannot take any step unless I had thee my Eliza for whose sake I live, to consult with" (267). And he thinks that with her there beside him he could "get up fast the hill of preferment, if [he] chose it" (267).

Persistently involved in these scenarios for himself and Eliza, he also projects them out upon others. His wife and daughter's planned visit is envisioned as an effort to "pillage" (238) him. This motif of his wife's return is repeated frequently (e.g., 243–44, 257). Curiously, the "plots" he creates around his wife Elizabeth reflect not only the anxiety he feels toward her but also an ambivalence he comes to feel for Eliza. As Arthur Cash points out, he writes that he must break off the journal on August 4 because Elizabeth and his daughter Lydia are arriving; they, in fact, did not come till October 1 (II 303). The final journal entry says that they stayed at Shandy Hall two months and that Elizabeth, more than half in love with Sterne again, has confessed to being ten years older than he thought. Again, as Cash has shown, both these "facts" are untrue; they stayed one month, and Elizabeth was fifty-four, one year younger than Sterne (II 310). Earlier in the *Journal* he makes a telling slip when he writes that he is at York, where he wants "to be employed in taking you a little house" (264). It is, of course, for Elizabeth and Lydia that he has to rent living quarters. The wish to distance himself from both women (Eliza by not writing; Elizabeth by making her older and sending her back to France) as well as the unconscious association of them with one another suggests that by the time of the last entry Sterne wants to distance himself as well from the "plots" and history he has associated with them. In the June 18 entry he specifically associates the word *history* with one of the scenarios he has been constructing: "How do you like the History, of this couple, Eliza?—is it to your mind?" (248).

Why should he wish this distance? In part, he finds that the pressure toward history which the women represent interferes with the book he wants to write. Rather than Eliza's serving as the inspiration for *A Sentimental Journey*, she was an influence Sterne had to suppress in order to get on with his work, as is clear from the entry for June 3: "Cannot write my Travels, or give one half hours close attention to them, upon Thy Acct my dearest friend—Yet write I must, & what to do with You, whilst I write—I declare I know not—I want to have you ever before my Imagination—& cannot keep you out of my heart or head—In short thou enterst my Library Eliza! (as thou one day shalt) without tapping—or sending for—by thy own Right of ever being close to thy Bramine—now I must shut you out sometimes—or meet you Eliza! with an empty purse upon the Beach" (239). Wanting to associate Eliza with the "golden age" (255), Sterne discovers that the plots she gives rise to (like the ill-health he associates with her [218, 220, 228]) tie him too closely to diachronic reality. In a scene remarkably reminiscent of Crusoe on his island, he describes how he could sit contentedly at supper with his cat, happy in a mythic state except for "all powerful Eliza, that has had this Magic authority over him; to bend him thus to the dust—But I'll have my revenge, Hussy!" (260). That revenge would be to break his obsessive tie to her and the historical conditions she represented for him.

He had asked her, in the July 18, 1767, letter to the Bramine affixed to the *Journal*, "Pray when you first made a conquest of T. Shandy did it ever enter your head what a visionary, romantic, kind of Being you had got hold of?" (270). While it is highly unlikely that they ever had a sexual relation (Cash II 279), Sterne did obsess about Eliza's physical presence, carrying her portrait about on his snuff box, continually showing it at social occasions, and apparently inflicting long descriptions of Eliza on anyone who would listen. As we have seen, rather than releasing his visionary side, this obsession seemed to tie him down to anxieties about health and separation, to jealousies about husbands and other lovers, to household renovations, to problematic relations with his wife and daughter, to, in short, all the everyday "plots" that are the antithesis of romance.

In *A Sentimental Journey* Yorick does not really "learn" to avoid plot; that, paradoxically, would involve him in a traditional Aristotelian praxis. Rather than undergoing a peripety, Yorick achieves a series of epiphanies whereby at the end of the novel he is able, as Tristram is not in volume 7, to accept the mythic implications of the peasant dance. The difference between growth through epiphany and insight acquired through peripety is foreshadowed in the opening of the novel. After refusing charity to the monk, Yorick reflects that he has "behaved very ill" but comforts himself that he "shall learn better manners as [he] get[s] along" (75). This idea of growth through travel seems oddly contradicted a few pages later in the "Preface" Yorick composes while sitting in the *Desobligéant*. There he satirizes the "inquisitive" traveler: "I am of opinion, That a man would act as wisely, if he could prevail upon himself, to live contented without foreign knowledge or foreign improvements, especially if he lives in a country that has no absolute want of either" (84). The contradiction is only apparent, however. Yorick does not want to pursue the kind of knowledge which derives from factual analysis or the examination of causal relations;[12] these would involve him in history. Rather, the "travels and observations" of the Sentimental Traveller "will be altogether of a different cast from any of [his] forerunners" (82). They will stress emotion rather than intellect, spontaneity rather than plan or sequence; they will be free from "closure" and the restrictions of time. Better manners involve a better way of *being* which may have little to do with knowing.

The difference between spontaneity based on feeling and plotting derived through reason is explored early in the text in Yorick's meeting with Mme de L——. Inspecting carriages with the innkeeper, Yorick takes the lady's willingly offered hand and continues to hold it after the innkeeper has been called away. He cannot help reflecting to her on the whimsicality of Fortune in thus joining two strangers. Whereupon the lady replies:

> And your reflection upon it, shews how much, Monsieur, she [Fortune] has embarassed you by the adventure.—
>
> When the situation is what we would wish, nothing is so ill-timed as to hint at the circumstances which make it so: you thank Fortune, continued she—you had reason—the heart knew it, and was satisfied; and who but an English philosopher would have sent notice of it to the brain to reverse the judgment? (96)

His "thinking" thus spoils a natural situation and the lady withdraws her hand. She allows him to reclaim it, however; and he reflects, "I had infallibly lost it a second time, had not instinct more than reason directed me to the last resource in these dangers—to hold it loosely and in a manner as if I was every moment going to release it, of myself" (98). And thus he does hold it all through the sentimental episode in which he exchanges snuff boxes with the monk. And he does not let it go till a query put to him by some "Inquisitive" English travelers starts him plotting to ask the lady to share his chaise to Amiens. This little plot is envisioned as a conflict between Avarice, Caution, Cowardice, Discretion, and the heart. The heart wins the debate, but unfortunately the lady "had glided off unperceived, as the cause was pleading" (106).

Yorick has another opportunity when the returned innkeeper, thinking to interest one or the other of his prospective customers in the *remise,* seats them both in it. When he is again called away and they are left alone, Yorick then seizes on the chance opportunity to make sentimental love to the lady. The arrival of the lady's brother ends their adventure, but Yorick sees what adventures are possible for "him who interests his heart in everything" (114). At Amiens, however, Yorick receives a letter from Mme de L—— inviting him to present himself to her friend Mme R—— in Paris and further to visit her if he should come to Brussels. At first, he plights himself to go to Brussels were it ten thousand posts out of his way. But the "plot" in which he has been involved with Eliza reminds him of his duty to her, and he pledges "That I would not travel to Brussels, unless Eliza went along with me, did the road lead me towards heaven" (148). This sequence establishes the pattern of the book with Yorick oscillating between the spontaneous movements of the heart which allow epiphanic insights that transcend time and those plots derived mostly through the intellect whose filiations tie one to the pattern of time.

Before looking at two major sequences, that of the passport, which emphasizes mythic spontaneity, and that of the beggar, which involves self-conscious plotting, it will be useful to trace some of Yorick's less consequential affairs. As his name suggests, the servant La Fleur serves as a model for liberated, mythic response. Yorick hired La Fleur spontaneously; he "hired him first—and then began to inquire what he could do" (124). When Wisdom discovers that La Fleur can in fact do nothing, Yorick's heart discovers that his being his cheerful self is enough. As with the comparable scene in the *Journal*, we are reminded of Robinson Crusoe at the height of his immersion in the mythic life of the island: "So supper coming in, and having a frisky English spaniel on one side of my chair, and a French valet, with as much hilarity in his countenance as ever nature painted in one, on the other—I was satisfied to my heart's content with my empire; and if monarchs knew what they would be at, they might be as satisfied as I was" (125). When the landlord tells Yorick that La Fleur is always in love, Yorick is pleased, for that is his own nature. He reflects, "if ever I do a mean action, it must be in some interval betwixt one passion and another: whilst this interregnum lasts, I always perceive my heart locked up" (128–29).

But, as we have seen, his involvement with Eliza has altered his receptivity to passion. Thus the gallant La Fleur, having told Mme de L—— that he has lost Yorick's reply rather than expose his master's want of gallantry, begs him to justify himself as a lover and write her a note. Unable to assimilate himself to La Fleur's spontaneous, unthoughtful mode, Yorick tries to please his servant but discovers he was "in no mood to write" (151). In the first of several lessons he learns from La Fleur, he copies a letter from a drummer to a corporal's wife. With a few minor alterations Yorick finds that it will do, for love in its archetypal form has a fine democracy.[13] In a later episode, having viewed La Fleur's new finery, Yorick plans to wait on Mme de R——, proud to have a servant who looks so well to attend him. Upon discovering that La Fleur wishes to spend this Sunday gallantly, Yorick spontaneously decides to forgo his own plans; for he says, "we must *feel*, not argue in these embarrassments" (247). In his apostrophe at the end of the chapter to the French people who "once a week at least are sure to lay down all your cares together, and dance and sing and sport away the weights of grievance" (248), Yorick seems to recognize the mythic reality of the holiday as a release from the everyday world of historical being.[14]

But while La Fleur sports, Yorick involves himself with a plot—this time not his personal plot but that in a story he finds in a fragment of paper. Written in old French, the story fascinates Yorick, and he translates it but must leave it permanently incomplete since his original is but a fragment. Melinda Rabb has pointed out that "most stories in *A Sentimental Journey*, including the narrator's, flagrantly lack closure" (546). In her feminist reading, she suggests that "unfinished stories, like incomplete transactions of money and unconsummated sexual acts, are part of the testing of personal power within the patriarchal hierarchy" (547). I would add that deliberately to eschew closure is not only to challenge patriarchy but also the history in which it manifests and transcribes itself. In this particular episode, Sterne seems to be making a comment on the possibilities of art as well. In devoting his attention to plot while La Fleur pursues spontaneity, Yorick seems to symbolize the value for art of plan, discipline, development, insight, and denouement—all the characteristics of Aristotelian praxis. Yet the plot can never be completed; for its ending is permanently lost—ironically because La Fleur has wrapped his flowers for his lady-friend in the other sheets of the paper. Nature and spontaneity have the last word over plan and art.

When he first arrives in Paris, Yorick plans to wait on Mme R——, but his barber detains him too long. So, he says, "I walked forth without any determination where to go—I shall consider of that, said I, as I walk along" (160). This spontaneity involves him in the famous pulse-feeling scene with the grisette who sells gloves, the first of a series of such scenes with such women in the book. Their function seems less bawdy than sentimental.[15] Plotting, the application of thought to one's action, can interfere with the capacity to feel. After Yorick has entertained (innocently) Mme R——'s *fille de chambre* in his room, the indignant hotel keeper asks him to leave—unless Yorick will entertain (and buy from) the publican's own grisette with her bandbox. Yorick first plans to repudiate the woman and triumph over the *maître d'hôtel;* but he recognizes "there was more of spleen than principle in my project, and I was sick of it before the execution" (242). He then plans to buy nothing as his act of retaliation. But the "poor creature . . . laid herself out to win me, and not so much in a manner which seem'd artful, as in one I felt simple and caressing" (242). Consequently, he says, "my heart relented, and I gave up my second resolution as quietly as the first" (242). Feeling triumphs over reason; spontaneity over plan. These episodes with the various grisettes help to free Yorick from the Eliza plot which was so obsessive in the *Journal*.

When Yorick is threatened with the Bastille because he has no passport, he responds with that insouciance which is his natural gift and which he has been cultivating since he came to France. The imagery he uses to downplay the value of rational concern is interesting: "Beshrew the *sombre* pencil! said I vauntingly—for I envy not its powers, which paints the evils of life with so hard and deadly a colouring. The mind sits terrified at the objects she has magnified herself, and blackened: reduce them to their proper size and hue, she overlooks them" (197). We see seemingly a collaboration between reason (mind) and art (the pencil) to create stories that exaggerate the real nature of life. At this point Yorick gleefully thinks he can escape involvement in such narratives. Ironically, an object from nature undercuts all Yorick's good cheer. The caged starling's cry, "I can't get out—I can't get out," forces him to face the real implications of imprisonment, and he plans to visit the Duc de Choiseul to try to arrange for a passport. On the way to Versailles, he composes a number of scenarios he might use to gain his ends, but then turns on himself with a sort of revulsion for doing so: "How many mean plans of dirty address, as I went along, did my servile heart form! I deserved the Bastille for everyone of them" (207). When the duke is too busy to see him right away, Yorick, who is "governed by circumstances" (114) rather than by plan, goes impulsively to throw himself on the goodwill of the unknown Count de B——, of whose interest in things English he has accidentally heard.

Asked his name, Yorick points to it in a copy of *Hamlet* which lies on the count's table. Apparently believing that Yorick *is* the character in the play, the count rushes off to secure a passport for him. The scene is worth quoting at length:

> Now whether the idea of poor Yorick's skull was put out of the Count's mind, by the reality of my own, or by what magic he could drop a period of seven or eight hundred years, makes nothing

> in this account—'tis certain the French conceive better than they combine—I wonder at nothing in this world, and the less at this; inasmuch as one of the first of our own church, for whose candour and paternal sentiments I have the highest veneration, fell into the same mistake in the very same case,—"He could not bear," he said, "to look into sermons wrote by the king of Denmark's jester."—Good, my lord! said I—but there are two Yoricks. The Yorick your lordship thinks of has been dead and buried eight hundred years ago; he flourish'd in Horwendillus's court—the other Yorick is myself, who have flourish'd, my lord, in no court—He shook his head—Good God! said I, you might as well confound Alexander the Great with Alexander the Coppersmith, my lord—'Twas all one, he replied—
>
> —If Alexander king of Macedon could have translated your lordship, said I, I'm sure your lordship would not have said so.
>
> The poor Count de B**** fell but into the same *error*—
>
> —*Et Monsieur, est il Yorick*? cried the Count.—*Je le suis,* said I. —*Vous?—Moi— Moi qui ai l'honneur de vous parler, Monsieur le Comte—Mon Dieu!* said he, embracing me—*Vous êtes Yorick*! (221–23)

Although we could speak of this interchange as reflecting an "example of the real world becoming quixotic, sharing or confirming Yorick's confusion of real and verbal, or real and fictional realms" (Loveridge 182), it seems more appropriate to suppose that Sterne wants the clergyman's and the count's error to symbolize their confusion of history and myth rather than that which is real and that which is verbal. In the mythic mode, time is not; and there is no difference between the prototype and its historical manifestation. For this reason, archaic peoples would welcome every year in the shape of different individuals the rebirth of their one, unchanging god. Like these peoples, the clergyman and the count do not respond to the individual Yorick (Sterne's) but to the prototype. They confuse not the real and the verbal but the individual and the archetype.

What is further interesting in this passage, and the one which follows two pages on when the count returns with Yorick's passport, is that Yorick tries to press a conception of historical reality on the clergyman and the count. It is they, not he, who turn quixotic. In fact, Yorick's reflections as he waits for the count to return suggest just how much his flights to mythic modes of perception are acts of will rather than of belief. "When evils press sore upon me, and there is no retreat from them in this world, then I take a new course—I leave it—and as I have a clearer idea of the elysian fields than I have of heaven, I force myself, like Eneas, into them" (225). We can see here a clear parallel with Leopold Bloom who, also lacking any clear idea of heaven, finds comfort in mythic memories when reality presses too hard.

And like Leopold Bloom, Yorick has a degree of practical cunning as we see in the other major episode I want to examine, the affair with the beggar. Yorick observes a beggar who asks only women for alms and who is never turned down. He puzzles over two things: "the first was, why the man should *only* tell his story to the sex—and secondly—what kind of story it was, and what species of eloquence it could be, which soften'd the hearts of the women, which he knew 'twas to no purpose to practise upon the men" (239–40). This "plot" seems to bother Yorick inordinately; he says, "it would have puzzled all the wise men of Paris, as much as those of Chaldea, to have given its interpretation" (245). Of course the answer to the riddle is simple, as Yorick discovers when he observes more closely the beggar at work; it is flattery. Yorick proceeds then to turn the secret to his own purposes: "I had got master of my *secret,* just in time to turn these honours to some little account" (261). In short, he practices flattery on the French aristocrats he encounters and becomes an enormous social success. His plot, in fact, works all too well; and soon he is sickened of the role he is playing: "The higher I got, the more was I forced upon my *beggarly system*—the better the *Coterie*—the more children of Art—I languish'd for those of Nature: and one night, after a most vile prostitution of myself to half a dozen different people, I grew sick—went to bed—order'd La Fleur to get me horses in the morning to set out for Italy" (266). With a surfeit of plot, Yorick's oscillation is ended, and in the few brief episodes that close the book he will seek mythic resonances in nature.

We will better understand those resonances if we recall the ending of volume 7 of *Tristram Shandy*, where Sterne ultimately took the path of history rather than myth. Although attracted to the "ring of pleasure," Tristram was not allowed to lose himself in the repetition of cyclic time. By the time Sterne came to the ending of *A Sentimental Journey*, this anxiety about myth seems to have relaxed. For one thing, he had already experimented with the mythic ending of *Tristram Shandy*. For another, historicity must have come to seem increasingly threatening to a man who had been dangerously ill for years. In all events, we discover a Sterne who is increasingly able to assimilate religious belief to a wider vision of nature. The episode in *Journey* comparable to the dance of volume 7 is made up of three chapters. In "The Bourbonnois," the first of these, Yorick addresses God as the "great SENSORIUM of the world!" (278); but in the second, "The Supper," he invokes not God but Nature (282). Stopping at a peasant house, Yorick observes their supper as a "feast of love" (281). R. F. Brissenden has finely said that although Sterne quite deliberately presents his scene as "a sacred occasion" (238) it is "not so much in its eucharistic sense" as in its "earlier sense of the feast of love and fellowship" (239). Perhaps for this reason, instead of drawing back from the communal scene as Tristram had in volume 7, Yorick can participate directly in it. He says, "my heart was sat down the moment I enter'd the room; so I sat down at once like a son of the family" (281).

In the chapter called "The Grace," the peasant sons and daughters dance before their parents and Yorick. Yorick remarks that, in "some pauses in the movement wherein they all seem'd to look up, I fancied I could distinguish an elevation of spirit different from that which is the cause or the effect of simple jollity.—In a word, I thought I beheld *Religion* mixing in the dance" (283–84). In the synchronic mode of these chapters religion seems more widely conceived than simply as Christianity. While the old, grey-haired peasant with his sons and daughters echoes some biblical patriarch, he also on a deeper archetypal level evokes Aeolus and his children whom Odysseus, another traveler, visited. That "The Grace" is danced rather than spoken suggests how the physical and the spiritual resonate together in this sequence. We seem to have moved from a purely historical world to the realms of myth.

A number of threats which Tristram had faced in the historical world of his novel have disappeared from this ritualized scene. For one, the sexual threat posed by the slit in Nannette's petticoat is gone; Yorick sits near the old peasant couple, able to observe in an uncompromised way the dance of the younger people. Then, there is no mention of Eliza who so obsessed Sterne in the *Journal*. With her gone, the need to plot has also disappeared; Yorick can live spontaneously, responding to events as they occur rather than trying to shape them to his will. Most consequentially, the theme of death is gone. As the motive force of volume 7, death constantly recalled Tristram to historical time and reality, generating considerable tension as it did so. Considering the perilousness of Sterne's health as well as his earlier obsessive response, perhaps the most startling thing about *A Sentimental Journey* is how far he has banished death from it. But he has not done so in Christian terms by positing an afterlife; nor does he rely on the plots he devised in the *Journal* to hold time at bay. Instead he generates here a cyclic world where event seems a part of an eternal pattern instead of some earthly plot. In this way he achieves at the end of the novel a fuller sense of the mythic vision which he had been adumbrating throughout its earlier parts.

As a text, however, *A Sentimental Journey* needs a sense of closure. Myths may eternally repeat; mere books need to finish. Sterne resolves the conflict between diachronic and synchronic narrative stances by resorting to comedy. Prevented from reaching his desired destination by a roadslide, Yorick takes refuge in a little wayside inn. Hardly settled in its one room, he is asked to share it with a Piedmontese lady and her maid who have also been delayed. The "Case of Delicacy" is how they are to sleep since the room offers only two beds and a draughty closet with a cot totally unsuited to Yorick's health. After much discussion, the lady and Yorick make a treaty which includes the provisions that the curtains on her bed are to be fastened up with corking pins, that Yorick will sleep in his black silk breeches, and that they shall not speak one word in the night. Unable to sleep, Yorick cries out; the lady argues that he has broken their treaty, in her earnestness causing the corking pins to fall out. Reaching out his hand, Yorick catches hold of an unnamed part of the fille de chambre who had crept out of her closet and between the beds upon hearing the noise.

The chapter begins in the mythic mode with an invocation to Nature, who offers "safety and protection" to the poor of Savoy (285). Moreover, the episode starts spontaneously as Yorick is driven to seek shelter through mischance on the road. Soon, however, we are immersed in the plot of the beds as the Piedmontese lady and Yorick plan what they can do about their sleeping arrangements. The inflated tone of this passage suggests its comic purposes: "We turn'd it every way, and debated and considered it in all kinds of lights in the course of a two hours negociation; at the end of which the articles were settled finally betwixt us, and stipulated for in form and manner of a treaty of peace—and I believe with as much religion and good faith on both sides, as in any treaty which as yet had the honour of being handed down to posterity" (288). In microcosm, Yorick and the lady form the oftentimes elaborate social contracts based on religion and goodwill by which humans try to cope with historical exigency. Though he tries to pass it off as a prayer, Yorick's "ejaculation" (290) reminds us how persistently nature undercuts those "treaties" people achieve by reason. Sterne comically undercuts the historical world by demonstrating how it creates forms (or structures "plots") which are far more elaborate than its real needs and then fails to be able to live up to these forms because of the realities of nature.

In fact, though "The Case of Delicacy" pulls us back from the more totally mythic world of "The Supper" and "The Grace," it does not return us entirely to the historical point of view, only enough to give us an ending which paradoxically remains unended. Most early editions of the *Journey* added a dash after the last phrase, "I caught hold of the Fille de chambre's—". Like most modern editors, Gardner Stout uses no punctuation, closing simply with "End of Vol. II." Whatever the punctuation, we can, of course, fill in the hiatus as our wit or salaciousness demands. One likely candidate is the word "hand." Since most of the actions of the novel take place as a meeting of hands (v. Rabb 542), this climactic (or anticlimactic) one could surely be that. If we remember that Yorick's encounter with Mme de L—— was largely a holding of hands and that his relations with the glove-selling grisette and Mme de R——'s maid also focused on hand holding, we see an important point in this scene. For the first time, Yorick encounters these two types of woman simultaneously. From a Freudian perspective, the obvious suggestion is that Yorick is overcoming what has been a crippling distinction between two types of woman which has prevented a mature sexuality from developing. From this angle we might argue that an insight based on a reversal is implied; a plot dealing with Yorick's relations to women has been worked out.[16] Sterne's ambiguity is more complex than this, however; for we remember that it was Eliza who tied Sterne to plots and to historical circumstances. We could also see the coming together of the two types of women in this final chapter as the ultimate killing off of the Eliza figure in Sterne's imagination, the release from obsession. In that reading, the last chapter leaves him not *in* history but finally free from it.

The other likely word to fill the hiatus after "Fille de Chambre's" is *pudenda* (or whatever variation of it one chooses). Arguing for this choice, Melinda Rabb explains that it represents "Sterne's joke on himself to have found his 'End' in the same anatomical place where he began" (558). Such a reading, of course, carries us directly to the cyclicity of myth with the female organ as the source from which life comes and to which it returns. The modern editorial practice of leaving out the dash in one way supports this reading and in another does not. If we assume the sexual double meaning of "End," then the absence of the dash underlines the implication that Yorick reaches toward the maid's pudenda. If, however, we take the "End" of "End of Vol. II" as a mark of closure, he reaches toward the death he has been evading. Sterne maintains here a fine balancing between those elements which suggest closure and give a sense of form to his work and those which suggest ongoingness and associate the book with myth.

There is another effect of leaving out the dash. It incorporates the phrase "End of Vol. II" *into* the text itself instead of leaving it separate. This suggests that not just the experiences within the text but the text itself has its elements of cyclicity, not simply closing in the sense of an Aristotelian action but also turning back upon its own beginning. Yorick's end is both his matured insight about women and his return to the womb; analogically, the book's closure describes both the completion of an Aristotelian action in which reversal has taught Yorick something and the ongoingness of a situation in which there is much to be felt but little to be learned. In short, the effect is both kinetic *and* static. I will argue that Joyce achieves the same effect of non-closing closure in Molly Bloom's soliloquy. Unlike those critics who see this soliloquy as pushing *Ulysses* over totally into myth, I believe it maintains the same fine balance between history and myth that we find in "The Case of Delicacy." It is one of the things that Joyce learned from Sterne.

5

Time, Language, and Plot in Ulysses

While some direct links between Joyce and these eighteenth-century novelists will inevitably appear, my intention in this chapter is not to try to show their "influence" on Joyce in traditional terms. Rather, examining ways in which Joyce mediates history and myth will show an affinity of form which, as Focillon has said (*Life* 52), can be found between masters who have never had the slightest acquaintance and whom nature, distance, and time have kept apart. Unlike post-structuralist critics, I do not believe that juxtaposed mythic and historic perspectives in Joyce dissolve "all possibility of a unified real underlying the fiction" (Topia 124). *Ulysses* instead is "a work of art which renders the bourgeois world in all its detail and potentiality, *uniting fact and myth* in a classic portrayal of Everyman as dispossessed hero" (Litz, *James Joyce's Ulysses* 405; my emphasis). The process of mediation itself forms the unity of the novel. And it was in a tradition of the novel fostered by Defoe, Smollett, and Sterne that Joyce could find the example of this particular sort of mediation.

From his study of the manuscripts and revisions of the novel, Michael Groden has concluded that Joyce "markedly altered many of his artistic goals while he was writing *Ulysses*, to such an extent that he wrote later episodes in a method vastly different from that of earlier ones" (18). While the techniques of the later chapters did grow greatly more complex, analysis of elements from all parts of the novel shows that one of Joyce's "goals" remained very much the same throughout the composition of his book. That goal was persistently to demonstrate that the artist can mediate the synchronic thrust of myth and the diachronic thrust of history. In this chapter I will show how we find such mediation in Joyce's use of time, language, and plot. For my analysis of time, I will focus on Stephen's riddle in Nestor and on a pattern of bodily functions throughout the novel. By looking at Cyclops, Nausicaa, and Oxen of the Sun, I shall explore the language motif. And, finally, Sirens and Penelope will demonstrate the conjoining of historic and mythic plots.

Stephen's riddle demonstrates his unconscious wish to mediate historical and mythical time. As Joseph Prescott has pointed out, the riddle forms a variant on a traditional one collected in P. W. Joyce's *English As We Speak It in Ireland* in 1910 (149). The original follows:

Riddle me, riddle me right:
What did I see last night?
The wind blew
The cock crew
The bells of heaven
Struck eleven
Tis time for my poor *sowl* to go to heaven.
Answer: The fox burying his mother under a holly tree.

Stephen's version differs in several ways. First of all, he does not include the first couplet in the riddle he presents the class. Either a significantly altered version of the couplet or more likely a different riddle does run through his mind, however. "Riddle me, riddle me, randy ro. / My father gave me seeds to sow." Then, he alters the elements within the actual riddle he presents the class:

The cock crew,
The sky was blue:
The bells in heaven
Were striking eleven
Tis time for this poor soul
To go to heaven.

Finally, the answer Stephen gives the class differs: "The fox burying his grandmother under a holly bush" (22).

In her essay "Covert Riddles in *Ulysses*: Squaring the Circle," Helen

Georgi distinguishes between covert and overt riddles in Joyce's fiction.[1] While Stephen's riddle is given openly and includes its own answer, I suggest that it conceals a covert riddle beneath its surface. Since the riddle is susceptible to two different readings—one in historical and the other in mythic time, the hidden question it poses is how these time patterns relate to each other. Although Stephen's answer to his riddle follows tradition and focuses on the mother, Joyce will suggest the answer to the covert riddle lies in the role of the father.

Although most modern commentators would assume a Christian reading of the riddle was mythic, Defoe's example shows how Joyce could associate Christian time with historical time. In this Christian/historical reading Stephen projects both Christ's mission and His passion and his own sense of identification with them. In these terms, God the Father has given Christ the task of sowing seeds of spiritual renewal. By censoring these lines from the class, Stephen conceals from them his own sense of deeper purpose. Similarly, as artist, he conceals the hidden spiritual purposes of his art. This reading finds collaboration in the Library scene, where Stephen, under attack for his theory about Shakespeare, thinks to himself: "Christfox in leather trews, hiding, a runaway in blighted treeforks, from hue and cry" (159). But Stephen identifies even more with Christ's persecution in historical time than with His mission. The riddle he gives the class figures forth Christ's crucifixion. The traditional riddle had clearly established its time as past in its second line, "What did I see last night?" Not only suppressing the time reference in favor of his seeds imagery, Stephen also suggests, by substituting the phrase "The sky was blue" for the traditional riddle's "The wind blew," that the action takes place in the daytime. We can then read the cock's crowing as that which warned Peter at Gethsemane, and the eleventh hour as marking the beginning of Christ's passion.[2] It is time for Him to go to heaven. In this reading, Stephen's alteration of the traditional answer from the fox's burying his mother to his grandmother makes sense. Christ's death does not "bury" or neutralize Mary but rather Eve, the grand mother and the co-partner in original sin. This identification of Eve with the grandmother is made explicit in the Oxen of the Sun episode, where Stephen identifies Mary as the second Eve who "won us, saith Augustine too, whereas that other, our grandam, which we are linked up with by successive anastomosis of navelcords sold us all, seed, breed and generation, for a penny pippin" (320).

While this interpretation suggests Stephen's alignment with the forces of diachronic, Christian time, clearly documented elsewhere in *Ulysses* is his antipathy to such history. In Nestor, Mr. Deasy articulates the Christian idea of time exactly: "All human history moves toward one great goal, the manifestation of God" (28). But, for the skeptical Stephen, the only goal is the boys' cry in their soccer game. With no sense of telos, or purpose, history can only become "a nightmare from which [he is] trying to awake" (28). Stephen's mode of awakening is associated with trying to revive various mythic visions where time is annihilated in perpetual cyclical renewal. He and Buck call their tower an "omphalos" (15); in the history lesson in Nestor he thinks of Blake's demolishment of history as something fabled by the daughters of memory (20); and in Proteus he experiments with the denial of historical time and space (31). As Jackson Cope has said, in his efforts in this scene to ring up "Edenville," the "telephone umbilical cords identify Stephen's nightmare as inverted dream, the ultimate dream of the primitivist: he would escape the endlessly bifurcated historical world of *beth* and enter not only into apotheosis, but into the uncreative unity of *aleph*. But this he envisions as retreat into the mythic paradise of Eve without a navel, the urMother's undifferentiating womb" (91).

An onanism theme suggests the counterhistorical, mythical reading of the riddle. Stephen's self-censored first couplet (or separate riddle juxtaposed to his public one) refers to himself as "randy ro," suggesting his sexual state. We can further interpret the seeds his father gave him as the semen of the ejaculate. This idea is reinforced by Stephen's placing the phrase "The cock crew" first in the riddle he does tell the class. This new position of importance stresses that what is on Stephen's mind is his penis. As we have seen, Stephen has switched the action of the riddle from night to eleven o'clock in the daytime. Now, that is precisely the hour when Stephen, having left the school, will walk upon the Strand. This is the time when his "poor soul" will go to the heaven of sexual climax.

Although most critics assume that Stephen urinates into Cock Lake in Proteus (see, for example, Moore, 46, and French, 80), at least two have suggested that he masturbates. David Hayman's is the most extended discussion, in "Stephen on the Rocks." Analyzing Stephen's movements and the sexual imagery within the chapter—but not drawing my connection between the riddle and Stephen at Cock Lake, Hayman concludes that Joyce carefully sets the scene for Stephen's masturbatory act as well as giving us "a full gestural presentation of a sexual climax" and "a suggestion of post-ejaculatory peace and lassitude" (11). Hugh Kenner accepts Hayman's interpretation and points out that in "one of the many parallels between 'Proteus' and 'Nausicaa,' Bloom on the rocks on the same beach does the same thing hours later" (57).

Like Sterne, Joyce associates masturbation with absorption in mythic reality. In his psychoanalytic reading of Joyce, Mark Shechner says that the "idea that one can find release from guilt and threat through narcissism or the total internalization of reality and sexuality pervades the book and organizes the psychic lives of both Stephen and Bloom—making them both versions of the creator-God" (48). Although I think Shechner undervalues the historical thrust of the novel,[3] I do believe his association of masturbation with narcissism and a synchronic vision of self is accurate. Joyce does use the onanistic act to symbolize an escape from historical time. Masturbating, Stephen as a "creator-God" does try to supersede the differentiated Father of Christian history. Under this reading, Stephen's answer to the riddle suggests his need to bury the Eve-figure who introduced heterosexuality and history into the world.

The covert riddle Joyce poses behind Stephen's asks what is the connection between these two, diametrically opposed attitudes toward time. We will discover the solution to this hidden riddle by considering the role of the father, not that of the mother as Stephen's overt riddle suggests. His riddle, in fact, comes to Stephen's mind as he listens to the student Talbot repeat the line, "Through the dear might of Him that walked the waves," from "Lycidas." Thinking about the power of the Christian God over his pupils and himself, Stephen defiantly tries to separate himself from that influence. "To Caesar what is Caesar's, to God what is God's" (22). We need to understand that there are two fathers for Stephen. One is God the Father, whom Stephen associates with the Roman Catholic Church, with history, and with the feminine. This is the father whom he fears and tries to defy. The other father is worldly (Caesar), mythic, and phallic. The line from the riddle, "My father gave me seeds to sow," demonstrates Stephen's conflict between the two fathers. The Christian father wants him to sow seeds of spiritual rebirth; in turning the riddle to sexual rather than spiritual purposes, Stephen wants to demonstrate his defiance of God the Father and his affirmation of the phallic father.

The theory of fatherhood Stephen develops in the library episode illustrates his idea of two fathers: "Fatherhood, in the sense of conscious begetting, is unknown to man. It is a mystical estate, an apostolic succession, from only begetter to only begotten. On that mystery and not on the madonna which the cunning Italian intellect flung to the mob of Europe the church is founded and founded irremovably because founded, like the world, macro and microcosm, upon the void. Upon incertitude, upon unlikelihood. *Amor matris,* subjective and objective genitive, may be the only true thing in life. Paternity may be a legal fiction. Who is the father of any son that any son should love him or he any son?" (170). The ideas here are sufficiently complex that one part of Stephen asks himself, "What the hell are you driving at?" The other part, his myth-oriented one, replies, "I know. Shut up. Blast you! I have reasons." What seems implied is this: fearing history, Stephen fears the Roman Catholic Church which espouses it and makes it palatable to the European "mob" through its cult of the Madonna. Stephen associates historical time with the feminine—whether it is his mother who, even in death, tries to tie him to the filiations of family or the Madonna who ensnares mankind in the historical coils of the church. Although he concedes that "*Amor matris,* subjective and objective genitive, may be the only true thing in life," he nevertheless envisions a church founded instead upon the principle of mythic fatherhood. Such a church would be founded "like the world, macro and microcosm upon the void. Upon incertitude, upon unlikelihood." Since there is no "conscious begetting" by fathers, there can be no historical continuity—fatherhood, Stephen tells us twice, is a mystical estate. One cycle after another emerges from the void, but there is no historical progression, only repetition.

This idea becomes clearer if we consider an earlier passage from the same episode. Having borrowed a pound from A.E., Stephen wonders not so much whether he should repay the debt as whether he actually owes it.

> Wait. Five months. Molecules all change. I am other I now. Other I got pound.
>
> Buzz. Buzz.
>
> But I, entelechy, form of forms, am I by memory because under everchanging forms.
>
> I that sinned and prayed and fasted.
>
> A child Conmee saved from pandies.
>
> I,I and I.I.
>
> A.E.I.O.U. (156)

Stephen's first response is a mythic one: his molecules have all changed; therefore he is no longer the old self but a cyclically reborn one. But his second thought takes a more historical view: memory provides continuity, which makes him the same person. Having weighed the historical view (I,I) against the mythic (I.I.), Stephen opts here for history, accepting the continuity of the self and his responsibility for the debt (A.E.I.O.U.).

While the vowels offer that kind of mysterious ratification that Joyce loved, Stephen would prefer the freedom from historical necessity found in mythic time, even if it means living in the void. Why? At this point, Stephen's thesis about Shakespeare and his theory of fatherhood converge. He thinks of Shakespeare the artist as a mythic father: "When Rutlandbaconsouthamptonshakespeare or another poet of the same name in the comedy of errors wrote *Hamlet* he was not the father of his own son merely but, being no more a son, he was and felt himself the father of all his race, the father of his own grandfather, the father of his unborn grandson who, by the same token, never was born, for nature, as Mr Magee understands her, abhors perfection" (171). In positing this mythic view of fatherhood, Stephen gives the artist complete freedom. Here, he seems much like the young artist at the end of *Portrait* who wanted to free himself of family, of religion, and of country in order to forge the conscience of his race. In addition to freedom, the artist as mystical father achieves enormous power. The Stephen of *Portrait* who was offered the priesthood felt chiefly the attraction of power; here he envisions powers for the artist that far exceed those of any priest. Finally, Stephen sees mystical fatherhood as an escape from historical time, where the son born "brings pain, divides affection, increases care. He is a new male: his growth is his father's decline, his youth his father's envy, his friend his father's enemy" (170).

The continuity between Stephen's riddle and his theory of fatherhood is established by Mulligan's satire of its masturbatory quality:

Everyman His Own Wife
or
A Honeymoon in the Hand
(a national immorality in three orgasms)
by
Ballocky Mulligan. (178)

While he does not take a conventionally moralistic attitude toward masturbation, Joyce does, through Mulligan's parody of Stephen's theory, suggest the basic limitations of a theory of art based purely on a mythic vision. Another riddle in Nestor reinforces this idea. Having asked his class what a pier is, Stephen gives the answer that it is "a disappointed bridge" (21). The pier would be "happier" or more "fulfilled" if it were a bridge—that is, if it mediated two points. The phallic father is like the pier in his incapacity to mediate. Consequently, his power, while considerable, is onanistic. Ironically, only through meeting another masturbator will Stephen learn to mediate historical and mythic time. In the complexities of that relationship, to which we now briefly turn, lies the implicit answer to Joyce's implicit riddle.

Although Robert Caserio argues that only "nostalgic commentators" import "idealizations of paternities and filiations, or father-son relationships" (239) into *Ulysses*, the text itself supports at least that idea of "fusion" which Joyce announced to Linati (v. the Linati schema and Ellmann UL 149–50, 154, 157, 183). For example, in the newspaper episode an unattributed thought occurs that is totally different stylistically from anything else in that chapter: "I have often thought since on looking back over that strange time that it was that small act, trivial in itself, that striking of that match, that determined the whole aftercourse of both our lives" (115). Although the thought may be Stephen's as he waits for J. J. O'Molloy's cigarette to be lit, it surely can have no reference to that particular action. Cope suggests that it is a "joke about fictional styles," but he also adds that it must have something to do with Bloom, "whose analogue is Moses and whose future duty is to inform Stephen" (88). The mystery is only resolved in Ithaca, where, as Bloom lights the fire to prepare their chocolate, Stephen thinks "of others elsewhere in other times who, kneeling on one knee or two, had kindled fires for him" (547). The stylistic differentiation in the earlier chapter suggests that a narrative voice which includes Stephen's but ranges beyond him is signaling readers a truth about the Bloom/Stephen relationship they will grasp only retrospectively.

Thus we must look to both indirect as well as direct relations between Stephen and Bloom to discover how Joyce covertly answers the riddle. Since my reading of that riddle (or riddles) has focused on the sowing of seeds and the crowing of cocks, tracing out these images further in the text should show that Joyce wanted us to read them both mythically and historically. An indirect connection between Bloom and Stephen concerns their telling stories of the sowing of seeds. To do so, both use styles which are not generally characteristic. In Aeolus, angry at the inflated rhetoric of the three "patriotic" speeches quoted to him, Stephen tells the story of the two old Dublin women who climb Nelson's pillar and spit plum pits over the edge. The story's title ("A Pisgah Sight of Palestine or the Parable of the Plums") indicates what Frye would call the mythos that lies beneath it. But, as Ellmann points out, Stephen's mode is "naturalism—things as they objectionally are—expressed in a style graceless but also windless, without figures of speech" (UL 70). In his anger at the political situation between England and Ireland, Stephen takes the matter of myth and translates it into a bitter response to historical time. Thus the image of the virgins spouting their seed is, as Lindsey Tucker suggests, "an inverted image of insemination that is a statement on sterility" (76).

Bloom's narrative is the opposite. Normally a reporter of or responder to historic event, Bloom opts to transform an event from his and Molly's life into a myth. Unhappy about Molly's upcoming adultery with Boylan as well as suffering from an increasing sense of personal alienation, Bloom seizes on the episode on Howth Hill when Molly passed chewed seed cake from her mouth to his before they made love for the first time. What would on a purely historic level be at least mawkish if not revolting (which is how some commentators read it) is transformed into a myth of power and beauty: "Ravished over her I lay, full lips full open, kissed her mouth. Yum. Softly she gave me in my mouth the seedcake warm and chewed. Mawkish pulp her mouth had mumbled sweetsour of her spittle. Joy: I ate it: joy. Young life, her lips that gave me pouting. Soft warm sticky gumjelly lips. Flowers her eyes were, take me, willing eyes" (144). Giving a synchronic reading to the experience, Bloom can create a more bearable present time for himself. Where Stephen pushed his sowing riddle toward harsh reality, Bloom creates a myth which offers escape from his own historical "nightmare."

But even elements within this generated myth push it back toward diachronic reality. The archetype behind Molly's giving the seed cake to Bloom is Eve's offering Adam the apple, and from that occurred their fall into history. Moreover, this paragraph of mythopoeia is anchored by the image of flies copulating: "Stuck on the pane two flies buzzed, stuck" at the beginning and "Stuck, the flies buzzed" (144) at the end. If the enclosure echoes the scene of Charles Bovary's introduction to Emma (Ellmann UL 79), it does so to contrast the insistence of historical time against the romances men and women create. Bloom's seed myth, real in its beauty and tender in its feeling, is juxtaposed to a carnality of a totally different order, one which insists on countering the synchronic vision with its diachronic action.

The repetition of the words "Buzz. Buzz" (156) in the scene where Stephen rationalizes that he does not owe A.E. the pound because he has been totally reconstituted molecularly suggests that Joyce wants to draw a connection between Bloom's seed cake myth and Stephen's situation. Stephen, after all, has no knowledge at this point of Bloom, nor do the words bear any relation to the syllogistic process going on in his mind at that point. They can only be a pointer from the narrator that we, as readers, must seek some connection between these two episodes. In both instances, the protagonist perceives that however agreeable an escape to mythic time would be (Bloom could forget Boylan; Stephen wouldn't have to worry about his debt), it must be mediated with a sense of one's historical role. The "Buzz. Buzz" phrase suggests that they also share a common world—not one of pure historical contingency as Stephen fears but one where linear time can be meliorated by synchronic vision.

Perhaps too much critical stress has been placed on the differences between the two men. Genuinely different personalities, Bloom and Stephen nevertheless have much in common. Lacking keys, they both urinate and masturbate; look at pornography; enjoy riddles; write poems; think of utopias; fear history; experiment with blocking out reality; and are capable of thinking on two levels of reality at once. In Oxen of the Sun, Stephen is genuinely, if drunkenly, pleased that Bloom shares his view, against that of all the medicals, that in difficult births the life of the child should take precedence over that of the mother (319). And, in Ithaca, Bloom reflects that "though they didn't see eye to eye in everything a certain analogy there somehow was as if both their minds were travelling, so to speak, in the one train of thought" (536). That train of thought leads to a mutual sense of the value of mediation.

Moving from the sowing of seeds to the crowing of cocks, we can see that an explicit example of mediation occurs when Stephen and Bloom, a "keyless couple," arrive from the cabman's shelter at number 7 Eccles Street. Granted the alternatives "To enter or not to enter. To knock or not to knock" (546), Bloom chooses to mediate by the stratagem of climbing over the area railing and dropping to the ground, thus achieving entry without a key and without awakening Molly. If we accept the metaphorical meaning of the cock as the penis, the questions that the narrator puts next seem particularly significant. "Did he fall?" and "Did he rise uninjured by concussion?" (546). Putting masturbation before sexual obligation to Molly, Bloom has fallen both in the sense of detumescence and in his agony over Molly's infidelity. In answer to the second question, the narrator responds: "Regaining new stable equilibrium he rose uninjured though concussed" (546). Though Bloom has been affected by Molly's act, he has not been permanently injured and will regain equilibrium. As Bloom's accomplice in entering, Stephen may also learn, through the practice of mediation, the value of falling to rise again.[4] The postcard sent to Breen contains the message "U.p.:up." As Ellmann suggests, the scurrilous import is that he emits urine rather than semen when he has an erection (UL 75). The phrase may have a different, happier import for Bloom, however. Ulysses and Penelope can come together ("up") when Bloom mediates linear and cyclic time. Stephen can achieve the status he wishes as an artist when he can unite both religious and secular time.

A final comment on Stephen's cock riddle seems hidden in the two men's mutual urination. Often taken as a contest, what occurs seems more important for its sense of mutuality. The dissimilarities of the "trajectories of their, first sequent, then simultaneous, urinations" (577) as well as the difference of their thoughts about each other's penis simply emblematize the differences between the two men which Joyce has developed throughout the novel. Stephen's trajectory is higher, suggesting his deeper involvement in the vertical world of myth; Bloom's is longer, as befits his horizontal view. Similarly, Bloom thinks only of the physical, scientific aspects of Stephen's penis while Stephen thinks only of the ritualistic implications of Bloom's. They maintain their differences, yet their acting in concert suggests they also mediate those differences. Urinating together joins them in contingent time; they have broken from the solipsistic world of masturbation after each has contemplated "the other in both mirrors of the reciprocal flesh of theirhisnothis fellowfaces" (577).[5]

Passages that stress bodily movements also reveal Joyce's emphasis on the need to integrate mythic and historical time.[6] The description of Thersites' urination in the Cyclops chapter reveals a structural pattern wherein two kinds of time, and actions, are juxtaposed to one another. As I will show, the episodes of bodily movement throughout the novel demonstrate the same structural juxtaposition. Involved in bodily acts which are repetitive or cyclic, the characters consistently think or respond both on that level and on another which is diachronic and irreversible.

The men in the bar have been speculating that Bloom has won a large amount of money on the "dark horse" Throwaway. Thus, Thersites thinks about Bloom as he relieves himself.

> Goodbye Ireland I'm going to Gort. So I just went round the back of the yard to pumpship and begob (hundred shillings to five) while I was letting off my *(Throwaway* twenty to) letting off my load gob says I to myself I knew he was uneasy in his (two pints off of Joe and one in Slattery's off) in his mind to get off the mark to (hundred shillings is five quid) and when they were in the (dark horse) pisser Burke was telling me card party and letting on the child was sick (gob, must have done about a gallon) flabbyarse of a wife speaking down the tube *she's better* or *she's* (ow!) all a plan so he could vamoose with the pool if he won or (Jesus, full up I was) trading without a licence (ow!) Ireland my nation says he (hoik! phthook!) never be up to those bloody (there's the last of it) Jerusalem (ah!) cuckoos. (275)

Even in a paragraph as unpromising as this one, we can discover evidence of Joyce's larger purposes. While the material within the parentheses at first relates to chronological time, it soon shifts to its own synchronic story of Thersites' bladder. Although Marilyn French has speculated that the passage ironically reveals that this unlovely narrator has the clap (147), it seems more simply to describe (with that kind of exactitude Joyce loved to show as, for example, in his spelling of a cat's Mkgnao in Calypso) the process of male urination. We notice that a complete story is narrated with cause (two pints off of Joe and one in Slattery's off), conflict (ow!), and happy resolution (ah!). In contrast to this cyclic pattern drawn from nature, Thersites' diachronic narrative suggests the incoherence and angry irresolution of history. Thinking that Bloom stole away to collect on his bet, Thersites' mind shifts to some story about the Blooms told him by pisser Burke. He apparently conflates in a manner incomprehensible to the reader several different anecdotes about the Blooms only to end with an angry anti-Semitic denunciation of those "bloody (there's the last of it) Jerusalem (ah!) cuckoos." The juxtaposing within this last phrase of the anger of diachronic narrative with the satisfaction of the mythic one suggests that Joyce saw dangers in the failure to mediate myth and history.

"Asquat on the cuck stool," Bloom also enacts two narratives, the cyclic one of defecation and the historic one of reading Philip Beaufoy's prize titbit which he regrets not having written himself (its nonreversible fate is made clear when Bloom tears away half the story to wipe himself). Unlike Thersites, Bloom can effect mediation between the two time sequences: "He glanced back through what he had read and, while feeling his water flow quietly, he envied kindly Mr. Beaufoy who had written it and received payment of three pounds, thirteen and six" (56). Because Bloom is persistently associated with processes of mediation—such as being able to read and to be worried about hemorrhoids at the same time, he finds it possible to regard life more kindly than does Thersites. The equanimity he achieves over his bowel movement prefigures the equanimity with which he will eventually regard Molly's adultery. In both instances, by relating a historical story (here his envy of Beaufoy's achievement) to a mythic experience, he achieves a solacing sense not of the defeat but the amelioration of time.

This repeated pattern of combining two modes of time or narrative while describing acts on the lower level of the body occurs also in Joyce's description of acts on the higher level. Bloom's letter to Martha Clifford is one example:

> Hope he's not looking, cute as a rat. He held unfurled his *Freeman*. Can't see now. Remember write Greek ees. Bloom dipped, Bloo mur: dear sir. Dear Henry wrote: dear Mady. Got your lett and flow. Hell did I put? Some pock or oth. It is utterl imposs. Underline *imposs*. To write today.
>
> Bore this. Bored Bloom tambourined gently with I am just reflecting fingers on flat pad Pat brought.
>
> On. Know what I mean. No, change that ee. Accep my poor litt pres enclos. Ask her no answ. Hold on. Five Dig. Two about here. Penny the gulls. Elijah is com. Seven Davy Byrne's. Is eight about. Say half a crown. My poor little pres: p.o. two and six. Write me a long. Do you despise? Jingle, have you the? So excited. Why do

> you call me naught? You naughty too? O, Mairy lost the string of her. Bye for today. Yes, yes, will tell you. Want to. To keep it up. Call me that other. Other world she wrote. My patience are exhaust. To keep it up. You must believe. Believe. The tank, It. Is. True. (229)

About half this passage represents Bloom's thoughts as he sits in the Ormond Hotel dining room having just finished his liver and bacon; for example, the passage beginning "Hold on" shows him figuring up his expenses for the day and determining how much money he wants to send Martha. The other half consists of Bloom's effort to involve himself in the self-titillation of his correspondence with Martha. Like his (and Stephen's) impulse to masturbate, the "affair" with Martha really represents an escape from historic time to a fantasy world. Obsessed as Bloom is at this point with Boylan's advances on Molly, he finds the letter writing a "bore." Although his later masturbation will demonstrate that he has not transcended such wishes to escape historical reality, Bloom's boredom with what has been a developed stratagem to find "weak pleasure" is a healthy sign.

The mythic, synchronic nature of the letter writing is made even more pointed by its association with music as Joyce has Bloom finish the letter:

> —Answering an ad? keen Richie's eyes asked Bloom.
>
> —Yes, Mr. Bloom said. Town traveler. Nothing doing, I expect.
>
> Bloom mur: best references. But Henry wrote: it will excite me. You know how. In haste. Henry. Greek ee. Better add postscript. What is he playing now? Improvising. Intermezzo. P.S. The rum tum tum. How will you pun? You punish me? Crooked skirt swinging, whack by. Tell me I want to. Know. O. Course if I didn't I wouldn't ask. La la la ree. Trails off there sad in minor. Why minor sad? Sign H. They like sad tail at end. P.P.S. La la la ree. I feel so sad today. La ree. So lonely. Dee. (230)

Instead of words, the letter becomes a series of notes, suggesting that Bloom recognizes it for what it is, a narrative whose time scheme escapes into synchronicity rather than confronts historical reality.

Like Robinson Crusoe, Bloom is able to slip easily between two kinds of time, finding consolation in synchronic vision when diachronic reality becomes too onerous. Also like Crusoe, he begins to reach back toward historical time as he faces up to his situation. Stephen, however, is more like Roxana, seeking escape from the nightmare of history in the worlds his mind can create. Yet, Joyce underlines for us that even the creation of high art is a consequence of the mediation of historical and mythic time. We notice that the one poem Stephen writes in *Ulysses* gets composed under much the same circumstances as Bloom's letter to Martha (or Bloom's defecation, for that matter): the action takes place on two different planes of time; at the same instant Stephen is creating his poem he reminds himself that he has forgotten to supply himself with paper taken from the library:

> Here. Put a pin in that chap, will you? My tablets. Mouth to her kiss. No. Must be two of em. Glue em well. Mouth to her mouth's kiss.
>
> His lips lipped and mouthed fleshless lips of air: mouth to her moomb. Oomb, allwombing tomb. His mouth moulded issuing breath, unspeeched: ooeeehah: roar of cataractic planets, globed, blazing, roaring wayawayawayawayaway. Paper. The banknotes, blast them. Old Deasy's letter. Here. Thanking you for the hospitality tear the blank end off. Turning his back to the sun he bent over far to a table of rock and scribbled words. That's twice I forgot to take slips from the library counter. (40)

In *Portrait* Joyce showed us, as many commentators have pointed out, that Stephen's villanelle could arise from a wet dream; the source of the aesthetic vision could be found in a very bodily response. Here, he seems more to suggest that both kinds of response can occur simultaneously. While Stephen is in the midst of poetic creativity (envisioned here in very mythic terms: "ooeeehah: roar of cataractic planets, globed, blazing, roaring wayawayawayawayaway"), he can be thinking at the same time of himself as Hamlet ("My tablets"); be aware of the irony of using the bottom of Mr. Deasy's letter on hoof and mouth disease; and remind himself to take slips of paper from the library counter in case of being "caught short." In fact, the affinity between poetic composition and defecation is brought out when Stephen presents Deasy's letter to Myles Crawford. "—That old pelters, the editor said. Who tore it? Was he short taken?" (109).

For Smollett and Joyce there must have been the sense that the English in which they wrote both was and was not their language. As a Scotsman, Smollett needed constantly to avoid solecisms, to adapt his native language to that of the society to which he had expatriated himself and where he sought to make his living as a writer. For Joyce, as for all Irishmen, there was the sense that English was a language imposed on his country—supplanting a native language which he could neither write nor find an audience for had he been able. English became, then, both the instrument by which they constructed their art and a symbol of perpetual alienation. The simulation of a mythic language thus has a double appeal for both these writers. First, as language became increasingly abstract, mythic-simulation was a means by which to restore "poetry" to expression. It could make language richer and more emotionally fulfilling. But mythic-simulation was also a means by which both writers could try to reach beyond a language imposed on them in part by hostile societies. It was a way of reaching back to roots and reclaiming for themselves the language which politics, ideology, economic determinism—history—had imposed on them. Their persistent linguistic experimentation demonstrates their reaction against English; it also demonstrates their triumph over English in the way they renewed the language by their experiments in mythic nostalgia.

As the Library scene focused on Stephen's theory of art, Cyclops centers around Bloom's theory of life. His heroic defense of love against the bile of the citizen takes as dim a view of historical process as Stephen had earlier: "Force, hatred, history, all that. That's not life for men and women, insult and hatred" (273). The instrument of history in this chapter is language; for it is through language that the English have mastered the Irish, and it is in language that the Irish might free themselves. One of the "inflated" passages describes the coming of John Wyse Nolan from a meeting where the "grave elders" at the city hall "had taken solemn counsel whereby they might, if so be it might be, bring once more into honour among mortal men the winged speech of the seadivided Gael" (266). While the nationalists in the pub associate independence with the regaining of their own language, Joyce's attitude, as we might expect from one whose artistic instrument is English, is more complex. A renewed English may more truly liberate Ireland than a resurrected Gaelic.

Joyce recognizes that he must accept the language history has given him; yet by attending to the mythic dimensions of English, he can subvert its authority more effectively than can the Nationalists who call for its overthrow. While this subversion reaches an extreme in *Finnegans Wake*, where myth creates a new English, in *Ulysses* Joyce works more conservatively. Here, he calls for a mediation of the language of history and that of myth. The climax of Cyclops comes when Bloom, after having defied the citizen, is apotheosized as Elijah:

> And the last we saw was the bloody car rounding the corner and old sheepsface on it gesticulating and the bloody mongrel after it with his lugs back for all he was bloody well worth to tear him limb from limb. Hundred to five! Jesus, he took the value of it out of him, I promise you.
>
> When, lo, there came about them all a great brightness and they beheld the chariot wherein He stood ascend to heaven. And they beheld Him in the chariot, clothed upon in the glory of the brightness, having raiment as of the sun, fair as the moon and terrible that for awe they durst not look upon Him. And there came a voice out of heaven, calling *Elijah! Elijah!* And He answered with a main cry: *Abba! Adonai!* And they beheld Him even Him, ben Bloom Elijah, amid clouds of angels ascend to the glory of the brightness at an angle of fortyfive degrees over Donohoe's in Little Green street, like a shot off a shovel. (282)

The sour voice of the first paragraph is that of a "historian" who persistently places events in the least-common-denominator mode. The other voice is that of a mythologizer, intent on raising Bloom from an ordinary person to a heroic archetype.[7] The last sentence of the passage (and the chapter) brings both tonalities together: "And they beheld Him even Him, ben Bloom Elijah, amid clouds of angels ascend to the glory of brightness ["inflated" style] at an angle of fortyfive degrees over Donohoe's in Little Green street like a shot off a shovel ["deflated" style]." It is the conjunction of voices here that lends credibility to "the magnificent flight of 'ben Bloom Elijah' into glory" (Cope 22). Joyce's own epiphany has to do with his realization of how the search into the mythic sources of English can lend freedom to his historical dependence on an "alien" language.

Having shown his language theme in Cyclops, Joyce proceeds to develop it in Nausicaa. He carefully establishes the mythic dimension of the chapter in his opening description: "The summer evening had begun to fold the world in its mysterious embrace. Far away in the west the sun was setting and the last glow of all too fleeting day lingered lovingly on sea and strand, on the proud promontory of dear old Howth guarding as ever the waters of the bay, on the weedgrown rocks along Sandymount shore and, last but not least, on the quiet church whence there streamed forth at times upon the stillness the voice of prayer to her who is in her pure radiance a beacon ever to the stormtossed heart of man, Mary, star of the sea" (284). The oxymoronic-like effect of the phrase "summer evening" creates the sense of life cyclically flowing into death, the static world of myth that folds the world with its mysterious embrace. The second sentence underlines the use of cliché that will characterize the chapter; but even as it does so, it adds a soothing and mollifying quality to the idea of temporality. Moreover, the personifications of the sentence ("fleeting day lingered lovingly" and the "proud . . . guarding" of dear old Howth Hill) break down the distinction between man and nature, creating a pastoral scene where human voices "streamed" forth. In the final metaphor of the paragraph human divinity (Mary) is first a lighthouse for the storm-tossed heart of man and then in the words of the litany the "star of the sea." Although the ironic tone keeps pushing the reader toward a historical skepticism, the metaphoric identifications lure him or her into a timeless world of pre-Christian pastoralism.

Frank Budgen, whose early work on his friend Joyce has proved so helpful to generations of critics, is useful here, too. He remarks on the "essentially pictorial" quality of the scene where everything "affirms the idea of space" and foreshadows "in conception though not in material, those mysterious dream glimpses of landscape in *Work in Progress*, where the earth comes to life and shares consciousness with its creatures" (213). Other elements as well underline the mythic quality of the scene. Master Tommy and Master Jacky Caffrey enact a comic variant of the Cain and Abel story in their struggle over the sand castle. Joyce again cleverly conflates Christianity and nature when the narrator sententiously remarks, "Boys will be boys and our two twins were no exception to this golden rule" (285). As Master Jacky's name clearly hints at the onanism Bloom practices later in the scene, this story of a fall foreshadows his own. And, of course, we have here not one but three virgins on the rocks, enacting variously not only three aspects of the Madonna but also the three archetypal roles of earth mother, temptress, and soul mate.

Although Cissy Caffrey's "word was law" (285), it is Gerty MacDowell, the waxen pallor of whose face "was almost spiritual in its ivorylike purity though her rosebud mouth was a genuine Cupid's bow, Greekly perfect" (286), who will be at once a temptress and soul mate for the errant Bloom. That is appropriate, for it is only she who has something to teach him. Commentators note Gerty's dependence on the clichés of pulp fiction; they do not, however, understand her persistent effort to mythologize her experience. During the long monologue focused through her eyes, we see Gerty consistently converting empirical reality, the "facts" of her history, into the stuff of romance, the myth of herself that she lives by. Having tacked up in the outhouse "Mr. Tunney the grocer's christmas almanac, the picture of halcyon days where a young gentlemen in the costume they used to wear then with a three-cornered hat was offering a bunch of flowers to his ladylove," Gerty "often looked at them dreamily when she went there for a certain purpose and felt her own arms that were white and soft just like hers" (291). She converts Reggie's indifference into a romantic image of herself as a forsaken sweetheart; and she will forgive Bloom's masturbation because "men were so different" (299). What she will remember is that "their souls met in a last lingering glance and the eyes that reached her heart, full of a strange shining, hung enraptured on her sweet flowerlike face" (301).

Although much fun has been made of Gerty's cliché-ridden speech, she has, as Ellmann has reminded us, some of the qualities of the poet (UL 130). And Barfield has helped us to see that clichés are, in effect, dead metaphors. True metaphor, Barfield explains, arises when the poet is able to recapture those unified meanings that inhered in words during the ages of myth. Gerty's language can be seen then as a weak but nevertheless real effort to speak in the language of myth. And to some extent she succeeds. Her role in the scene to a degree parallels that of the Virgin Mary, to whom prayers are offered at the men's temperance retreat conducted at the same time by Reverend John Hughes, S.J. In conceiving Christ, Mary does, in Christian theology, bring together the worlds of history and myth in the Incarnation. So does Gerty in the incandescence of the fireworks. Although one might well say that Gerty's parallel to the Virgin was a part of Joyce's persistent effort to undercut the church, to parody the very notion of the Incarnation, we noticed at the beginning that Joyce showed Mary as, in effect, another nature goddess in the larger pastoral world of myth. And it would seem likely that he is using the parallel here to suggest the real attractions of the mythic mode whether realized on the high spiritual plane of the Virgin or in the commonplace romanticism of Gerty. Certainly, Joyce's attitude toward Gerty is not unsympathetic.

Bloom's language in his ensuing monologue is quite different. He calls Gerty a "hot little devil" and supposes she is near "her monthlies" (301); expresses satisfaction over his fart earlier in the day: "Good job I let off there behind coming out of Dignam's. Cider that was. Otherwise I couldn't have. Makes you want to sing after" (303); and, in one of the book's funnier passages, empirically attempts to ascertain the smell of semen: "Mr. Bloom inserted his nose. Hm. Into the. Hm. Opening of his waistcoat. Almonds or. No. Lemons it is. Ah no, that's the soap" (307). Although he prefers not to think of Molly and Boylan, he can not evade doing so. "O, he did. Into her. She did. Done" (303). In contrast to Gerty's myth-making, Bloom indulges in a crudely empirical historicizing, perhaps in consequence of his sense of the crudity of his response to Gerty: "Begins to feel cold and clammy. Aftereffect not pleasant. Still you have to get rid of it someway" (303).

Their modes of consciousness and narrative discourse seemingly alien, Bloom and Gerty have nevertheless achieved a kind of union. Bloom thinks, "Still it was a kind of language between us" (305). And it really is in terms of language that Joyce shows their having come at all together. Although Bloom will not adopt such a consistent mythic language as that of Gerty, he will modify the crudely reductive historical language he uses early in his monologue. His movement into mythic expression will be primarily seen in terms of syntax rather than words as Gerty's was. The language of Bloom's interior monologue which follows Gerty's exit is remarkable for its closeness to ordinary syntax. It follows the usual sentence pattern of subject, verb, and object. This sentence "plot" suggests a diachronic action which extends itself forward into time. And, indeed, for most of the passage Bloom's syntax does serve as a historical foil against the synchronic pressure of Gerty's pseudoarchaic vocabulary. His earlier speech patterns thus reinforce his position in this scene as the historian who undercuts Gerty's mythic posturing.

A later passage in his monologue shows a different kind of syntax, however. It is one which Roy K. Gottfried has demonstrated as being characteristic of Bloom in other sections of the novel. It occurs as Bloom looks at Howth Hill and thinks of his sexual experience with Molly there: "All quiet on Howth now. The distant hills seem. Where we. The rhododendrons. I am a fool perhaps. He gets the plums, and I the plumstones. Where I come in. All that old hill has seen. Names change: that's all. Lovers: yum yum" (308). Gottfried points out that Joyce paid particular attention to the *order* of his words in his sentences and that one of his efforts was to twist that order to new purposes. Establishing a pattern of sentence order, Joyce would then vary it by omitting words, leaving the sentence incomplete, and/or twisting syntax. Gottfried concludes that "the entelechy embodied in certain of Joyce's constructed sentences represents a profound statement in favor of life. The incomplete sentences generate their own ends, growing from what exists inherently within them. This growth at the level of syntax, the development and coming-to-be of meaning, is not merely a metaphor but actually imparts a corresponding sense of development and growth to the material it treats: the character, plot, world of the novel" (167). I would extend Gottfried's analysis and suggest that Joyce, in creating these incomplete, seemingly fractured sentences, actually seeks a more synchronic sense of syntax than is found in the usual subject-verb-object pattern, a pattern which lends itself, as I have suggested, to the diachronic forward thrust into time. There is growth in such incomplete sentences, but it is not so much growth *in* time as *through* time, creating not so much the sense of progression forward as the timelessness of events, their repetitive and cyclic aspects.

Bloom's paragraph on Howth Hill shows thus a slipping in and out of synchronic, mythic speech. "All quiet on Howth now" works progressively, and the adverb marks the time clearly in the present (although the absence of a verb suggests the continuing time of myth). The next incomplete sentences create a timeless sense that brings out more fully the idea of *place* Budgen noticed. "The distant hills seem. Where we. The rhododendrons." The affair between the Blooms seems as eternal as the earth itself. The straightforward syntax of the next sentence reflects the bitterness he feels as he returns to the linear reality of the time world where Boylan has cuckolded him. "He gets the plums and I the plumstones." The next sentence unit is peculiarly poignant; in one sense it is syntactically complete (as a clause), in another it is not (as a sentence). "Where I come in." Where, in fact, does Bloom come into time? The paragraph ends with a concession to the cyclic world of myth. "All that old hill has seen. Names change; that's all. Lovers: yum yum." In accepting the cyclicity of life, yet retaining the syntax of history (these last sentences do form complete syntactic units, however small), Bloom may be achieving a kind of mediation of history and myth that can tell him where he does come in.

His next paragraph is filled with contradictory thoughts about cyclicity and return: "Take the train there tomorrow. No. Returning not the same." "The new I want. Nothing new under the sun." "So it returns. Think you're escaping and run into yourself." "Circus horse walking in a ring" (308–9). The paragraph ends, however, on the image of Rip van Winkle in the charade Bloom acted out before Molly early in their relationship. "Then I did Rip van Winkle coming back. She leaned on the sideboard watching. Moorish eyes. Twenty years asleep in sleepy hollow. All changed. Forgotten. The young are old. His gun rusty from the dew" (309). In a way, Rip van Winkle also mediates between myth and history; his story is both in and beyond time. In that sense he might serve as a model for Bloom as he too must try to work himself into his new situation with Molly where all is "changed."

Some mythic readings of *Ulysses* have suggested that the question of whether Bloom will change is irrelevant. Bloom, and Stephen and Molly too, are at the end of the novel no longer so much characters in whose "growth" we are interested as parts of eternity—elements in a mythic unity which is larger than their individual selves (Ellmann UL 167). Joyce's intention, however, is not to transform his novel into a myth but to infuse it with mythic feeling and language. It remains a novel although not the novel of despair and alienation high modernist critics claimed it to be. Much in Nausicaa itself points to a more hopeful conclusion. After masturbating, Bloom had remarked, while watching Gerty move off with the others to watch the fireworks: "My fireworks. Up like a rocket, down like a stick" (304). His sexual problem appears to have been temporarily relieved, but not resolved. But later he decides not to try to leave a message for Gerty in the sand and tosses aside the stick he has been using to write with: "The stick fell in the silted sand, stuck. Now if you were trying to do that for a week on end, you couldn't. Chance" (312). The upright, phallic posture of the stick seems to bode well for Bloom's resumption of conjugal relations with Molly.

Chance will certainly play a part in any reconciliation he will achieve; but chance will only be able to operate effectively if Bloom can from time to time suspend the laws of causality, put himself in the position to receive grace. While his broad role in Nausicaa has been to offer a realistic, historical opposition to the "jammy marmalady" myth world of Gerty MacDowell, we have also seen in Bloom (and Joyce) a sympathy for Gerty's idealization process and an attunement to her language. Bloom will never mythologize himself in the manner of Gerty, but he grows increasingly toward a recognition of his need to mediate between the languages of history and myth. For that reason, we ought to accept the last paragraph of the chapter that is focused through his eyes not as the mindless, infantile gurglings of a man in despair but as the assimilation of Gerty's mythologizing to his own needs. "O sweety all your little girlwhite up I saw dirty bracegirdle made me do love sticky we two naughty Grace darling she him half past the bed met him pike hoses frillies for Raoul de perfume your wife black hair heave under embon *senorita* young eyes Mulvey plump bubs me breadvan Winkle red slippers she rusty sleep wander years of dreams return tail end Agendath swooney lovey showed me her next year in drawers return next in her next her next" (312). Although Gerty's unchanging use of mythic language suggests that she will be trapped in the stasis of her fantasy and cut off from growth, Bloom's forays into mythic speaking are sporadic and suggest that he will, in fact, achieve growth through his ability to mediate synchronic and diachronic modes of expression.

The next section, Oxen of the Sun, gives us a historical picture of the development of language which parallels the gestation and birth of the Purefoy baby. Joyce parallels each stage of the development of the embryo with a stage in the development of English language and literature, though these relations are hard to establish and at times seem chronologically contradictory. In a more general sense, Joyce traces the development of language from its more mythic, emotive, synchronic period through its giving way to more rationalistic, abstract speech. The outburst of jive talk, slang, and nearly incoherent babble at the end of the chapter reflects, on one level, the drunkenness of the characters; but in another way, it suggests possibilities for language in a resurgence of less rational and logical, more emotive modes of communication. In this way, the chapter ends with a *re*-birth of Vico's sense of the richness of the earliest phase of mythic language (and, of course, thus parallels the ideas about language of Barfield and Cassirer).

As shown in the "encyclopaedic" (341) language with which they debate the question of whether the mother's or the unborn child's life should have precedence in cases of difficult birth, the medicals accept unquestioningly the dominance of an abstract language. Only Bloom and Stephen support the child's right to life over that of the mother. The narrator comments that "the perverted transcendentalism to which Mr. S. Dedalus' [Div. Scep.] contentions would appear to prove him pretty badly addicted runs directly counter to accepted scientific methods" (341). Symbolically, he and Bloom favor the effort to renew the spiritual, emotional resources of language rather than to continue it as it is. The only way the medical/scientific community can attempt renewal is through the parodic national fertilizing farm to be named *Omphalos* where Buck Mulligan will offer himself to all women comers. Stephen, however, will renew language by being born as a poet, by "the utterance of the word" (345). Like Bloom in Nausicaa, Stephen thus achieves a new awareness of the need to mediate history and myth. The word he actually utters is "Burke's!" (345) which, historically, is the bar to which they scatter, but which, mythically, is the burp of the newborn child-poet and which introduces the four pages of irrational babble that concludes the chapter but also suggests how the artist can renew language for artistic expression. "Just you try it on," the chapter ends.

Throughout Sirens Joyce explores the tensions between diachronic and synchronic plotting as well as looking at the possibility of achieving a mediating narrative form. By creating three variations on one passage, Joyce makes these three narrative modes quite obvious to us. Bloom and Richie Goulding have been listening to Simon Dedalus sing "M'Appari" while dining at the Ormond Hotel.

> Goulding, a flush struggling on his pale, told Mr.Bloom, face of the night, Si in Ned Lambert's, Dedalus house, sang *'Twas rank and fame*.
>
> He, Mr. Bloom, listened while he, Richie Goulding, told him, Mr. Bloom, of the night he, Richie, heard him, Si Dedalus, sing *'Twas rank and fame* in his, Ned Lambert's house.
>
> Brothers-in-law: relations. We never speak as we pass by. Rift in

> the lute I think. Treats him with scorn. See. He admires him all the more. The night Si sang. The human voice, two tiny silky chords, wonderful, more than all others. (227)

As I have suggested, the usual subject-verb-object structure of the ordinary English sentence suggests a time-oriented, historical "plot." Joyce's manipulations of syntax are efforts to break up this plot and to suggest other modes of perceiving reality. In the first paragraph of this quotation, we see a deliberate effort to break the word order of English in favor of a pattern like that of more highly inflected languages. By constantly interrupting historical pattern ("a flush struggling in his pale, told Mr. Bloom, face of the night" for "a flush struggling in his pale face, told Mr. Bloom of the night"), the narrative mode cuts synchronically into reality, creating a spiral rather than linear movement, savoring depth rather than extension.

The second paragraph operates in the historic mode, where the "plot" is laid out all too clearly in front of us. Our reading thrusts forward instead of circling around as in the first paragraph. The insistence upon defining each pronoun lends an almost excessive rationalism to a sentence that tries to insist that reality can be represented in a causal plot. In contrast, the third paragraph moves freely from subjective to objective modes, mingling Bloom's statements of fact ("Brothers-in-law: relations.") and of speculation ("Rift in the lute I think") with recollections of Goulding's past words ("We never speak as we pass by.") and of his present story ("The night Si sang."). The third paragraph mixes complete sentences or syntactical units which suggest complete historical action with incomplete ones ("The night Si sang.") which suggest repetitive, synchronic movement. The third passage, then, mediates between the first two in its mode of emplotment. Although Joyce came to rely more and more on this mediating narrative perspective in the stylistic complications of the later chapters, it oversimplifies too much to say that it was his preferred mode in this chapter. While Joyce wanted to show that Stephen's riddle could be mediated, in this chapter he is more concerned to explore possibilities of plotting than to choose between them.

This does not mean, of course, that certain possibilities were not quickly ruled out. In the sixty-two lines of phrases and sentences that open the chapter, Joyce apparently tries to create a verbal imitation of an opera overture. While we may recognize a lack of logical coherence in this passage, we cannot say that in using these fragments he is trying to show the void at the center of language;[8] rather, he experiments with an extreme mode of mythic narration to demonstrate what it can and cannot do to tell a story. What these "chords" can do, as C. H. Peake points out, is to convey "various general emotional connotations" (227). What they cannot do is to organize these connotations in any coherent narrative fashion. While Joyce is having fun putting on the conventions of the overture, he is also pushing to its furthest extreme synchronic, mythic telling.

Although the "overture" demonstrates the unsuitability of purely mythic narrative to the novel, Joyce does not, in this chapter, eschew mythic plotting altogether. In the diachronic narrative which opens the chapter proper, Miss Douce and Miss Kennedy talk about men and particularly about a pharmacist who seems to have made some sort of advance to Miss Douce. Further, they can't imagine being married to some greasy-eyed person. Since the males have been unclearly specified, since numerous references to Bloom have been woven into the text, and since the narrator intersperses the phrase "Married to Bloom, to greaseabloom" (214), the reader almost inevitably thinks the women have been talking about Bloom. Actually, what Joyce does is to pause in his diachronic narrative of Miss Douce and Miss Kennedy and to cut synchronically to Bloom's contemporaneous adventures on the street. We have, then, two plots going on at once. While the primary mode is the diachronic "history" of events at the Ormond bar, we also see a synchronic view of the action. Frequently, the two modes are merged, as in the following: "In came Lenehan. Round him peered Lenehan. Mr. Bloom reached Essex bridge. Yes, Mr. Bloom crossed bridge to Yessex. To Martha I must write. Buy paper. Daly's. Girl there civil. Bloom. Old Bloom. Blue bloom is on the rye" (215). The first sentence is in the historical mode as is the second, though the "him" is unspecified. Is it Simon (but he is at the bar already)? Is it Bloom (but he is on the street)? We interrupt our narrative in the Ormond bar to cut synchronically to Bloom on the Essex bridge. The narrative is objective till the speaker tells us that Bloom crossed the "bridge of Yessex." The coined word "Yes/sex" clearly makes a subjective comment pertinent to Bloom's sexual condition. We switch then to Bloom's own mind as he thinks of Martha, his mythic love. The passage then ends back in the mind of the narrator, but not apparently in the barroom.

Three main refrains are used throughout the chapter to show us that we must envision a plot that works vertically in addition to the one which proceeds horizontally. The first of these is the word "jingle" and its variations. Although Bloom associates the word with Boylan as he leaves the bar, I do not think we are to assume the jingle references occur in his mind as he imagines Boylan's advance to Molly. Rather, the narrative is telling two stories at once—the one in the bar is presented largely as history; the other, Boylan and Molly's, is presented in its mythic aspect in a manner similar to that of the overture. Although the word *jingle* is associated with the tram car, we have already learned that the quoits in the Blooms' bed jingle (46). And Molly in her soliloquy talks of this "damned old bed too jingling" till she suggested that she and Boylan continue their love making on a quilt on the floor (633). The jingle refrain, then, symbolizes simultaneously Boylan's journey to Molly's bed, the archetypal promise of that bed, and Boylan's success in that bed. All this is conveyed by the repetition of simple, concrete words like "jingle" or "jaunty jingle."

When the narrator does on occasion try to develop this refrain into a more elaborated plot, it results in an awkward narrative style for which he apologizes. "Blazes Boylan's smart tan shoes creaked on the barfloor, said before. Jingle by monuments of sir John Gray, Horatio one handled Nelson, reverend father Theobald Mathew, jaunted as said before just now. Atrot, in heat, heatseated" (227). At this point in the Ormond bar narrative, Boylan has long since made his exit. The mythic plot seems to be trying to collapse linear time, seeing Boylan *in* the bar and *in* the tram at the same time. Yet the phrases "said before" and "as said before just now" suggest a self-consciousness that undercuts the effect of synchronicity. Interspersed as phrases within a diachronic narrative telling a different story, a mythic mode of telling creates a more satisfying effect than when developed extensively on its own as in the overture.

The other refrains within the Ormond bar scene are the "tap" and the developing gas within Bloom's intestines. Intensifying after the narrative mythologizes Boylan's knock on Molly's door, the "tap" seems to suggest (like "jingle") their sexual intercourse.

> One rapped on a door, one tapped with a knock, did he knock Paul de Kock with a loud proud knocker with a cock carracarracarra cock. Cockcock.
>
> Tap. (232)

Each successive single or multiple tap thus suggests a synchronic sexual story. While that story primarily is that of heterosexual intercourse between Molly and Boylan, the following passage suggests it has affinities with Stephen's and Bloom's masturbation, too:

> On the smooth jutting beerpull laid Lydia hand, lightly, plumply, leave it to my hands. All lost in pity for croppy. Fro, to: to, fro: over the polished knob (she knows his eyes, my eyes, her eyes) her thumb and finger passed in pity: passed, reposed, and gently touching, then slid so smoothly, slowly down, a cool firm white enamel baton protruding through their sliding ring.
>
> With a cock with a carra.
>
> Tap. Tap. Tap. (235)

The narrator of the opening is Bloom, but a Bloom who seems able to understand and project the implicit action (Miss Douce's symbolic masturbation) beneath the overt situation (her listening with Lidwell to Dollard's singing "The Croppy Boy"). The accuracy of Bloom's projection is underlined by the mythic refrain "With a cock with a carra. / Tap. Tap. Tap."

It is not till the refrain has occurred thirteen times (out of a total of eighteen) that we discover that it tells another story as well: "Tap blind walked tapping by the tap the curbstone tapping, tap by tap" (236). The blind youth whom Bloom had helped in Lestrygonians is tapping his way back to the Ormond bar where he had left his tuning fork. Although the "tap" story of the blind boy's return to the Ormond bar seems more realistic than the sexual narrative implied by the repetition of this refrain, even he—as a figure of death or time—has archetypal associations. Moreover, the fact that the piano tuner is described as an unseeing stripling reverberates on the synchronic axis of the novel. At the very end of Circe, Bloom has a vision of his dead son as an eleven-year-old fairy who "gazes, unseeing" into Bloom's eyes and "holds a slim ivory cane with a velvet bowknot" in his left hand (497). It is not unlikely that that mythic vision was partially prepared for in Sirens, for the tapping sequence encompasses several narrative levels within one synchronous moment.

The last sequence of mythic plotting begins even more mysteriously than the other two: "Rrr." Then, "Rrrrrrrsss." Although a hint is given us as Bloom thinks how gassy cider is, the reader is unlikely to understand that the narrator is describing the beginning of Bloom's flatulence till it is made more explicit: "Pwee! A wee little wind piped eeee. In Bloom's little wee" (237). As the synchronic story of "jingle" had merged with that of "tap" until the latter formed the other story of the blind boy's journey, so that story merges with the narrative of Bloom's gas.

> Far. Far. Far. Far.
> Tap. Tap. Tap. Tap. (236)

If we read these lines horizontally, they suggest a kind of minimal sequential pattern. The tapping of the cane seems to be going on a far journey. Even such strictly synchronic elements can give some suggestion of plot. If we remember Sterne and look at the lines vertically, we have an even more complete synchronic plot; for the "t" of tap completes the "far" and foreshadows Bloom's fart. (Lest I be accused of overingenuity, let me point out that the tap of the *blind* boy's cane reverses to the name Pat of the *deaf* waiter in the scene; Joyce delighted in drawing these strands of his story together.) Throughout the ending of Sirens the refrain of Bloom's flatulence suggests that mythic narrative cannot be written off, even if the overture did display its limitations.

Indeed, the last episode of the chapter sums up what Bloom might have called the "triliteral" aspect of Joyce's commentary on narratology within Sirens.

> Seabloom, greasabloom viewed last words. Softly. *When my country takes her place among.*
> Prrprr.
> Must be the bur.
> Fff! Oo. Rrpr.
> *Nations of the earth.* No-one behind. She's passed. *Then and not till then.* Tram kran kran kran. Good oppor. Coming. Krandlkrankran. I'm sure it's the burgund. Yes. One, two. *Let my epitaph be.* Kraaaaaa. *Written. I Have.*
> Pprrpffrrppffff.
> *Done.* (238–39)

Robert Emmett's last words, which Bloom has just read on a picture in Lionel Mark's window and which Joyce reproduces in the italicized passages, form the historical narrative. Although history is given the last word here (Emmett's "done"), mythic perception, expressed in Bloom's fart, speaks out powerfully, too. But Bloom's own words suggest the third narrative possibility. They are perfectly expressive of his personality—scientific, receptive to objective reality, anxious about appearances, concerned for others and their subjective natures, able (sometimes) to seize the right moment. Mingling complete and incomplete syntactical units, Bloom's language mediates, as he does himself, synchronic and diachronic vision.

I want to conclude my discussion of *Ulysses* by considering the relation between plot and closure in Penelope. Joyce's comment to Harriet Weaver that Ithaca was "in reality the end" of his novel and that Penelope had "no beginning, middle, or end"[9] has led to a variety of misconceptions about Penelope (both the chapter and the character). At issue is the question whether the characters are involved in a linear plot leading to a peripety or in a cyclical, repetitive action.[10] As I have suggested, Bloom does not resolve the tension between linear and cyclic plot but rather mediates it. While the insight he achieves suggests resolution and closure to his plot, this insight itself was built upon the acceptance of incompleteness. Similarly, while Molly's soliloquy may tilt toward mythic repetitiveness, it does have more structure than Joyce suggested to Weaver. Like Sterne's *A Sentimental Journey*, Penelope mediates between plot and plotlessness, closure and openness, history and myth. Among the things Joyce learned from Sterne, the most important for *Ulysses* was how to reconcile the concept of plot associated with history with the cyclic pattern of myth. As in Sterne's case, a key element is the concept of peripety. I will argue that, rather than achieving insight based on peripety, Molly (like Yorick) reaches epiphanic insight which allows for both continuation and closure.

Alternative views of women are suggested in the riddle Molly remembers the cornerboys saying. The answer to Uncle John's putting his thing long into Aunt Mary's thing hairy turns out to be putting the handle into a sweeping brush (639). The image of woman as a brush is as much a patriarchal construct as the implied image of woman as vulva. Historically, women's inferior social and economic position has made them drudges to male privilege; one path to female empowerment has been to emphasize her archetypal power of sexuality. Neither alternative is a good one. As with Stephen's and Bloom's riddles, Joyce is searching for a way of mediating undesired alternatives in order to discover a more human way of being. I argue, then, that Molly enacts the same struggle as Bloom and Stephen. She is not "already at home, fulfilled" in her life (Caserio 242), but like her male counterparts searching for her place. Our conditioning as to sex roles undoubtedly makes it seem that Joyce is denigrating Molly by describing her bodily functions. But her urinating, farting, and (remembered) masturbating are only parallels to the same acts in Bloom and Stephen; these bodily functions are not male or female but merely human. Molly's menstruation, of course, is a female act. As such, it heightens the mediation of myth and history found in Bloom at the cuckstool. The blood of the menses is both cyclic and ordinary.[11]

The other bodily function Molly performs on Bloomsday that the men do not is sexual copulation. The real plot of the chapter involves tracing the pattern from Molly's satisfaction with Boylan's physical prowess to her recognition of the larger satisfactions of her remembered relationship with Bloom, and we see Molly thinking her way through to that understanding. Although her thought shows a strong circular dimension, that should not blind us to its linear aspect because it is that progressive side which allows her to achieve her epiphany. An extended quotation demonstrates both the linear and circular patterns in Molly's monologue. She reflects on being sent by Bloom to try to get him reinstated in a job he has lost:

> he could have been in Mr Cuffes still only for what he did then sending me to try and patch it up I could have got him promoted there to be the manager he gave me a great mirada once or twice first he was as stiff as the mischief really and truly Mrs Bloom only I felt rotten simply with the old rubbishy dress that I lost the leads out of the tails with no cut in it but theyre coming into fashion again I bought it simply to please him I knew it was no good by the finish pity I changed my mind of going to Todd and Burns as I said and not Lees it was just like the shop itself rummage sale a lot of trash I hate those rich shops get on your nerves nothing kills me altogether only he thinks he knows a great lot about a womans dress and cooking mathering everything he can scour off the shelves into it if I went by his advices every blessed hat I put on does that suit me yes take that thats alright the one like a weddingcake standing up miles off my head he said suited

> me or the dishcover one coming down on my backside on pins and needles about the shopgirl in that place in Grafton street I had the misfortune to bring him into and she as insolent as ever she could be with her smirk saying Im afraid were giving you too much trouble what shes there for but I stared it out of her yes he was awfully stiff and no wonder but he changed the second time he looked Poldy pigheaded as usual like the soup but I could see him looking very hard at my chest when he stood up to open the door for me it was nice of him to show me out in any case Im extremely sorry Mrs Bloom believe me without making it too marked the first time after him being insulted and me being supposed to be his wife I just half smiled I know my chest was out that way at the door when he said Im extremely sorry and Im sure you were (619–20)

The linear part of Molly's thinking occurs at the beginning and end of the passage as she remembers a mortifying act. Only by following the convolutions of Molly's thought do we understand her deeper anxieties and embarrassment. She displaces how rotten her task makes her feel onto her feeling for her dress. This allows her to question Bloom's judgment in a way she can safely manage. In a similar way, her anxiety about rich shops suggests how insecure she finds the Bloom financial boat. Her reflections on Bloom's interest in women's dress and cooking suggest that unconsciously she fears he fulfills a woman's role rather than a man's; and by deriding him for making her stand up to the shopgirl she really reflects how embarrassed she is by having to plead for his reestablishment. We thus see her concentration on the way Cuffes stared at her breasts as he turned down her request as a face-saving device for her rather than as simply a reflection of her egoistic sensuality. We need to be aware of the complexity of Molly's thought processes, working diachronically as well as synchronically, to understand her fully.

Behind this passage we see a pattern in which Molly's thought works on two levels. It moves forward, telling a story; but it also circles around the implications of the story, allowing a synchronic dimension to emerge. As I have suggested, Molly in part lapses into mythic thinking as a defense mechanism. Avoiding the real issue of Bloom's qualifications as a provider and displacing her anxieties onto such comparatively trivial issues as his taste in women's clothing, she of course avoids any real growth in understanding. With one exception, the pattern of this passage provides the pattern of the chapter as a whole. Molly's story both progresses as well as cuts synchronically into a timeless reality. The exception is that within the larger unit of the chapter Molly reaches a fuller insight. Since this insight does not lead to an ordinary plot closure, we could say that Molly, like Yorick in *A Sentimental Journey*, achieves epiphanic awareness rather than insight derived from true peripety.

Beginning with Bloom as inadequate husband, Molly's thought proceeds, as Peake has suggested (314ff.), from Boylan as physical lover to Mulvey as romantic lover. Imagining Stephen as her poetic lover, she returns finally to Bloom as the good lover. Molly's "plot" involves her discovery of the nature of love. Her well-founded anger at Bloom's inadequacies is qualified even at the start by her thoughts of his appeal to other women. Moreover, as a foreshadowing of her eventual attitude, she remembers how he sent her the eight poppies for her birthday and kissed her heart at Dolphin's barn (615). Similarly, her satisfaction with Boylan's "tremendous big red brute of a thing" (611) is qualified from the beginning by the memory of how he slapped her on the rear (610). Although they have full sexual intercourse, the care with which she washes suggests that full communication, even between their bodies, has not occurred. Boylan's suckling her dry breasts (620) is suggestive of the lack of real interchange; when Bloom nursed her over-full breasts, he ingested her milk, and even wanted to put it in his tea.

Molly's reflection on the inadequacy of Boylan's love letter effects the transition to Mulvey, her romantic lover. Unlike Boylan's phlegmatic missive, Mulvey's first letter still lives for Molly as the embodiment of romance. The magic of Boylan's body begins to recede before the magic of the word. While the memory of their kisses thrills Molly, her sexual interchange with Mulvey has been even more incomplete than that with Boylan. Having masturbated him into her handkerchief, she smells it as a memory of him (626)—a pale parody of the flower imagery she will associate with Bloom. The cluster of images of bodily movements at this point in the text (she is flatulent [628]; she menstruates [632]; and she urinates [633]) signifies at the same time Molly's ties to the world of her body and, as each is an act of elimination, her release to a more mental-spiritual world. In this frame of mind she becomes responsive to her idea of Stephen as a poetic lover. As her thoughts of performing fellatio on Bloom's statue of Narcissus symbolize, Stephen's "seed" would fertilize her head, not her body. Unrealistic as this is, the idea of Stephen causes Molly to dismiss Boylan as a "joke" (638).

Her thoughts of being "damned well fucked" (641) by Boylan do not suggest renewed satisfaction in sexuality as much as the use of sexuality as a form of retaliation at Bloom's inadequacy as lover. This anger, which has built in the course of the chapter, gives way however to kindlier feelings, which have also persisted amidst the rising anger. Throughout the chapter she has associated love with flowers; she has told Mulvey that she was engaged to a wealthy Spaniard named Don Miguel de la Flora (625), and she reflects how much she would rather be named Bloom than Ramsbottom (626)—associatively a rejection of Boylan's penis and his slapping her bottom. The final change in her attitude toward Bloom begins as she looks at the flowers in the wallpaper as she tries to go to sleep and remembers the "nicer" paper in their rooms in Lombard street. This reawakens a sense of their "history" together, and Molly achieves her epiphany, remembering the same "seed cake" scene Bloom so memorably recalled in Lestrygonians:

> the sun shines for you he said the day we were lying among the rhododendrons on Howth head in the grey tweed suit and his straw hat the day I got him to propose to me yes first I gave him the bit of seedcake out of my mouth and it was leapyear like now yes 16 years ago my God after that long kiss I near lost my breath yes he said I was a flower of the mountain yes so we are flowers all a womans body yes that was one true thing he said in his life and the sun shines for you today yes that was why I liked him because I saw he understood or felt what a woman is and I knew I could always get round him and I gave him all the pleasure I could leading him on till he asked me to say yes (643)

Having considered her various lovers—present, past, and imaginary—Molly finds Bloom the best. The seed they share orally symbolizes the real communion of mind and body, past and present, history and myth.

Had Molly's unconscious anxieties continued to affect her, as in the shorter passage I analyzed, she would have been caught in an eternal pattern of repetition. But in the larger unit of the chapter, she is able to resolve anxiety and achieve growth. Her epiphany is of a curious nature, however, as it allows repetition at the same time that it suggests change. Although some affirmative hints have been dropped, we have no assurance that the Blooms' married life will alter, no certainty that Molly will not resume her sexual relation with Boylan. In fact, the strongly mythic nature of her narrative suggests that repetition will continue to play a large part in Molly's life. Yet a strong undercurrent in her chapter moves her to recognize, as Bloom had earlier, that their love is the truest thing in her life. Though her soliloquy is tinged with some of the despair Defoe's Roxana felt at the tension between linear and cyclic reality, it also shares some of Yorick's cheerfulness. Her meditations do not so much close the novel as provide it with an epiphanic vision of the eternal "yes," at once an end and a continuing.

Frank Kermode has written that the "provision of accommodations between Greek and Hebrew thought is an old story, and a story of concord-fictions" which is "necessary, as Berdyaev says, because to the Greeks the world was a cosmos, but to the Hebrews a history" (68). Simply substituting Stephen Dedalus for the word Greek and Leopold Bloom for the word Hebrew gives us a clear sense of Joyce's major concern in *Ulysses*. Joyce had no need to search in the eighteenth-century novelists for this theme; it was a concern that was innately congenial to him.[12] But these novelists could offer him examples of technical ways of dealing with questions of time, language, and plot as he sought to effect mediations that were similar to theirs. Without denying *Ulysses* any of the vast originality that lends it a unique status in the tradition of the English novel, we can find affinities of form with these earlier works that show us that it too is not merely a cosmos but also a history.

Conclusion

In serving as our key to Joyce's concerns in *Ulysses*, Bloom's ad also became our key to Joyce's reading of his eighteenth-century predecessors. Expanding the implications of that passage will more fully illustrate the complex grandfather-grandson relationship between Joyce and Defoe, Smollett, and Sterne. It will also address the implications of this tradition of the novel for larger questions of narrative form.

The crossed keys represent Bloom and Stephen met together within the circle of the female Molly. Like his eighteenth-century predecessors, Joyce does not cringe from the bodily implications of his symbols representing the characters' sexual as well as their intellectual and spiritual roles. Joyce told Frank Budgen that the "four cardinal points" of the Penelope chapter were "the female breast, arse, womb and cunt" (*Letters* I 170). Analysis of the sexual implications of the keys and circle in the ad suggests that some cardinal points of *Ulysses* are the penis as in Stephen's cock riddle, Bloom's masturbation, Boylan's "great red brute of a thing," etc.; the womb/cunt imagery developed most specifically in Nighttown; and the anus (Lindsey Tucker argues convincingly that the black dot that ends the Ithaca chapter is Molly's anus [155]).

Where would Joyce have found models in the English novel for such preoccupations? Moll Flanders and Roxana with their multiple lovers and children clearly project "cunt/womb" significance, but Crusoe's fortification and cave are equally prominent womb symbols. Day theorizes a "deeply buried homosexual/excremental myth" (241) in Smollett, and certainly throughout Smollett's fiction there is a fascination with the bowels perhaps only equaled in Joyce. Penises, both limp and otherwise, abound in both *Tristram Shandy* and *Ulysses*. This is a relatively minor but unmistakable thread connecting Joyce with his eighteenth-century grandfathers rather than with Austen, Eliot, or even Dickens. We are, moreover, quite ready to find symbolic significance in Joyce's use of sexual and bodily images. Reading the eighteenth-century writers through Joyce's eyes can make us more responsive to such implications in their works.

On another level of interpretation, the symbols in Bloom's ad suggest the cross of Christian historical time within the larger circle of mythic timelessness. The symbolic crossing of Stephen and Bloom's urine under the shadow cast by Molly's bedside light in Ithaca brings together these different levels of interpretation and offers the final answer to Stephen's riddle. As they urinate and think about each other's penis, Stephen appropriately focuses on the ritualistic aspects of Bloom's, and Bloom thinks of the physiological, material aspects of Stephen's. Each character remains caught in his static preoccupations; yet that they think of the other, the non-self, that they act in concert, and that they act within the shadow of Molly's circular light suggests an interaction leading toward change and growth. In indicating, through the action of the novel, his characters' capacity *both* to be and to become—to exist both synchronically and diachronically—Joyce indicates what he learned from his eighteenth-century grandfathers and what, reading through his eyes, we can learn about them and about larger questions of narrative within the novel.

However we try to understand the novel, we should remember that it tells a story and that there are varied types of story. If we think of a chess game broken off in mid-play, we can understand two different kinds of stories. If, to use Bloom's words, we "divine" (559) the vertical implication of the broken-off game, we interpret the passion of what the pieces tell us, the despair of a nearly lost, bitterly unequal fight, the tension of evenly matched, strategically marshaled forces, etc. Our story, on this axis, brings us sharply into the immediacy of a present, single time. If, however, we read the story of the chess board diachronically, if we "decipher" (559) it, we will engage ourselves in trying to reconstruct how the players reached, from the given of the opening, their present situation; and, unless we are very much without curiosity, we will think through the next moves which are possible and will even speculate about who will win the game. The novel lends itself more naturally to this diachronic kind of story-telling, but there is also a place in it for the synchronic, frozen story which works not in time, but timelessly.[1]

All novels have to be concerned with both synchronic and diachronic axes in their story-telling. During the nineteenth century, the realistic tradition predominated, and writers gave central emphasis to historical continuity, although the mythic lay just beneath its surface. Contrastingly, after World War II a great deal of attention was paid to the "failure" of diachrony in fiction, and some modern novelists gave up the realistic tradition and sought to forge purely synchronic fictions. James Joyce is often taken as the "forefather" of such writers; but close attention to his complex relationship to his own eighteenth-century forefathers convinces one that Joyce, like them, created his fiction out of the tensions between myth and history.

In Joyce's critical reshaping of *Stephen Hero* into *A Portrait of the Artist* we can see his initial reaction to the "decadence" of nineteenth-century realism. The abandonment of *Stephen Hero* testifies to the novelist's sense of the impossibility of continuing in these (for him) sterile traditions. *Portrait*, written in a modified Flaubertian/ aestheticist manner, points to Joyce's effort to find a more viable tradition in foreign models. The uneasiness of its ending testifies to Joyce's *dis*-ease with such models. In these earlier English novelists, who—unlike the realists—did not try to conceal the tensions between the synchronic and diachronic thrusts of their fiction but rather explored them openly, unafraid of jagged edges and cacophonous effect, Joyce found his models for *Ulysses*. In effect, he created a tradition for himself. Recognizing the sterility for his time of the realistic tradition, he was led to writers who similarly offered challenges to that mode. In them he found a revolutionary nostalgia for myth that paralleled his own response to the sterility of his rationalist culture. But shaping and controlling these revolutionary gestures were larger acts of submission to historical necessity; and these also suited Joyce's nature, which adroitly mixed conformity with rebellion.

In compelling *us* to look backward and see what he has seen in these eighteenth-century novelists, Joyce "re-creates" them for us. We see things in these writers that we have not seen before. It was a tradition created out of need, yet it could not have been created had not the tension between myth and history existed in these earlier novels. Primary evidence lies, of course, in the analysis—seen through Joyce's eyes—of the novels themselves. External evidence lies in the parallel epistemological crises affecting the eighteenth and early twentieth centuries. In a period when "history" in the modern positivist or empirical sense had replaced myth, "revolutionary nostalgia" manifests itself in a wide variety of writers from Vico, the abstract thinker who gives it conceptual status, to certain novelists who try to rescue myth in narratives that mingle that older perception of the world with new historicist attitudes.

"History is not like a river on whose waters the events, and fragments of events, are carried along at the same pace and in the same direction," writes Henri Focillon. "In fact," he continues, "what we call history consists precisely in the diversity and unevenness of its currents. It should remind us rather of geological strata, laid one on top of the other, at various angles, broken here and there by sudden faults; here we can grasp in one place and at one time several of the earth's ages; and every moment of the time that has gone by is here at once past, present, and to come" (*The Year 1000* 1). Reminding us that true history is not based on a uniform continuous time, the metaphor of history as a geological strata has implications for this study both in terms of idea and form. Instead of recognizing a contrast between a fallen modern world and a past, far-off golden age (as had the Renaissance), we see that our landscape encompasses mythic remnants and progressive ideologies in one space.[2] Jarring against the historic present, these mythic residues remind us of warmer, more unified visions of reality without deluding us into believing we can escape our contingent existence. When he came to write *Ulysses*, Joyce understood the need to express the hunger for myth without succumbing to mythicity, the lure of unrecoverable golden ages. In my reading, he achieved an understanding of history like that Focillon describes—a stratum of the present interspersed with traditions, survivals, metamorphoses of the past.

This was not an insight his eighteenth-century forebears had easily or completely achieved. The Renaissance concept of the golden age still operated powerfully on them, offering the image of an ideal age which radically separated itself from the modern materialist one. On the other hand, the modern age offered a new view of history as both chronological and progressive. Intuiting the tension, these early novelists were rarely able to achieve the concord fictions that would resolve, or at least suspend, the oppositions. Defoe most clearly articulates this dilemma when he tries to substitute mythic paradises for a lost Christian telos. Roxana's failure to find satisfaction in modern positivism and economics leads her to try to mythicize her world, but the attempt is leaden rather than golden. Unable to reconcile the progressive histories of his earlier heroes to their romantic conclusions, Smollett does achieve convincing closure in *Humphry Clinker,* but only after he lets go of the idea of a static Scottish paradise for one based more realistically on the social changes embodied in Humphry and Win. Like Joyce, Sterne was probably more interested in the human than the historical dimensions of this problem, and Yorick—if not Tristram—finds, without the aid of Christianity, a way to solace historical contingency with some of the fruits of myth.

Focillon tells us that "the historian who reads events in sequence also reads them in breadth, synchronously, as the musician reads a full orchestral score. History is not unilinear; it is not pure sequence" (*Life* 55). This passage actually sounds like a description of Joyce's method in Sirens, where he combines chronology and synchronicity into true history. Joyce achieves, in my reading, a true concord fiction in *Ulysses,* where we remain suspended between the chronology of positivist history and the timelessness of myth. Joyce's novel, Frank Kermode tells us, may be said to unite "the irreducible *chronos* of Dublin with the irreducible *kairoi* of Homer" (58). But in achieving this accommodation, it drew upon the dialectical tensions experienced by its eighteenth-century grandfathers.[3]

Focillon's metaphor of history as geological strata is particularly apt in speaking of Joyce's formal relation to these grandfathers. *Ulysses* demonstrates his search for juxtapositions—his need to give creative coexistence to opposing tendencies in his treatment of time, language, and structure. In doing so, Joyce was deliberately exploding a landscape most novelists in the nineteenth century had smoothed over. The tidiness of their scene did not suit Joyce so well as the earlier novelists' craggy, disrupted vistas, which were more convincing as images of the world in time and time in the world. Defoe's baldfaced lapsing out of Christian historical time into myth surely had its impact on *Ulysses.* If the double ending of *Roxana* shows that Defoe was unable to weld myth and historic time into one place where he could stand as a novelist, Joyce could understand how to create his own more satisfying ground through the earlier example. Until *Humphry Clinker,* Smollett's experiments with synchronic effect in language are scarce, and even in that novel they are intermittent, if brilliant. For Joyce, they would have been effective models of the deliberate use of heteroglossia. Sterne was the most extravagantly experimental of these earlier novelists; and he achieved, tentatively in the ending of *Tristram Shandy* and more confidently in that of *A Sentimental Journey*, a structure that could encompass both the progressivist ideology of his day and the nostalgia for the world of myth that seemingly had passed.

Hovering at the edge of the novel tradition instead of occupying its center, these writers form a kind of tradition of their own. Instead of reducing the importance they have for our understanding of the novel as a form, their liminality, paradoxically, enhances that role; for they enact in extreme forms, which clarify our vision, those acts of disjunction and mediation that all novels perform. Their deliberate exaggerations, their implosions and explosions, their defiances of norms of narrative decorum allow us to perceive more readily than in more carefully homogeneous works how the novel is always telling us two stories at once, spinning us on both its diachronic and synchronic axes. In fiction we are perpetually "out far" and "in deep."

Notes

1 *Myth, History, and Mediation*

1 Ellmann points out that Bloom's and Stephen's being "keyless" in effect makes them "keys" to the meaning of the novel (UL 65).
2 This summary undervalues the richness of MacCaffrey's approach to Milton's text and language. While I cannot broadly illustrate that reading, perhaps one brief example will demonstrate the quality of her insight. She feels Milton's "celebrated description of poetry as 'simple, sensuous and passionate' was made to distinguish it from logic and rhetoric, the discursive forms of expression" (40). In Cassirerean terms, Milton's poetry emerges from the unified consciousness of myth rather than from the language of logic.
3 In *Paradise Regained: Recreations of Eden in Eighteenth- and Nineteenth-Century England*, Max F. Schulz argues for the continuation of the Christian impulse in the eighteenth-century effort to re-create landscape as a "hieroglyph of divine order," but he recognizes that effort combines "its archaic instincts with more historical and immediate motives calculated to realize paradisal bliss in the here and now rather than in the there and then" (2–3).
4 Burton Feldman and Robert D. Richardson's collection *The Rise of Modern Mythology, 1680–1860* is a useful gathering. Other studies include James Engell, "The Modern Revival of Myth: Its Eighteenth-Century Origins," in *Allegory, Myth, and Symbol*, ed. Morton W. Bloomfield; also Alex Zwerdling, "The Mythographers and the Romantic Revival of Myth," *PMLA* 79: 447–56. See also various essays in *Giambattista Vico's Science of Humanity*, ed. Giorgio Tagliacozzo and Donald Phillip Verene, and in *Giambattista Vico: An International Symposium*, ed. Giorgio Tagliacozzo and Hayden V. White.
5 Most Enlightenment thought, Feldman and Richardson tell us, not only "did not admire myth" but in fact "sought ways to disarm and denature it, to undercut its

popularity with artists and writers, and to belittle or deny its curious and long-lived hold on the imagination" (3–4).

6 In *Myth and Reality*, Mircea Eliade differentiated between the cyclic time of the pagan past and the linear view of time that developed within the Judaeo-Christian tradition. Archaic man gave paradigmatic value to his life by repeating the divine archetypes within his own actions. Thus he lived in an eternal present which perpetually repeated the original divine beginnings. Judaeo-Christian man, however, lived within the framework of Creation-Fall-Incarnation (for the Christian)-and final judgment. Such a pattern freed him from the repetition of archetypal patterns but awakened him to time and history. The terrible burdens these created for him were assuaged by the recognition of the final end that gave meaning and purpose to history. See also H. and H. A. Frankfort, "The Emancipation of Thought from Myth," in their *The Intellectual Adventure of Ancient Man*, 363–88.

7 In *Feeling and Form* Suzanne Langer speaks of the remarkable coincidence in Barfield's and Cassirer's developing such similar ideas in total separation from one another and at the same time (237).

8 I am not trying to establish a direct influence of Vico's work on either Smollett or Sterne. In "The Supposed Influence of Vico on England and Scotland in the Eighteenth Century," René Wellek appears to demolish Max H. Fisch's argument that the Vichian ideas scattered through the writings of "Blackwell, Fergusson, Hume, Wollaston, Warburton, Hurd, Monboddo, Wood, Blair, Duff, Mason, Brown, Lowth, Warton, and Burke" attested to direct Vichian influence on these writers. Wellek argues that these "Vichian" ideas "were known before Vico and were developed by English writers from sources other than Vico" (218). One of these ideas is the importance of the early ages of society. This idea could be found in Hume, Hugh Blair, Monboddo, and Fergusson's *Essay on the History of Civil Society*. Wellek quotes Blair's view that "the times which we call barbarous [were] most favorable to the poetic spirit," and that "imagination was most glowing and animated in the first ages of society" (Hugh Blair, *Critical Dissertation on the Poems of Ossian* [London, 1763], 3–5). Moreover, Wellek states that the view that the imagination was strongest in the earliest ages of history was a commonplace of the Renaissance. The idea that language arose from the expression of emotion dates back to Epicurus and Lucretius and could be found developed in Warburton (Wellek 219). If not through Vico, the ideas I am speaking of were available to Smollett and Sterne through English as well as continental sources.

9 As H. and H. A. Frankfort point out in "The Emancipation of Thought from Myth," "Not cosmic phenomena, but history itself, has here become pregnant with meaning; history has become a revelation of the dynamic will of God" (370).

10 That Joyce admired Defoe we know from his Trieste lecture and from Budgen's claim that Joyce "possessed his [Defoe's] complete works and had read every line of them" (181). Swift and Sterne are the two authors most frequently referred to in *Finnegans Wake*. Although there are fewer references to Smollett, the use of the name Humphry Chimpden Earwicker is suggestive, and the references to Roderick Random in the same text (381.11–12) certainly indicates Joyce's awareness of Smollett. Hermione de Almeida feels that "Joyce acknowledged Smollett as

his direct forerunner in the use of misspellings to suggest another, usually bawdy, meaning" (125).

Earlier critics made brief attempts to relate Joyce to the eighteenth-century novel. The relation with Sterne has often been commented on (see, e.g., Louis D. Rubin and Lodowick Hartley). V. S. Pritchett first raised the question of Smollett's influence in *The Living Novel* (22). Building on Pritchett, Giorgio Melchiori suggested a deeper connection with Fielding, Smollett, Swift, and Sterne (52). In *The Novel as Family Romance: Language, Gender, and Authority from Fielding to Joyce*, Christine van Boheemen describes how *Ulysses* rebels against yet remains responsive to the patriarchal values found in *Tom Jones* and, more attenuatedly, in *Bleak House*.

11 "Victorian Mythography and the Progress of the Intellect," *Victorian Studies* (1975) and "The Journey beyond Myth in *Jude the Obscure*," *Texas Studies in Literature and Language* (1973).

12 Although the archetypalist response to Joyce tends to emphasize the "perdurability of patterns of human behavior and of the quasi-vestigial persistence of customs and beliefs that no longer retain their original cultural functions" (Vickery 355), other critics have suggested a fuller role for myth in Joyce's work. The structuralist approach, in fact, goes a good deal further than I in claiming that "no less than Homer, Joyce was intent on making a myth" (Gould *Sub-Stance* 76). Since Lévi-Strauss sees myth's function as a mediating one, that approach might seem perfect for my purposes. When one of the binary elements is, however, the agent itself which does the mediating, an impasse is reached. How can myth mediate between myth and history? Other factors distinguish the idea of myth I am developing from Lévi-Strauss's. For one, Lévi-Strauss does not postulate a "period of myth." According to his view, myths are always being created. Then, he conceives myth essentially in an etiological way; as Gould states, "the central function of myth . . . is to incorporate problem solving thought, not simply in a particular instance, but in such a way that problems can be restated and 'resolved' over and over again" (*Sub-Stance* 76). The view of myth I espouse tries to understand it from an epistemological perspective rather than viewing it as an etiological activity.

13 Joseph Frank, for example, identifies the novel's vertical and horizontal planes with the mythic and the historical: "These prototypes are created by transmuting the time-world of history into the timeless world of myth. And it is the timeless world of myth, following the common content of modern literature, which finds its appropriate esthetic expression in spatial form" (653).

14 See particularly Ralph W. Rader, "Exodus and Return: Joyce's *Ulysses* and the Fictions of the Actual."

2 *Mythic and Historic Time in Defoe*

1 In his centrally important book on time in Defoe, Paul K. Alkon stresses the interaction of the "timeless (whether of the Christian eternity or of archetypal situations and personalities) with events located within time" (42). My own reading of the

time theme in Defoe will focus more on concepts developed by Vico and Cassirer.

2 The preface to the third volume, *Serious Reflections During the Life and Surprising Adventures of Robinson Crusoe*, is often cited to support the idea of Defoe's allegorical intention. "I Robinson Crusoe . . . do affirm, that the story, though allegorical, is also historical; and that it is the beautiful representation of a life of unexampled misfortunes, and of a variety not to be met with in this world, sincerely adapted to, and intended for the common good of mankind" (v). Damrosch has said that "*Robinson Crusoe* is a novel that intermittently tries to revert into allegory" (10). I find more consistent allegory throughout the book.

3 Thus, we might understand a deeper significance of Friday's name: it was on Friday that Christ was crucified in order that He might redeem historical time.

4 Without raising the idea of myth, Robert Erickson makes a similar point about this "giants" passage: "He has transformed the 'Island of Despair' into his own imaginative empire, a creation which I think precedes in importance, but certainly does not displace, the 'economic kingdom' or the 'religious kingdom' others have discerned in his possession of the island" (68).

5 This attunement had been foreshadowed earlier in the novel when Crusoe speculated whether to take the gold coins from the wrecks. After thinking how useless they were to him, Crusoe nevertheless in both instances takes the gold away with him. Pat Rogers has commented that doing so "acknowledges the dimension beyond immediate necessity (hatchets and crowbars), the fact that civilization is going on although Crusoe is condemned to a bare island where gold is a superfluous commodity" (82). I would add that the act confirms Crusoe's commitment to history at the very time he lives primarily within a mythic context.

6 *The Farther Adventures of Robinson Crusoe* takes on a much more historical cast than the first part had. (See Maddox 683 and Boardman 67.) Only when Crusoe visits an exiled Russian prince in Tobolski is there a brief recurrence of the attraction to myth. The latter tells Crusoe that "he would not have exchanged such a state of life as mine [on the island], to have been Czar of *Muscovy;* and that he found more felicity in the retirement he seem'd to be banish'd to there, than ever he found in the highest authority he enjoy'd in the court of his master the Czar" (*Farther Adventures* 315).

Critics have been puzzled why Crusoe remarks casually that the island colony began to fall apart not long after he left it for the second, final time. The answer seems clear: in the fallen world of Christian historical time, we do not live happily ever after. In his book *Imagining the Penitentiary*, John Bender makes a similar point that after Crusoe's departure, "the island and its furniture exchange their metaphorical standing as prison for that of an actual penal colony with his fortress as its civic center and his story as its master narrative" (56). This analysis ignores the freedom of the mythic condition of the island but correctly understands how history turns it into a prison.

7 Since I argue for a pluralistic sense of the novel, I may seem to contradict myself in refusing to treat *The Memoirs of a Cavalier*, written during the same period as *Singleton*, as a novel when other scholars have done so. I find, however, that

the mythic elements of the *Memoirs* are totally sunk in history. It is not just that the book is "essentially a compilation based on previously printed biographies, memoirs, and histories" (Secord 130–31), but that Defoe's *method* of presenting his material follows the pattern of a historian. Even though the narrator of the *Memoirs* did not exist as a real person (Sutherland 158), his method of presenting fact is historical. A persona obviously selects the material and makes comments on it, but we as readers believe "history controls the point of view, subdues the emotional force when personality interacts with events, and even makes possible the referential significance of the account" (Boardman 71).

8 Without trying to turn Defoe into an early Conrad, we can see the naked Englishman as a symbol of the regression to the primitive mind. Freud has described this process in a way that shows its relevance to mythic states: "When a village grows into a town or a child into a man, the village and the child become lost in the town and the man. Memory alone can trace the old features in the new picture . . . It is otherwise with the development of the mind. Here we can describe the state of affairs, which has nothing to compare with it, only by saying that in this case every earlier state of development persists alongside the later stage which has arisen from it; here succession also involves coexistence, although it is to the same materials that the whole series of transformations has applied. . . . The extraordinary plasticity of mental developments is not unrestricted as regards direction; it may be described as a special capacity for involution—for regression—since it may well happen that a later and higher state of development, once abandoned, cannot be reached again. But the primitive mind is, in the fullest meaning of the word, imperishable" (*Complete Works* XIV 285).

9 In other words, I agree in a qualified way with those critics who have stressed the nonreligious aspect of Newgate. We can consider, for example, John J. Richetti's analysis: "Newgate is simply pure compulsive circumstances, a place where the self is so restricted and oppressed by the other that it loses all independence and becomes habituated to an environment which embodies personal destruction" (133).

10 Thus I differ from Richetti, who argues that Jack "transforms a larger and more generalized environment than any of his predecessors, history itself rather than any of the locales the others master" (191). Crusoe commanded the island; Moll as thief dominated London; but Jack surveys all of history. *Colonel Jack* becomes, in this argument, one of Defoe's most unified and powerful works as its hero reduces history itself to the self's subjective need. Attractive as this idea is to my idea of myth, I am unconvinced that the novel is a unified and powerful work. Instead, I see it as a work which flails about as it seeks unsuccessfully to find some other means to order its narrative than the concept of providential history.

11 Jack lists "*Livy's* Roman History, the History of the *Turks,* the *English* History of *Speed,* and others; the History of the *Low Country* Wars, the History of *Gustavus Adolphus,* King of *Sweden,* and the History of the *Spaniard's* Conquest of *Mexico*" (157).

12 Maximillian Novak suggests that, in trying to create "a quintessential courtesan rather than any single historical mistress," Defoe "seemed reluctant to place her in

any definite time between his own period and that of the Restoration. As a result he resorted to a curious combination of mythic synchronic time and the particular social chronology of history" (116).

13 James Maddox says that Amy is "a ready-made doppelgänger, responsible both for the shameful thought and often for its execution" (671).

14 Maddox's answer is economic and sociological, suggesting that recognition would "plunge her back into that despised, vulnerable position of helplessness which was her condition when her first husband left her" (678). But Zimmerman, correctly I think, argues that the possible economic effects "do not justify the rage, despair, and near madness of both Roxana and Amy" (164). Roxana cannot acknowledge her daughter, he suggests, for psychic reasons: "Admitting her evil only to herself, while changing public identities, is her way of retaining a sense of inner coherence and of partially denying the reality of her actions" (164).

15 Zimmerman says: "Amy and Susan are opposites: one representing the interests of the narcissistic world, the other, the demands of larger responsibility" (169).

3 *Mythic and Historic Language in Smollett*

1 Although a few of Smollett's critics have declared him a univocal writer (Copeland, Rosenblum, and especially Sekora), most have seen his work expressing deep tensions. These have been interpreted variously as those between the country and the city (Evans), sensibility and violence (Daiches), Augustan values and the expressive and affective theories of the later eighteenth century (Grant), Christian and secular world views (New), and, most interestingly for my study, between realism and mythopoeia in Byron Gassman's reading of *Humphry Clinker*.

2 As innumerable scholars have demonstrated, the texture of the world Smollett has created for Roderick can be traced directly to sources in eighteenth-century politics, law, medicine, etc. To indicate just one example, John F. Sena has shown that Smollett's picture of Narcissa's strange aunt is "derived almost entirely from contemporary medical theories of hysteria" (270).

3 The introduction of Melopoyn's story differs somewhat from Smollett's use of the Carthagenean material. While in prison, Roderick listens to the difficulties the poet has had in trying to get his tragedy on the stage. The two chapters Smollett devotes to this story are based on his own experiences with his play *The Regecide*. Much like Joyce, then, Smollett is using biographical reality as the basis for fiction. "Earl Sheerwit" is a thinly veiled picture of Lord Chesterfield, and "Marmozet" clearly reflects a satiric image of David Garrick himself. Thus we know that the story *is* history; yet the way the story is colored and told keeps us from believing its historical reality. What does emerge as "true" is the indignation in the language of the "I" who responds to the story. We sense that it is Smollett rather than the fictional character Roderick whose anger we hear.

4 David Green maintains that Smollett's *History* is a "greatly underestimated work"

which emphasizes not the grand movements of history as did his contemporary historians but rather the psychology and motivation of individuals (301).

5 See, for example: Rosenblum, "Smollett and the Old Conventions," 389–401; New, " 'The Grease of God': The Form of Eighteenth-Century Fiction," 240–43; Treadwell, "The Two Worlds of *Ferdinand Count Fathom*," 144–49; and Copeland, "*Humphry Clinker*: A Comic Pastoral Poem in Prose?," 493–501.

6 *Peregrine Pickle* is Smollett's closest approach to the traditional novel as Watt defines it. As Rufus Putney demonstrated more than forty years ago, there is a "plan" to the novel that involves Peregrine's overcoming a false pride (1051–65). One of the central features of plot, as we have seen, is the idea of peripety, upon which the moral development of the main character depends. In this novel, Smollett tries to demonstrate such growth in Peregrine. Confined to jail, Peregrine, as Boucé suggests, confronts both the reality of the social world whose false values have misled him and his own flaws which are ultimately responsible for his downfall. Although Peregrine is rescued by the deus ex machina of his father's death intestate, Smollett clearly tries to show his hero's moral growth under the face of circumstances. This tighter plot leads to a more intense emphasis upon a small group of characters who figure consistently in Peregrine's growth rather than the more miscellaneous relationships Roderick has. These characters are also more fully individualized than those in Smollett's first novel.

7 Although rumors circulated from the first that Smollett was well paid for publicizing Lady Vane's story, James L. Clifford doubts this was so. Instead, he suggests that for Smollett Lady Vane "may have symbolized the rebel condemned by society. Her very frankness in admitting her many affairs, and her insistence that it was love which had been her undoing, evidently made an immediate appeal" (xxvi).

8 Damian Grant says that "Smollett has succeeded in colouring Trunnion's whole expression with a dense network of images, until it seems almost another created language" (139).

9 In an extended discussion of Smollett's blending of historical detail and fiction, Thomas R. Preston points to this scene to demonstrate that it is "not the individual items, factual or fictional, but the new mixture, the comic fusion of historical, factual, and fictional elements that constitutes the reality" ("Introduction" xlv). Preston's discussion helps one to see how Joyce could have found in Smollett a model in incorporating historical personages into his fiction.

10 In his study of Smollett's work in the *Critical Review*, James Basker points out a critique of Warton's language, whose "insistence on purity and correctness links Smollett to a century-long tradition of linguistic conservatism" (94). Lismahago's view of language is clearly the one held by Smollett himself in 1756. The novels themselves, however, demonstrate the breaking away from a unitary language toward heteroglossia.

11 Cunningham himself did not believe these six essays from *The British Magazine* were Goldsmith's, although he included them in his edition. Caroline Tupper, on the basis of both internal and external evidence, attributed them to Smollett (325–

42). While accepting that the essays are not Goldsmith's, Ronald S. Crane feels that Tupper's "suggestion that the real author was Smollett is hardly more than a plausible guess" (xix).

12 The history of the response to these letters reads like a microcosm of Smollett scholarship, moving as it does from more literal, historical responses to freer considerations of Smollett's artistic purposes. W. Arthur Boggs first approached these letters from a linguistic angle, attempting to describe the realism of their idiolect. He concluded that unlike Scott, Mrs. Gaskell, and Thackeray, who "have recorded actual dialects with remarkable fidelity," Smollett has created "a rich and persuasive speech which turns out to be no speech at all" (337). When V. S. Pritchett suggested in *The Living Novel* (1946) that Joyce and Smollett might "have had not dissimilar obsessions" in their chamber pot humor and that there was "some hint of Anna Livia in the Welsh maid's letters in *Humphry Clinker*" (22), ground was broken, if only superficially, for a less literal, more "poetic" reading of the letters. Damian Grant's reading shows affinities with modern deconstructionist theory. For him, Win and Tabby's letters are "a significant testimony to the willfulness of words, and a spirited exposure of the simple model of language proposed by the empirical tradition." Smollett's distortion of language has been "pushed beyond the point where it has any significant moral implications, into the sphere of pure linguistic virtuosity" (94–95). Eric Rothstein returns to a historical view, suggesting that Smollett has been using these women's speech to overcome an English prejudice against the "outlandish jargon" of the Scots (70). Perhaps rounding out a cycle in Smollett scholarship, Thomas R. Preston extends Bogg's analysis of dialectical usage in the letters ("Introduction" xxxv–xxxvii), though he draws our attention to Sherbo's critique of such efforts (li).

13 Owen Barfield points out that in the twentieth century "the expression 'I have no stomach to the business' is still by no means purely psychic in its content. It describes a very real sensation, or rather one which cannot be classified as either physical or psychic." He continues by suggesting that, on the general model of language development this meaning of this word will also split into two, and "the physico-psychic experience in question will have become as incomprehensible to our posterity, as it is incomprehensible to most of us today that anyone should literally feel his 'bowels moved' by compassion" (80n). Robert Adams Day ("Sex, Scatology, Smollett") and William Park ("Fathers and Sons—*Humphry Clinker*") have pointed out an excremental motif in Smollett's work. Rather than following their psychological explanations, I would suggest that some of the same physico-psychic feeling we have for the metaphor "stomach to the business" persisted in Smollett's response to "bowels moved by compassion." The persistent emphasis on excrement in Smollett's fiction functions as part of an effort to recall an earlier unity of body and spirit.

14 Grant, in fact, argues that Smollett demonstrates the "wilfulness" of words, that his "imagination has gone to work, picking at the seams of language, revealing the abyss that opens (or is temporarily concealed) under our everyday handling of words" (96).

15 From one perspective or another, a wide variety of critical studies have stressed the archetypal, mythic aspect of *Humphry Clinker*. Many have called attention to its circular movement (one of the earliest of these was B. L. Reid's "Smollett's Healing Journey"). Paul-Gabriel Boucé also notes this pattern (202), while Byron Gassman argues that a "mythic kingdom" materializes in the last pages of the novel (*Criticism* 107). Accepting that romance archetypes lie behind Smollett's fiction, Michael Rosenblum suggests, however, that in his last novel Smollett parodies these conventions (393). And Melvyn New finds Smollett "most solidly within the romance tradition, except for his final work . . . which thrusts the romance further from the center of consideration than any previous fiction" (240).

4 *Mythic and Historical Plotting in Sterne*

1 Caserio argues that unlike Dickens, Conrad, and late James, Joyce loses faith in plot, giving preference to Molly Bloom's formless mode of narrative (243–46). In my chapter on Joyce, I shall want to qualify this view.

2 Arthur H. Cash has fully explored in his biography the origins of *Tristram Shandy* in Sterne's personal, social, and religious context. He traces, as random examples, the house servants of the novel to the humble parishioners Sterne served (I 123); he suggests Toby's and Walter's origins among the Demoniacs (I 190); he describes for us Sterne's sources in Chamber's *Cyclopedia* and in Tindall (I 201ff.).

3 Some question in fact has arisen about how seriously we can judge volume 7 as a work of art. Melvyn New says that it "appears to be Sterne's travel notes, hastily worked into the Shandy world in order to have adequate material for publication" (171). Although he qualifies this judgment in his own analysis, William Holtz notes that volume 7 "is generally regarded as an excrescence upon the main body, an attempt by Sterne to patch together enough material to make another installment of his book" (130). From this perspective, the biographical or historical materials have been inadequately assimilated to the novel form. Others, like Martin Price, have defended the volume precisely for its truth to life: "In the remarkable seventh volume of *Tristram Shandy* the apparent artlessness of uncontrollable feeling breaks into the structure of the book" (377). Unfortunately, when we read such chapters as chapter 18, which describes for us how Paris's nine hundred streets are divided up among the different quarters, we are all too aware that other things than passionate feelings have entered the novel.

4 W. B. Carnochan believes that Tristram's "talk of inconvenience" in having to choose between these roads is "a red herring" (121). But if we think of them as narrative options, we understand Sterne's difficulty in choosing between the different routes.

5 Max Byrd says that Tristram's commitment to what is intensely and authentically alive in volume 7 "frequently gives the impression of being willed, deliberately summoned to repel the cold authority of numbers and forms" (*Tristram Shandy* 126).

6 Byrd notes that Tristram enters "into a pagan dance where sexuality revives . . .

social forms collapse and time yields" (*Tristram Shandy* 128), while Carnochan more accurately says that Tristram "finds a transient paradise in an open plain" (120).

7 New argues that "faced with the reality of fulfillment, Tristram flees from it, repeating the process all along the southern coast of France" (178).

8 Byrd agrees with me about the tension "between Christian and pagan values" in volume 7. He, however, believes that to meet Sterne's anti-Catholic prejudices "Tristram will praise Jupiter and other heathen gods and will end the volume with a pagan dance" (*Tristram Shandy* 125).

9 Applying the ideas of Joseph Frank about "modernist" literature, K. G. Simpson (155) and John Stedmond (22) have discussed the notion of "spatial form" in *Tristram Shandy.*

10 Neil Isaacs has discussed the autoerotic metaphor in Joyce and Sterne (as well as in Lawrence, Stevens, and Whitman). He, however, focuses on volume 5, chapter 15, the violin-playing scene (94–97).

11 Critics have widely differed in responding to the novel's tone. Some have discovered life-affirming comedy (Lanham 100) while others see the "use of laughter as the defense-action of an embattled psyche" (Alter 10). Still others have noted behind the comedy "something very cold, something more like nihilism than rationalism" (Nuttall 78–79). It has even been suggested that we come to a "tragic view" of the work (Francis 101).

12 If the *Journey* were conceived as a response to Smollett's *Travels,* it would have been in reaction to Smollett's overemphasis on the "historical" aspects of his trip.

13 The parallel episode in *Peregrine Pickle* serves primarily as a device of plot. As a consequence of Pipes's action of replacing a lost letter with a false one, a serious misunderstanding occurs between Peregrine and Emilia. In Sterne the episode has no relation to plot at all; it serves to illustrate Yorick's need to achieve greater spontaneity and, indeed, release from the Eliza plot he is involved in.

14 For a full discussion of the implications of holiday, see C. L. Barber, *Shakespeare's Festive Comedy*, and M. M. Bakhtin, *Rabelais and Folk Culture of the Middle Ages and Renaissance.*

15 Although R. F. Brissenden argues that the *Journey* is in some ways "more deliberately and provocatively sexual" (224) than *Tristram Shandy*, he is surely more correct in seeing that this last novel emphasizes that "man must always keep alive in himself the capacity to feel" (216).

16 In her insightful reading of the novel, Rabb makes a similar argument. Caught in the "linear configuration of the 'male' metaphor of the journey" (549), Yorick nevertheless tries to gain entrance to the feminine "ring of pleasure." Doing so involves becoming aware, as an author, of his androgynous nature. In the last episode, "he remains, reaching out to what is female, beyond himself, and beyond the power of language and money" (558).

5 *Time, Language, and Plot in* Ulysses

1 The answer she suggests to the covert riddle she explores in *Ulysses* is "that the shadow of Bloom's impotence has lifted, and the sexual union correlates in microcosm to the sense of squaring the circle in macrocosm, namely, unity in the material and spiritual world" (334).

2 Robert Adams Day reminds us that Joyce doubtlessly knew that the cock was also a "type of Christ dispelling the darkness—a famous early Christian hymn makes it explicit that the cock's crowing is *figura judicis nostri*. The blue sky and the bells striking eleven suggest the virgin and resurrection" (*Literary Monographs* 165).

3 Jackson Cope more accurately reflects Stephen's tension between myth and history. "Stephen's dilemma is insoluble. Wanting the private ahistoricity of the unbifurcated paradise, a world static from everlasting to everlasting, he still finds that he must shuffle on the shells of history (sea wrack) which threatens him with limitation, with a heritage at one end and death at the other" (91).

4 Cope comments on Stephen's growth: "In the course of his difficult day Stephen passes from the rejection of history as a pedagogical burden in the classroom overshadowed by that anti-Semite Deasey to the epiphany of the past stimulated by Leopold Bloom's Hebraic chant" (98–99).

5 In "Deacon Dedalus: The Text of the *Exultet* and its Implications for *Ulysses*," Day says that the "blessing of the water is concelebrated by Bloom and Stephen. The sexual symbolism of the candle and font having been perceived, Joyceans at least should not be too sensitive about urination as creation, consecration, or baptism; nor should they be puzzled further about Stephen's association of his own penis with that of Christ triumphant" (163).

6 In *Stephen and Bloom at Life's Feast: Alimentary Symbolism and the Creative Process in James Joyce's "Ulysses"* (1984), Lindsey Tucker describes how the novel's emphasis on bodily processes and excremental images is a "manifestation of Joyce's larger artistic concerns about the creative process" (115 et passim). Elliott Gose's *The Transformation Process in Joyce's "Ulysses"* emphasizes that Joyce "gives a sense of the time of day during which each incident occurs . . . More subtly, he provided another time sense, a legendary-mystical one, by the main clue of his title" (198). In a way, I am combining the insights of these two important books by suggesting that Joyce associates the transformative acts found in bodily functions with the idea of this double time sense.

7 It is an oversimplification to identify the chapter's alternative passages of inflation and deflation (narrated by men Ellmann aptly calls Pangloss and Thersites) with myth and history. Indeed, within these passages Joyce parodies both mythic and historic vision. In one of the inflated passages Joyce parodies myth by describing how the dog Garryowen's poem bears a "*striking* resemblance (the italics are ours) to the ranns of ancient Celtic bards" (256). Joyce mocks here Vichian ideas of the origins of language by associating them with dogs. Similarly, Joyce mocks the mode of history by having the citizen read a skit from the *United Irishman* which describes a Zulu chief's visit to England. Events that are too absurd to be possible

are treated as real in the mode of reportage. History has a language which confers a credibility even on the patently absurd. (We are reminded here of Smollett's "historical" account of Lismahago's experiences among the American Indians. The reportorial language of these passages led to much research by scholars to discover historical sources for what were clearly fabricated events.) Still, the very existence of these parodies suggests that Joyce was preoccupied with this issue, if not so exclusively as my topic forces me to suggest.

8 French argues that Joyce thrusts "in the reader's face the arbitrariness of language, the void at its core" (127). Stanley Sultan also says that the "overture makes no sense and has no unity" (220). Fritz Senn argues, however, that the phrases "turn out to be a prospective arrangement for the pages to follow, both a thematic preparation *for* and a variation *of* the composition which they precede" (130). C. H. Peake has the fullest discussion of the opening of Sirens. Agreeing with Stuart Gilbert that the phrases prepare the reader for the chapter, he does not understand "why their meanings have been disguised, or why false relationships have been established between them" (226). He suggests that we think more profitably of the opening section as a "prelude [where] the separate fragments may correspond to chords" (227).

9 See Sultan 415–17 for a full discussion of Joyce's comments and their relation to the novel.

10 Ellmann feels Molly's is a timeless, mythic world where the characters awaken from "the Circean nightmare of history by drawing the past into the present (a timeless present) and making it an expression of love instead of hatred" (UL 175). Caserio thinks Joyce associates Stephen and Bloom with the patriarchal need to "plot" (243), whereas Molly's monologue is "not shaped by male purposive direction or by structures of willful creation" (243). In contrast, Sultan believes Molly achieves a peripety in a clearly defined action where she decides to honor Bloom's request for breakfast in bed. Molly, he says, "arrives at her attitude—her stream of consciousness is not merely content but process" (419). As usual, my reading would unite these contrary perspectives by suggesting that in Molly's soliloquy Joyce meditates between historical and mythical plot.

11 Ellmann argues similarly: "In allowing Molly to menstruate at the end Joyce consecrates the blood in the chamberpot rather than the blood in the chalice, mentioned by Mulligan at the beginning of the book. For this blood is substance, not more or less than substance. The great human potentiality is substantiation, not transubstantiation, or subsubstantiation" (UL 171).

12 Stanislaus Joyce has written that his brother "felt very forcibly both the attraction of mysticism and the call of reality, and for a while he was interested in the figure of Paracelsus, scientist and mystic, who had laboured somewhat too boldly in both spheres" (132).

Conclusion

1 I have altered here the basic idea of Frederick Pottle in his plea for the use of Saussure's terms *synchrony* and *diachrony* in literary analysis.
2 In "Préhistoire et Moyen Age," his Dunbarton Oakes Inaugural Lecture, 1940, Focillon concludes that "Traditions passives, metamorphoses, réveils, avec leur interférences selon les âges et selon les lieux, nous aident à comprehendre comment le plus lointain passé, avec une vitalité tantôt ralentie, tantôt intense et continue tantôt explosive, ondule à travers l'évolution" (23).
3 Michael McKeon's more rigorously Marxist sense of the dialectical character of the novel is appropriate to his historical study of its origins which he can relate to the social and economic dynamics of a particular period. Working synchronically as well as diachronically, my study requires a looser sense of the idea of the dialectic. The oppositions I speak of in the novel are always there irreducibly yet always being mediated in one way or another.

Bibliography

Primary Texts

DEFOE

The Farther Adventures of Robinson Crusoe Being the Second and Last Part of His Life. London: Constable & Company, 1925.

The Fortunes and Misfortunes of the Famous Moll Flanders. Edited by G. A. Starr. New York: Oxford University Press, 1971.

The History and Remarkable Life of the Truly Honourable Col. Jacques. Edited by Samuel Holt Monk. New York: Oxford University Press, 1970.

The Life, Adventures, and Pyracies, of the Famous Captain Singleton. Edited by Shiv K. Kumar. New York: Oxford University Press, 1969.

The Life and Strange Surprizing Adventures of Robinson Crusoe, of York, Mariner. Edited by J. Donald Crowley. New York: Oxford University Press, 1972.

Roxana: The Fortunate Mistress. Edited by Jane Jack. New York: Oxford University Press, 1964.

Serious Reflections during the Life and Surprising Adventures of Robinson Crusoe with His Vision of the Angelick World. London: Constable & Company, 1925.

JOYCE

Daniel Defoe. Edited and translated by Joseph Prescott. *Buffalo Studies* 1, no. 1. Buffalo: State University of New York, 1964.

Ulysses: The Corrected Text. Edited by Hans Walter Gabler with Wolfhard Steppe and Claus Melchior. New York: Random House, 1986.

SMOLLETT

The Adventures of Ferdinand, Count Fathom. Introduction and notes by Jerry C. Beasley, text edited by O. M. Brack, Jr. Athens: University of Georgia Press, 1988.

The Adventures of Peregrine Pickle. Edited by James L. Clifford. New York: Oxford University Press, 1964.

The Adventures of Roderick Random. Edited by Paul-Gabriel Boucé. New York: Oxford University Press, 1979.

The Adventures of Sir Launcelot Greaves. Edited by George Saintsbury. London: n.d.

The Expedition of Humphry Clinker. Introduction and notes by Thomas R. Preston, text edited by O. M. Brack, Jr. Athens: University of Georgia Press, 1990.

STERNE

The Life and Opinions of Tristram Shandy, Gentleman. Edited by Melvyn New and Joan New. Vols. 1–2. Gainesville: University Press of Florida, 1978. Vol. 3, The Notes. Edited by Melvyn New, with Richard A. Davies and W. G. Day. Gainesville: University Press of Florida, 1984.

A Sentimental Journey through France and Italy by Mr. Yorick. Edited by Gardner D. Stout, Jr. Berkeley: University of California Press, 1967.

A Sentimental Journey through France and Italy with Selections from the Journals, Sermons, and Correspondence. Edited by Wilbur L. Cross. New York: Liveright, 1926.

Secondary Texts

Alkon, Paul K. *Defoe and Fictional Time*. Athens: University of Georgia Press, 1979.

Alter, Robert. "Sterne and the Nostalgia for Reality." *Far Western Forum* 1 (1974): 1–21.

Attridge, Derek. *Peculiar Language: Literature as Difference from the Renaissance to James Joyce*. Ithaca: Cornell University Press, 1988.

Bakhtin, M. M. *The Dialogic Imagination: Four Essays*. Translated by Caryl Emerson and Michael Holquist. Austin: University of Texas Press, 1981.

Barfield, Owen. *Poetic Diction: A Study in Meaning*. New York: McGraw Hill, 1964.

Barlow, Sheryl. "The Deception of Bath: Malapropisms in Smollett's *Humphry Clinker*." *Michigan Academician* 2 (1970): 13–24.

Basker, James G. *Tobias Smollett: Critic and Journalist*. Newark: University of Delaware Press, 1988.

Beebe, Maurice. "*Ulysses* and the Age of Modernism." *James Joyce Quarterly* 10 (1972): 172–88.

Begnal, Michael H. "James Joyce and the Mythologizing of History." In *Directions in Literary Criticism*, ed. S. Weintraub and P. Young. University Park: Pennsylvania State University Press, 1973.

Bell, Ian A. *Defoe's Fiction*. London: Croom Helen, 1985.

Bender, John. *Imagining the Penitentiary: Fiction and the Architecture of Mind in Eighteenth-Century England*. Chicago: University of Chicago Press, 1987.

Berthoff, Warner. "Fiction, History, Myth: Notes toward the Discrimination of Narrative Forms." In *The Interpretation of Narrative: Theory and Practice*, ed. Morton W. Bloomfield. Cambridge, Mass.: Harvard University Press, 1970.

Blewett, David. *Defoe's Art of Fiction*. Toronto: University of Toronto Press, 1979.

Boardman, Michael M. *Defoe and the Uses of Narrative*. New Brunswick: Rutgers University Press, 1983.

Boggs, W. Arthur. "Dialectical Ingenuity in *Humphry Clinker*." *Papers in English Language and Literature* 1 (1965): 327–37.

Booth, Wayne. "Did Sterne Complete *Tristram Shandy?*" *Modern Philology* 48 (1951): 172–88.

Boucé, Paul-Gabriel. *The Novels of Tobias Smollett*. Translated by Antonia White. New York: Langman, 1976.

Bradbury, Malcolm. *Possibilities*. New York: Oxford University Press, 1973.

Brissenden, R. F. "Trusting to Almighty God: Another Look at the Composition of *Tristram Shandy*." In *The Winged Skull*, ed. Arthur H. Cash and John M. Stedmond. Kent, Ohio: Kent State University Press, 1971.

———. *Virtue in Distress*. Totowa, N.J.: Barnes and Noble, 1974.

Brivic, Sheldon. *Joyce between Freud and Jung*. Port Washington, N.Y.: Kennikat Press, 1980.

Brown, Richard. *James Joyce and Sexuality*. Cambridge: Cambridge University Press, 1985.

Budgen, Frank. *James Joyce and the Making of "Ulysses"*. 1933. Reprint. Bloomington: Indiana University Press, 1960.

Bulhof, Ilse. "Imagination and Interpretation in History." In *Literature and History*, ed. Leonard Schulze and Walter Wetzels. Lanham, Md.: University Press of America, 1983.

Bunn, James H. "Signs of Randomness in *Roderick Random*," *Eighteenth Century Studies* 14 (1980–81): 452–69.

Burke, John J., Jr. "History without History: Henry Fielding's Theory of Fiction." In *A Provision of Human Nature*, ed. Donald Kay. University, Ala.: University of Alabama Press, 1977.

———. "Observing the Observer in Historical Fictions by Defoe." *Philological Quarterly* 61 (1982): 13–32.

Burstein, Janet. "The Journey beyond Myth in *Jude the Obscure*." *Texas Studies in Literature and Language* 15 (1973): 499–515.

———. "Victorian Mythography and the Progress of the Intellect." *Victorian Studies* 18 (1975): 309–24.

Byrd, Max. "Sterne and Swift: Augustan Continuities." In *Johnson and His Age*, ed. James Engell. Cambridge, Mass.: Harvard University Press, 1984.

———. *Tristram Shandy*. London: George Allen & Unwin, 1985.

Byrd, Don. "Joyce's Method of Philosophic Fiction." *James Joyce Quarterly* 5 (1967): 9–21.

Cantelli, Gianfranco. "Myth and Language in Vico." In *Giambattista Vico's Science of Humanity*, ed. Giorgio Tagliacozzo and Donald Phillip Verene. Baltimore: Johns Hopkins University Press, 1976.

Carnochan, W. B. *Confinement and Flight*. Berkeley: University of California Press, 1977.

Caserio, Robert. *Plot, Story, and the Novel from Poe to the Modern Period*. Princeton: Princeton University Press, 1979.

Cash, Arthur H. *Laurence Sterne: The Early and Middle Years*. London: Methuen & Co., 1975. Referred to as Cash I.

———. *Laurence Sterne: The Later Years*. London and New York: Methuen & Co., 1986. Referred to as Cash II.

Cassirer, Ernst. *Language and Myth*. Translated by Suzanne K. Langer. New York: Dover Publications, 1946.

———. *The Philosophy of Symbolic Forms*. Vol. 2, *Mythical Thought*. Translated by Ralph Manheim. New Haven: Yale University Press, 1955.

Cixous, Helene. "Joyce: The (R)use of Writing." In *Post-Structuralist Joyce*, ed. Derek Attridge and Daniel Ferrer. Cambridge: Cambridge University Press, 1984.

Connolly, Thomas E., ed. *The Personal Library of James Joyce*. Buffalo: University of Buffalo Monographs in English, no. 6, 1955.

Cope, Jackson I. *Joyce's Cities: Archeologies of the Soul*. Baltimore: Johns Hopkins University Press, 1981.

Copeland, Edward. "*Humphry Clinker*: A Comic Pastoral Poem in Prose?" *Texas Studies in Language and Literature* 16 (1974–75): 493–501.

Crane, Ronald S., ed. *New Essays by Oliver Goldsmith*. Chicago: University of Chicago Press, 1927.

Cunningham, Peter, ed. *The Works of Oliver Goldsmith*. Vol. 3. Boston: Little, Brown & Co., 1854.

Curtis, Laura A. *The Elusive Daniel Defoe*. London: Vision and Barnes & Noble, 1984.

Daiches, David. "Smollett Reconsidered." In *From Smollett to James*, ed. Samuel I. Mintz, Alice Chandler, and Christopher Mulvey. Charlottesville: University Press of Virginia, 1981.

Damrosch, Leopold. *God's Plot and Man's Stories: Studies in the Fictional Imagination from Milton to Fielding*. Chicago: University of Chicago Press, 1985.

Davis, Robert Gorham. "Sterne and the Delineation of the Modern Novel." In *The Winged Skull*, ed. Arthur H. Cash and John M. Stedmond. Kent, Ohio: Kent State University Press, 1971.

Day, Robert Adams. "Deacon Dedalus: The Text of the *Exultet* and Its Implications for *Ulysses*." In *The Seventh of Joyce*, ed. Bernard Benstock. Bloomington: Indiana University Press, 1982.

———. "Joyce, Stoom, King Mark: 'Glorious Name of Irish Goose.'" *James Joyce Quarterly* 12 (1975): 211–50.

———. "Joyce's Waste Land and Eliot's Unknown God." In *Literary Monographs* 4, ed. Eric Rothstein. Madison: University of Wisconsin Press, 1971.

———. "Sex, Scatology, Smollett." In *Sexuality in Eighteenth-Century Britain*, ed. Paul Gabriel Boucé. Manchester, Eng.: Manchester University Press, 1982.

De Almeida, Hermione. *Byron and Joyce through Homer*. New York: Columbia University Press, 1981.

Donoghue, Denis. *The Ordinary Universe: Soundings in Modern Literature*. London: Oxford University Press, 1968.

Eagleton, Terry. *Literary Theory: An Introduction*. Minneapolis: University of Minnesota Press, 1983.

Eliade, Mircea. *Myth and Reality*. New York: Harper & Row, 1963.

———. *The Myth of the Eternal Return*. Translated by Willard R. Trask. Princeton: Princeton University Press, [1954] 1971, 1974.

Ellmann, Richard. *James Joyce*. New and Revised Edition. New York: Oxford University Press, 1972.

———. "The Limits of Joyce's Naturalism." *Sewanee Review* 43 (1955): 567–75.

———. *Ulysses on the Liffey*. New York: Oxford University Press, 1972.

Engell, James. "The Modern Revival of Myth: Its Eighteenth-Century Origins." In *Allegory, Myth, and Symbol*, ed. Morton W. Bloomfield. Cambridge, Mass.: Harvard University Press, 1981.

Erickson, Robert A. "Starting Over with *Robinson Crusoe*." *Studies in the Literary Imagination* 15 (1982): 51–73.

Ermarth, Elizabeth Deeds. *Realism and Consensus in the English Novel*. Princeton: Princeton University Press, 1983.

Evans, David L. "*Humphry Clinker*: Smollett's Tempered Augustanism." *Criticism* 9 (1967): 257–74.

Feldman, Burton, and Robert D. Richardson. *The Rise of Modern Mythology, 1680–1860*. Bloomington: Indiana University Press, 1972.

Focillon, Henri. *The Art of the West in the Middle Ages*. Edited by Jean Bony. Vol. 1, *Romanesque Art*. London: Phaidon, 1963.

———. *The Life of Forms in Art*. Translated by Charles Beecher Hogan. New York: Wittenborn, Schultz, 1948.

———. "Prehistoire et Moyen Age." *Dumbarton Oaks Inaugural Lectures*, November 2 & 3, 1940. Cambridge, Mass.: Harvard University Press, 1941.

———. *The Year 1000*. New York: Harper & Row, 1971.

Francis, C. J. "Sterne: The Personal and the Real." In *A Festschrift for Edgar Ronald Seary*. St. John's, Newfoundland: Memorial University of Newfoundland, 1975.

Frank, Joseph. "Spatial Form in Modern Literature." *Sewanee Review* 53 (1945): 2, 3, 4, 221–40, 433–56, 643–53.

Frankfort, H. and H. A. *The Intellectual Adventure of Ancient Man*. Chicago: University of Chicago Press, 1946.

French, Marilyn. *The Book as World: James Joyce's "Ulysses."* Cambridge, Mass.: Harvard University Press, 1976.

Freud, Sigmund. *Complete Psychological Works*. Vol. 14. Translated by James Strachey. London: Hogarth Press, 1953–74.

Frye, Northrop. *The Great Code*. New York: Harcourt Brace Jovanovich, 1982.

———. "History and Myth in the Bible." In *The Literature of Fact*, ed. Angus Fletcher. New York: Columbia University Press, 1976.

———. "Quest and Cycle in *Finnegans Wake*." *James Joyce Review* 1 (1957): 39–47.

———. *The Secular Scripture*. Cambridge, Mass.: Harvard University Press, 1976.

———. *Spiritus Mundi*. Bloomington: Indiana University Press, 1976.

Gassman, Byron. "The Economy of *Humphry Clinker*." In *Tobias Smollett Bicentenial Essays*, ed. G. S. Rousseau and Paul-Gabriel Boucé. New York: Oxford University Press, 1971.

———. "*Humphry Clinker* and the Two Kingdoms of George III." *Criticism* 16 (1974): 95–108.

Georgi, Helen. "Covert Riddles in *Ulysses*: Squaring the Circle." *Journal of Modern Literature* 13 (1986): 329–39.

Goldberg, Milton A. *Smollett and the Scottish School*. Albuquerque: University of New Mexico Press, 1959.

Goldberg, S. L. *The Classical Temper*. New York: Barnes & Noble, 1961.

Gose, Elliott B. *The Transformation Process in Joyce's "Ulysses."* Toronto: University of Toronto Press, 1980.

Gottfried, Roy K. *The Art of Joyce's Syntax in "Ulysses."* Athens: University of Georgia Press, 1980.

Gould, Eric. "Condemned to Speak Excessively: Mythic Form and James Joyce's *Ulysses*." *Sub-Stance* 22 (1979): 67–83.

———. *Mythical Intentions in Modern Literature*. Princeton: Princeton University Press, 1981.

Grant, Damian. *Tobias Smollett: A Study in Style*. Manchester, Eng.: Manchester University Press, 1977.

Graves, Lila V. "Locke's Changling and the Shandy Bull." *Philological Quarterly* 60 (1981): 257–64.

Green, David. "Smollett the Historian: A Reappraisal." In *Tobias Smollett: Bicentennial Essays Presented to Lewis M. Knapp*, ed. G. S. Rousseau and P. G. Boucé. New York: Oxford University Press, 1971.

Groden, Michael. *"Ulysses" in Progress*. Princeton: Princeton University Press, 1977.

Hamlin, Cyrus. "The Conscience of Narrative: Toward a Hermeneutics of Transcendence." *New Literary History* 13 (1982): 205–30.

Hampshire, Stuart. "Joyce and Vico: The Middle Way." In *Giambattista Vico's Science of Humanity*, ed. Giorgio Tagliacozzo and Donald Phillip Verene. Baltimore: Johns Hopkins University Press, 1976.

Hartley, Lodowick. "Swiftly-Sterneward: The Question of Sterne's Influence on Joyce." *Studies in the Literary Imagination* 3 (1970): 37–47.

Hay, John A. "Rhetoric and Historiography: Tristram Shandy's First Nine Calendar Months." In *Studies in the Eighteenth Century* II, ed. R. F. Brissenden. Toronto: University of Toronto Press, 1973.

Hayman, David. "Stephen on the Rocks." *James Joyce Quarterly* 14 (1977): 5–17.

Heath, Stephen. "Ambiviolences: Notes for Reading Joyce." In *Post-Structuralist Joyce*, ed. Derek Attridge and Daniel Ferrer. Cambridge: Cambridge University Press, 1984.

Holtz, William V. *Image and Immortality*. Providence: Brown University Press, 1970.

Horwitz, Howard. "'I Can't Remember': Skepticism, Synthetic Histories, Critical Action." *South Atlantic Quarterly* 87 (1988): 787–820.

Hughes, Peter. "From Allusion to Implosion: Vico, Michelet, Joyce, Beckett." In *Vico and Joyce*, ed. Donald Phillip Verene. Albany: State University of New York Press, 1987.

Hunter, J. Paul. *The Reluctant Pilgrim: Defoe's Emblematic Method and Quest for Form in "Robinson Crusoe."* Baltimore: Johns Hopkins University Press, 1966.

———. "Studies in Eighteenth-Century Fiction, 1976." *Philological Quarterly* 56 (1977): 498–539.

Hunter, Richard A., and Ida Macalpine. "Smollett's Reading in Psychiatry." *Modern Language Review* 51 (1956): 409–11.

Isaacs, Neil D. "The Autoerotic Metaphor in Joyce, Sterne, Lawrence, Stevens, and Whitman." *Literature and Psychology* 15 (1965): 92–106.

Joyce, Stanislaus. *My Brother's Keeper*. New York: Viking Press, 1958.

Jung, Carl. "*Ulysses*: A Monologue." *Nimbus* 2 (1953): 7–20.

Kahler, Erich. *The Inward Turn of Narrative*. Translated by Richard and Clara Winston. Princeton: Princeton University Press, 1973.

Kellogg, Robert, and Robert Scholes. *The Nature of Narrative*. New York: Oxford University Press, 1966.

Kenner, Hugh. *Ulysses*. London: George Allen & Unwin, 1980.

Kermode, Frank. *The Sense of an Ending: Studies in the Theory of Fiction*. New York: Oxford University Press, 1967.

Knapp, Lewis M. *Tobias Smollett: Doctor of Men and Manners*. Princeton: Princeton University Press, 1949.

Knapp, Lewis M., and Lillian de la Torre. "Smollett, Mackercher, and the Annesley Claimant." *English Language Notes* 1 (1963): 31–33.

Langer, Suzanne. *Feeling and Form*. New York: Scribners, 1953.

Lanham, Richard A. *Tristram Shandy: The Games of Pleasure*. Berkeley: University of California Press, 1973.

Levitt, Morton P. "A Hero for Our Time: Leopold Bloom and the Myth of *Ulysses*." *James Joyce Quarterly* 10 (1972): 132–46.

Litz, A. Walton. "The Genre of *Ulysses*." In *The Theory of the Novel: New Essays*. New York: Oxford University Press, 1974.

———. "Ithaca." In *James Joyce's "Ulysses": Critical Essays*, ed. Clive Hart and David Hayman. Berkeley: University of California Press, 1974.

———. "Pound and Eliot in *Ulysses*: The Critical Tradition." *James Joyce Quarterly* 10 (1972): 5–18.

———. "Vico and Joyce." In *Giambattista Vico: An International Symposium*, ed. Giorgio Tagliacozzo and Hayden V. White. Baltimore: Johns Hopkins University Press, 1969.

Lodge, David. *The Novelist at the Crossroads*. Ithaca: Cornell University Press, 1971.

Lotman, Jurij M. "The Origin of Plot in the Light of Typology." *Poetics Today* 1 (1979): 161–84.

Loveridge, Mark. *Laurence Sterne and the Argument about Design*. Totowa, N.J.: Barnes and Noble, 1982.

———. "Liberty in *Tristram Shandy*." In *Laurence Sterne: Riddles and Mysteries*, ed. Valerie Grosvenor Myer. Totowa, N.J.: Barnes and Noble, 1984.

MacCaffrey, Isabel Gamble. *Paradise Lost as "Myth."* Cambridge, Mass.: Harvard University Press, 1959.

Macksey, Richard. " 'Alas, Poor Yorick': Sterne Thoughts." *Modern Language Notes* 98 (1983): 1006–20.

Maddox, James. "On Defoe's *Roxana*." *English Literary History* 51 (1984): 669–91.

Manuel, Frank E. *The Eighteenth Century Confronts the Gods*. Cambridge, Mass.: Harvard University Press, 1959.

Mayoux, Jean-Jacques. "Variations on the Time-Sense in *Tristram Shandy*." In *The Winged Skull*, ed. Arthur H. Cash and John M. Stedmond. Kent, Ohio: Kent State University Press, 1971.

McCarthy, Patrick A. "The Riddle in Joyce's *Ulysses*." *Texas Studies in Literature and Language* 17 (1975): 193–205.

McKeon, Michael. *The Origins of the English Novel, 1600–1740*. Baltimore: Johns Hopkins University Press, 1987.

Melchiori, Giorgio. *The Tightrope Walkers*. London: Routledge and Kegan Paul, 1956.

Miller, Henry Knight. "Augustan Prose Fiction and the Romance Tradition." In *Studies in the Eighteenth Century* III, ed. R. F. Brissenden and J. C. Ende. Canberra: Australian University Press, 1976.

New, Melvyn. " 'The Grease of God': The Form of Eighteenth-Century English Fiction." *PMLA* 91 (1976): 235–43.

———. *Laurence Sterne as Satirist*. Gainesville: University of Florida Press, 1969.

Novak, Maximillian E. *Realism, Myth, and History in Defoe's Fiction*. Lincoln: University of Nebraska Press, 1983.

Nuttall, A. D. *A Common Sky*. Berkeley: University of California Press, 1974.

Park, William. "Fathers and Sons—*Humphry Clinker*." *Literature and Psychology* 16 (1966): 166–74.

Parreaux, André, ed. *The Expedition of Humphry Clinker*. Boston: Houghton Mifflin, 1968.

Pater, Walter. *Greek Studies*. 1895. Reprint. London: Macmillian, 1967.

Paulson, Ronald. "Fielding in *Tom Jones*: The Historian, the Poet, and the Mythologist." In *Augustan Worlds*, ed. J. C. Hilson, M. M. B. Jones, and J. R. Watson. Leicester, Eng.: Leicester University Press, 1978.

———. "The Pilgrimage and the Family: Structures in the Novels of Fielding and Smollett." In *Tobias Smollett: Bicentennial Essays*, ed. Paul-Gabriel Boucé and George Rousseau. New York: Oxford University Press, 1971.

———. "Satire in the Early Novels of Smollett." *Journal of English and Germanic Philology* 59 (1960): 381–402.

Peake, C. H. *James Joyce: The Citizen and the Artist*. London: Edward Arnold, 1977.

Peck, H. Daniel. "*Robinson Crusoe*: The Moral Geography of Limitation." *Journal of Narrative Technique* 3 (1973): 20–31.

Pottle, Frederick A. "Synchrony and Diachrony: A Plea for the Use in Literary Studies of Saussure's Concepts and Terminology." In *Literary Theory and Structure*, ed. Frank Brady, John Palmer, and Martin Price. New Haven: Yale University Press, 1973.

Prescott, Joseph. "Notes on Joyce's *Ulysses*." *Modern Language Quarterly* 13 (1951): 149–62.

Price, Martin. *To the Palace of Wisdom*. Garden City, N.Y.: Doubleday, 1964.

Pritchett, V. S. *The Living Novel*. London: Chatto & Windus, 1946.
Putney, Rufus. "The Plan of *Peregrine Pickle*." *PMLA* 60 (1945): 1051–65.
Qualls, Barry V. *The Secular Pilgrims of Victorian Fiction*. New York: Cambridge University Press, 1982.
Rabb, Melinda Alliker. "Engendering Accounts in Sterne's *A Sentimental Journey*." In *Johnson and His Age*, ed. James Engell. Cambridge, Mass.: Harvard University Press, 1984.
Rader, Ralph W. "Defoe, Richardson, Joyce and the Concept of Form in the Novel." In *Autobiography, Biography, and the Novel: Papers Read at a Clark Library Seminar, May 13, 1972*. Los Angeles: University of California Press, 1973.
———. "Exodus and Return: Joyce's *Ulysses* and the Fiction of the Actual." *University of Toronto Quarterly* 48 (1978–79): 149–71.
Radford, F. L. "King, Pope and Hero-Martyr: *Ulysses* and the Nightmare of History." *James Joyce Quarterly* 15 (1978): 275–323.
Reid, B. L. "Smollett's Healing Journey." *Virginia Quarterly Review* 41 (1967): 549–70.
Restuccia, Frances L. *Joyce and the Law of the Father*. New Haven: Yale University Press, 1989.
Richetti, John J. *Defoe's Narratives: Situations and Structures*. Oxford: Clarendon Press, 1975.
Rogers, Pat. *Robinson Crusoe*. London: George Allen and Unwin, 1979.
Rosenblum, Michael. "Smollett and the Old Conventions." *Philological Quarterly* 55 (1976): 389–401.
Rothstein, Eric. "Scotophilia and *Humphry Clinker*: The Politics of Beggary, Bugs, and Buttocks." *University of Toronto Quarterly* 52 (1982–83): 63–78.
———. *Systems of Order and Inquiry in Later Eighteenth-Century Fiction*. Berkeley: University of California Press, 1975.
Rousseau, G. S. *Tobias Smollett: Essays of Two Decades*. Edinburgh: T & T Clark, 1982.
Rubin, Louis D. "Joyce and Sterne: A Study in Affinity." *Hopkins Review* 3 (1949): 14–22.
Rymer, Michael. "Another Source for Smollett's Lismahago." *Notes & Queries* 21 (1974): 57–59.
Schiffer, Paul. " 'Homing, upstream': Fictional Closure and the End of *Ulysses*." *James Joyce Quarterly* 16 (1979): 283–97.
Scholes, Robert, and Robert Kellogg. *The Nature of Narrative*. New York: Oxford University Press, 1966.
Schulz, Max F. *Paradise Regained: Recreations of Eden in Eighteenth- and Nineteenth-Century England*. London: Cambridge University Press, 1985.
Secord, Arthur W. *Robert Drury's Journal and Other Studies*. Urbana: University of Illinois Press, 1961.
Seidel, Michael. *Epic Geography: James Joyce's "Ulysses."* Princeton: Princeton University Press, 1976.
Sekora, John. *Luxury: the Concept in Western Thought, Eden to Smollett*. Baltimore: Johns Hopkins University Press, 1977.

Sena, John F. "Smollett's Portrait of Narcissa's Aunt: The Genesis of an 'Original.'" *English Language Notes* 14 (1971): 270–75.

Senn, Fritz. *Joyce's Dislocutions: Essays on Reading as Translation*. Edited by John Paul Requelme. Baltimore: Johns Hopkins University Press, 1984.

———. *Nichts gegen Joyce* [Joyce Versus Nothing]. Zurich: Hoffmans Verlag, 1983.

Schechner, Mark. *Joyce in Nighttown*. Berkeley: University of California Press, 1974.

Sherbo, Arthur. "Win Jenkins' Language." *Papers in English Language and Literature* 5 (1969): 199–204.

Simpson, K. G. "At This Moment in Space: Time, Space and Values in *Tristram Shandy*." In *Laurence Sterne: Riddles and Mysteries*, ed. Valerie Grosvenor Myer. Totowa, N.J.: Barnes and Noble, 1984, 142–58.

Spacks, Patricia Meyer. *Imagining a Self*. Cambridge, Mass.: Harvard University Press, 1976.

Starr, G. A. *Defoe and Spiritual Autobiography*. Princeton: Princeton University Press, 1965.

Stedmond, John M. *The Comic Art of Laurence Sterne*. Toronto: University of Toronto Press, 1967.

Stovel, Bruce. "*Tristram Shandy* and the Art of Gossip." In *Laurence Sterne: Riddles and Mysteries*, ed. Valerie Grosvenor Myer. Totowa, N.J.: Barnes and Noble, 1984.

Sultan, Stanley. *The Argument of "Ulysses."* Athens: Ohio State University Press, 1964.

Survant, Joseph. "The Idea of History in James Joyce's *Ulysses*." *Perspectives on Contemporary Literature* 1 (1975): 3–19.

Sutherland, James. *Daniel Defoe*. Cambridge, Mass.: Harvard University Press, 1971.

Swearingen, James E. *Reflexivity in Tristram Shandy*. New Haven: Yale University Press, 1977.

Symonds, John Addington. "Nature Myths and Allegories." In *Essays Speculative and Suggestive*. 1890. Reprint. London, 1907.

Topia, André. "The Matrix and the Echo: Intertextuality in *Ulysses*." In *Post-Structuralist Joyce*, ed. Derek Attridge and Daniel Ferrer. Cambridge: Cambridge University Press, 1984.

Trachtenberg, Allen. "The Journey Back: Myth and History in *Tender Is the Night*." In *Experience in the Novel*, ed. Roy Harvey Pearce. New York: Columbia University Press, 1968.

Treadwell, T. O. "The Two Worlds of *Ferdinand, Count Fathom*." In *Tobias Smollett: Bicentennial Essays*, ed. Paul-Gabriel Boucé and George Rousseau. New York: Oxford University Press, 1971.

Tucker, Lindsey. *Stephen and Bloom at Life's Feast: Alimentary Symbolism and the Creative Process in James Joyce's "Ulysses."* Columbus: Ohio State University Press, 1984.

Tupper, Caroline. "Essays Erroneously Attributed to Goldsmith." *PMLA* 39 (1924): 325–42.

Turner, Victor. *The Ritual Process: Structure and Anti-Structure*. Chicago: Aldine, 1969.

van Boheemen, Christine. *The Novel as Family Romance: Language, Gender, and Authority from Fielding to Joyce*. Ithaca: Cornell University Press, 1987.

Verene, Donald Phillip. "Vico as a Reader of Joyce." In *Vico and Joyce*, ed. Donald Phillip Verene. Albany: State University of New York Press, 1987.

———. "Vico's Science of Imaginative Universals and the Philosophy of Symbolic Forms." In *Giambattista Vico's Science of Humanity*, ed. Giorgio Tagliacozzo and Donald Phillip Verene. Baltimore: Johns Hopkins University Press, 1976.

Vickery, John B. *The Literary Impact of "The Golden Bough."* Princeton: Princeton University Press, 1973.

Vico, Giambattista. *The New Science of Giambattista Vico.* Translated from the third edition (1744) by Thomas Goddard Burgin and Max Harold Fisch. Ithaca, N.Y.: Cornell University Press, 1948.

Voegelin, Eric. *Order and History*, 5 vols. Baton Rouge: Louisiana State University Press, 1956–87.

———. "Postscript: On Paradise and Revolution." *Southern Review* 7 (1971): 25–48.

Wardropper, Bruce. "*Don Quixote*: Story or History?" *Modern Philology* 63 (1965): 1–11.

Warner, John M. "Myth and History in Joyce's 'Nausicaa' Episode." *James Joyce Quarterly* 24 (1986): 19–31.

———. "Smollett's Development as a Novelist." *Novel* 5 (1972): 148–61.

Watt, Ian. *The Rise of the Novel.* London: Chatto and Windus, 1957.

Waugh, Patricia. *Feminine Fictions: Revisiting the Postmodern.* New York: Routledge, 1989.

Wellek, René. "The Supposed Influence of Vico on England and Scotland in the Eighteenth Century." In *Giambattista Vico: An International Symposium*, ed. Giogio Tagliacozzo and Hayden V. White. Baltimore: Johns Hopkins University Press, 1969.

White, Hayden. "The Fictions of Factual Representation." In *The Literature of Fact*, ed. Angus Fletcher. New York: Columbia University Press, 1976.

———. "The Tropics of History: The Deep Structure of the *New Science*." In *Giambattista Vico's Science of Humanity*, ed. Giorgio Tagliacozzo and Donald Phillip Verene. Baltimore: Johns Hopkins University Press, 1976.

Zimmerman, Everett. *Defoe and the Novel.* Berkeley: University of California Press, 1975.

Zwerdling, Alex. "The Mythographers and the Romantic Revival of Myth." *PMLA* 79 (1967): 447–56.

Index